S0-ACL-630

STORY STRUCTURE
STRUCTURE
architect

STORY
STRUCTURE
architect

a writer's guide to building
dramatic situations & compelling characters

Victoria Lynn Schmidt, Ph.D.

WRITER'S DIGEST BOOKS
Cincinnati, Ohio
www.writersdigest.com

Story Structure Architect© 2005 by Victoria Lynn Schmidt. Manufactured in Canada.
All rights reserved. No other part of this book may be reproduced in any form or by any
electronic or mechanical means including information storage and retrieval systems
without permission in writing from the publisher, except by a reviewer, who may quote
brief passages in a review. Published by Writer's Digest Books, an imprint of F+W Publications, Inc., 4700 East Galbraith Road, Cincinnati, Ohio 45236. (800) 289-0963. First
edition.

09 08 07 06 05   5 4 3 2 1

Distributed in Canada by Fraser Direct
100 Armstrong Avenue
Georgetown, ON, Canada L7G 5S4
Tel: (905) 877-4411

Distributed in the U.K. and Europe by David & Charles
Brunel House, Newton Abbot, Devon, TQ12 4PU, England
Tel: (+44) 1626 323200, Fax: (+44) 1626 323319
E-mail: mail@davidandcharles.co.uk

Distributed in Australia by Capricorn Link
P.O. Box 704, Windsor, NSW 2756 Australia
Tel: (02) 4577-3555

Library of Congress Cataloging-in-Publication Data

Schmidt, Victoria
  The story structure architect : a writer's guide to building dramatic
situations and compelling characters / by Victoria Lynn Schmidt.-- 1st ed.
      p. cm.
  Includes bibliographical references and index.
  ISBN 1-58297-325-3 (pbk. : alk. paper)
  1. Fiction--Technique. 2. Plots (Drama, novel, etc.) 3. Characters and
characteristics in literature. I. Title.

PN3378.S36 2005   2005000590
  808.3--dc22

Edited by Michelle Ruberg
Designed by Lisa Buchanan-Kuhn & Claudean Wheeler
Cover design by Lisa Buchanan-Kuhn
Production coordinated by Robin Richie

Printed in Canada

fw
F+W PUBLICATIONS, INC.

Dedication

To my second family—Mike, Cathy, Cindy, Mike, Kevin, and Matt. Thanks for being there.

To Cyndi, Cathy, Carol, and Maggie. Thanks for creating stories with me all those years ago. Wally, Anne, Eileen, and Paul, too!

And also to Mom, Dad, Tom, Oliver, Angie, Kim, and Barbie. Bobby, Ada, Debbie, Randall, Randy, and Pam

About the Author

Victoria Schmidt is the author of the popular book *45 Master Characters: Mythic Models for Creating Original Characters*. She is a graduate of the film program at UCLA and the MFA screenwriting program at Loyola Marymount University, and she holds a Ph.D. in psychology. Visit her Web site at www.CharactersJourney.com for more information on upcoming books and writing resources.

Table of Contents

Part 4: Finishing Touches

Introduction

"Trust that still, small voice that says, 'This might work,' and try it."

—DIANE MARIECHILD

*S*tory Structure Architect has really been a labor of love for me, and I am honored to share it with you. While creating this book, it almost seemed as if it existed in the ether just waiting to be plucked down and written. Many times I thought I would write about one subject only to have several other subjects reveal themselves. Once the Writer's Digest team suggested the addition of story structures, as opposed to standard plots, the book really took off in some exciting directions.

I guess this is what writing is all about—plotting a story, or in the case of nonfiction, mapping a direction to go in and then leaving room to allow the story to take you in the direction it wants to go. There's a certain balance to be found between demanding control over a piece of work and surrendering to the writing process and seeing what develops organically.

There are many writers who choose sides between control and surrender, which may compromise their work. They strictly obey plotting rules and structure or they strive to not have plot or direction at all.

But, as yoga philosophy teaches, I have always found the middle path between two extremes to be the most advantageous. The middle path is what granted the Buddha enlightenment, after all! When the Buddha first participated in extreme meditation practices that did not grant him enlightenment, he left his teachers and sat by the side of a lake praying for guidance on what to do next. Suddenly a man and his son in a small boat paddled past the Buddha. The father was teaching his son how to play a sitar, and his words floated toward the Buddha, answering his dilemma:

Tune the sitar neither low nor high.
The string overstretched breaks, the music flies, The string over slack is dumb, and the music dies.

When you over-plot your story, you may lose spontaneity and feel like a slave to your overly detailed outline. When you build your story as you go, you tend to end up with a ton of subplots and loose ends that can't be tied up and a character arc that flatlines.

You need to have some direction as to where you are going, but you also need to feel free to write what your heart tells you to write. One way is no better or worse than the other, but together they can compliment and enhance each other.

I hope this book helps you discover your own writing style, somewhere in the middle path, so you can express your unique vision to the world.

> There is a vitality, a life force, an energy, a quickening, that is translated through you into action, and because there is only one of you in all time, this expression is unique. And if you block it, it will never exist through any other medium and will be lost.
>
> —MARTHA GRAHAM

Part 1

DRAFTING A PLAN

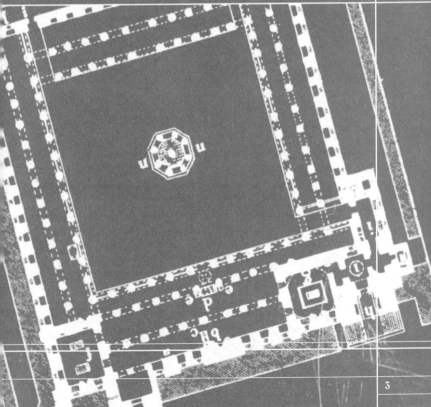

How to Use This Book

> "Life consists of small things, just your ego goes on saying these are small things. You would like some great thing to do—a great poetry. You would like to become Shakespeare or Kalidas or Milton. It is your ego that is creating the trouble. Drop the ego and everything is creative."
>
> —OSHO

Within these pages you will find 5 Dramatic Throughlines, 6 Conflict Types, 21 Genres, 11 Master Plot Structures, 55 Master Dramatic Situations, and several Research guidelines. In short, you will find all the assistance you need to be the architect of a wonderful yet unique story.

Throughout these chapters you will also find many questions to answer when developing your story. I present a lot of information in the form of questions to allow you the creative room to make your story unique, to make it from who you are as you answer these questions. Questions make you think, after all, and they get the creative juices flowing as you explore possibilities. I find this to be a much more effective teaching tool than espousing rules to be memorized and followed.

There are also sections on anti-structure stories such as Metafiction and Slice of Life. These sections may be challenging for some. I strongly encourage those who judge these types of stories as "wrong" or "lacking" to watch the film examples given.

When you grow up in a westernized culture, the traditional plot structure becomes so embedded in your subconscious that you may have to work hard to create a plot structure that deviates from it. Sometimes just watching a film created in another culture can be tough for westerners because it usually deviates from the traditional westernized Aristotelian structure.

Understand this and keep your mind open when reading these sections. Just because a piece doesn't conform to the model you are used to does not make it bad or wrong.

Plot Driven vs. Character Driven

Since many new writers have a hard time understanding the difference between plot-driven and character-driven pieces, I want to go over it here before we get started since I use these terms many times throughout this book.

PLOT DRIVEN

In a plot-driven story the events of the story move the story forward and cause the character to react to those events. Characters are secondary to the plot. They act in accordance with the plot and do not create events or situations on their own.

In a sense, the plot takes over like a tornado. If a tornado suddenly comes through a town out of nowhere, the characters can't stop it; they have to brace themselves and react to what ever happens around them. They don't cause the tornado—the tornado causes them to react to it.

CHARACTER DRIVEN

In a character-driven story the character moves the story forward through action and choices. She initiates the events of the story and causes the events to happen. Each scene is instigated by the characters within it.

If a character chooses to stay home one day and work in her garden, no event or situation will stop her from doing so, but another character may try to make her feel guilty for it. This may cause her to decide not to garden, but it is totally her choice even if it seems like someone else is manipulating her.

If a tornado comes through town, the characters will always have the time needed to decide what to do. The focus is on the characters and how and why they make their decisions to stay or leave. These decisions have the power to move the plot in different directions. The characters have options and choices that affect the outcome.

INDEPENDENCE DAY VS. SIGNS

Think of the films *Independence Day* and *Signs*. Both are about aliens coming to take over Earth. At first glance this type of story may seem like a plot-driven story, pure and simple. It's very high-concept.

But while the characters in *Independence Day* react to the events around them (plot driven), the characters in *Signs* create the events around them and are the main focus of the story (character driven). They even have issues and problems to deal with outside of the aliens coming to visit. They learn lessons from their experience and grow stronger as a family. The faith of Mel Gibson's character plays a huge role in the film, and all characters are asked to confront deep issues about what is happening around them. I encourage you to rent both films to really understand the difference between plot- and character-driven stories.

Using This Book

Within this book are six decisions for you to make to create a wonderfully well-developed structure for your story. These six decisions are ones you have probably made before when writing a story but just weren't conscious you were making them at the time. Now that you will be conscious of them, you can make more informed decisions and perhaps flesh out your story much more quickly when you know the right questions to ask yourself:

1. What Dramatic Throughline should I use?
2. What type of Conflict works best for my story?
3. Which Genre should I select?
4. What Structure Model works best?
5. How many Situations will I use?
6. How much Research should I conduct?

Selecting a Dramatic Throughline

A Dramatic Throughline is the main direction of the story. It is not the goal, story, or theme but the basic thrust of the plot. It asks the central question that keeps the reader reading.

Every time you come up with a story idea you already have decided on a Dramatic Throughline. You know if you want the main character to be successful or not; you just may not have known this was called a Dramatic Throughline or that there were other options available. Although most stories are about happy, successful characters, you can choose to have your characters fail in the end.

There are five types of Dramatic Throughlines:

1. The main character succeeds.
2. The main character is defeated.
3. The main character abandons his goal.

4. The main character's goal is undefined.

5. The reader creates the goal.

Even if the story you are working on is plot driven, the Dramatic Throughline is still all about the character and his goal.

Jurassic Park is very plot driven, yet it is the characters' goal of surviving that keeps the story alive.

There would be no story at all without characters. The character's goal is in direct relationship to the plot. The goal is either conceived by the character (character driven) or the goal is pushed upon the character by the plot (plot driven), but either way it is still the character's goal.

Selecting a Conflict

Once you know your Dramatic Throughline you can then select the Conflict you would like to predominately use throughout your story. Conflicts sustain and reinforce the theme. There are six Conflicts:

1. Relational Conflict

2. Situational Conflict

3. Inner Conflict

4. Paranormal Conflict

5. Cosmic Conflict

6. Social Conflict

Conflict, at its core, is the opposition of forces that serve to advance the plot. It can be between people, about ideas, or from natural or man-made circumstances. In some stories and even individual scenes, several different types of Conflict are present at the same time:

Perhaps a young man wants to move away from his family and they are very upset with him about it (Relational Conflict). He is torn by feelings of guilt about his decision (Inner Conflict). He wants to move in with his girlfriend but the society he lives within shuns such a thing (Societal Conflict) and so does his religion (Cosmic Conflict).

Selecting a Genre

Twenty-one Genres are listed, beginning on page twenty, to help you decide what type of Genre, or combination thereof, would be best for your story. Perhaps you have had one type of Genre in mind and now find a different one more suited to your story. The choice of Genre will greatly influence your story. Think of dark comedies, for example: When a serious, often morbid horror story is treated like a comedy, the whole feel and subtext of the story changes.

Selecting a Structure

Eleven Master Structures are outlined in detail for you to explore. The first six structures—Roller Coaster, Replay, Fate, Parallel, Episodic, and Melodrama—are more traditional in nature, closely following Aristotle's three-act structure design.

The next two—Romance and Journey—are based on structure content rather than structure design. The beginning, middle, and end are there, but how they develop is the "content" difference.

The final three—Interactive Fiction, Metafiction, and Slice of Life—are somewhat anti-structure in design.

Selecting a Situation

Next you will find chapters on the 55 Dramatic Situations. As you will see in the introduction to this section, these are based on Georges Polti's work, where he found thirty-six dramatic situations to use in plotting. An explanation on how I developed the additional nineteen situations will be found there.

These situations are used to add drama and spice to the often-lagging second act. They can be used as a story, subplot, or incident—whatever you need at the time.

Conducting Research

Finally you will see a section on Research that will help you make the most of the story you have created. Punching up the setting, tone, and character to full effect is what will make your story stand out from all the rest.

For example, instead of writing about a young man in a suit just starting his career, Research can lead you to write about a more specific type of character whose father grew up during the Great Depression and instilled a deep mistrust of financial institutions and the government into his son. Now we have some conflict brewing. Perhaps this mistrust comes into direct conflict with something his boss is asking him to do.

Together these six decisions will help you find new and interesting elements to add to your story.

The 5 Dramatic Throughlines

> "There are basically two types of people. People who accomplish things, and people who claim to have accomplished things. The first group is less crowded."
>
> –MARK TWAIN

The first decision to make when creating a great work of fiction is to figure out what your overall Dramatic Throughline is. A throughline asks the central question that keeps the reader reading and the main character moving forward:

"Will the main character succeed? Fail? Give up?"

Once you know the answer to this question you know how to design your story, especially the dreaded second act that most writers have trouble with. If the character will succeed, the second act is filled with scenes testing her resolve and putting obstacles in her path that later serve to help her succeed.

You will know what type of situations to use to bring out and support this Success Throughline. This helps you to keep your story on track. All events and obstacles will push the character toward success:

- He will learn the skills he needs to learn to be successful. Perhaps in the second act the villain pushes the hero to jump over a creek filled with snakes. The hero doesn't want to do it, but little does he know that doing this now will help him later when he has to jump over something far worse.

- He will meet supporting characters that will help him succeed. Perhaps in the second act he is forced into hiding in a home for the elderly and winds up making friends.

- He will find the information he needs to win. Perhaps in the second act he is stuck in library for the night and sees it as a chance to do some research.

There are 5 Dramatic Throughlines. The first three are Traditional Throughlines that work well with Traditional Structure, and the remaining two work well with Nontraditional Structure:

1. The main character succeeds.
2. The main character is defeated.
3. The main character abandons her goal.
4. The main character's goal is undefined.
5. The reader creates a goal.

Traditional Dramatic Throughlines

Traditional Dramatic Throughlines have a clear-cut beginning, middle, and end that allow them to fit nicely into traditional types of structures with a clear-cut beginning, middle, and end.

The best way to illustrate the first three Dramatic Throughlines is to think of an episodic television show; since it is on every week, a strong Dramatic Throughline is needed to hold it together and keep it focused. The Dramatic Throughline in episodic television is never resolved until the series is over. (In traditional feature films and novels, the Dramatic Throughline is resolved by the end of the story, regardless if the character succeeds, is defeated, or abandons the throughline goal.)

In the television show *Monk*, for example, the main character has two goals in life: One is to find out who murdered his wife, and the other one is to get back on the police force. So the overall Dramatic Throughline is to see the character succeed at these two goals.

The Dramatic Throughline presented is in every episode whether written into the episode directly or just briefly touched upon. He may succeed or fail in each episode's storyline, but his overall goal is to succeed at finding his wife's killer and get back on the force.

THE CHARACTER SUCCEEDS THROUGHLINE

Here the main character has a goal to achieve or a question to answer, and he succeeds in doing so. Most novels and films have this type of Dramatic Throughline, especially action-driven stories. Happy endings abound here.

An example of "question- to answer-driven" character success, besides the obvious mystery/detective story, is *It's a Wonderful Life*. The main character doesn't have a major outward goal to achieve but a question to answer: "Will George Bailey escape from his boring life in Bedford Falls to a life of adventure and riches or will he find satisfaction in his own hometown?"

Some Examples of the Character Succeeds Throughline

Problem $\rightarrow$ Solution
Mystery $\rightarrow$ Solution
Conflict $\rightarrow$ Peace
Danger $\rightarrow$ Safety
Confusion $\rightarrow$ Order
Dilemma $\rightarrow$ Decision
Ignorance $\rightarrow$ Knowledge
Question $\rightarrow$ Answer

(Artsedge.kennedy-center.org/content/)

Donna Lee of the Hollywood Scriptwriting Institute states that the hero accomplishes his goal through one of four ways:

1. BY MEANS OF COURAGE: The hero uses his courage to solve his problem and achieve his purpose. Great for dramas.

2. BY MEANS OF INGENUITY: The hero uses his brains and creativity to solve his problem. Great for mysteries.

3. BY MEANS OF A SPECIAL CAPACITY: The hero has a special ability or acquires a new skill. Great for superheroes.

4. BY MEANS OF A SPECIAL WEAPON: The hero has a special weapon to bring about the villain's defeat. Great for action stories.

I would also add that characters can succeed by means of Self-sacrifice. The hero is able to endure anything in order to reach his goal. This is great for melodramas.

Characters can also succeed through receiving help and working in partnership with others. How successful would Gandhi or Martin Luther King have been if no one else stood with them and believed in their goals? This is great for inspirational stories.

THE CHARACTER IS DEFEATED THROUGHLINE

Here the main character is defeated by the events of the story and can't achieve her goal. It is as if life itself is out to get her. She just can't catch a break. The character may even be the richest woman alive, yet she still can't have the one thing she truly wants. Money can't buy everything.

Think of *Death of a Salesman* or *Moby-Dick* as examples. In *Death of a Salesman*, Willy Loman just can't get it together. Try as he might he is unsuccessful in life, so he tries to be successful in death. He sacrifices everything, yet it still doesn't garner the result he hoped for.

What defeats the character is usually not a villain but the character himself. He is his own worst enemy. Perhaps he gives up or doesn't take the time he should take to prepare himself for his task, or he sabotages himself and refuses to see he's doing it. This is similar to the Masculine Journey Rebellion Stage (discussed in Part 3), in which the hero refuses to face his demons and therefore fails to grow as a person, though any structure can be used for this throughline.

Here the Character Succeeds Examples Are Reversed

Solution	$\rightarrow$ Problem
Solution	$\rightarrow$ Mystery
Peace	$\rightarrow$ Conflict
Safety	$\rightarrow$ Danger
Order	$\rightarrow$ Confusion
Decision	$\rightarrow$ Dilemma
Knowledge	$\rightarrow$ Ignorance
Answer	$\rightarrow$ Question

The character tries to come up with solutions but only creates more problems. The character has some sense of peace and winds up creating more conflict than he started out with. Many comedies utilize this. Struggle is the most important element in this Dramatic Throughline when creating the main character.

Donna Lee states that the hero is defeated by one of two ways:

1. **DUE TO CIRCUMSTANCES:** The hero deserves to achieve his goal but in the end he doesn't because that's the way life is.

2. **DUE TO WEAKNESS OR OBSESSION:** The hero is likable but has a dark side that clashes with the circumstances of the plot and drives him to destruction.

The above two ways are very plot driven, so I would add that the hero can be defeated due to Choices, which is character driven. The hero has the ability to be successful—he just keeps making mistakes. He can't seem to get it right. It's as if he's been cursed. Every decision he makes goes haywire. The circumstance he is in does not cause his failure (which would be plot driven); he causes it by making the wrong decisions (which is character driven).

THE CHARACTER ABANDONS GOAL THROUGHLINE

Here the main character abandons her original goal and may or may not pick up a new one. "The main character either realizes that if her goal is achieved it will not bring her the happiness she seeks and may bring misfortune upon others" (Lee), or she realizes she was lied to or betrayed and accomplishing the goal no longer suits her—it was all a lie or an illusion.

Think of *Bridget Jones's Diary*—Bridget wants to marry her boss and she will do whatever it takes to win his affection. In the end she realizes he is not good enough for her (her idea of him was an illusion) and she doesn't want to settle (she won't be happy with him).

Nontraditional Throughlines

Throughlines four and five are Nontraditional Throughlines, often breaking with traditional three-act structure altogether.

THE CHARACTER'S GOAL IS UNDEFINED THROUGHLINE

When a character's goal is undefined, the story takes on an ethereal quality. One has to view the story outside of traditional narrative form. The events are not dramatically determined but instead flow with a natural rhythm that reflects true-life experience. Anton Chekhov's work fits this Dramatic Throughline, especially *An Upheaval.*

A story written without Traditional Structure and Dramatic Throughline is *not* a story written without planning, focus, and effort, as some may think. In fact, these stories can take more crafting than traditional stories, making them more intellectual and thought provoking. The reader or audience has to participate in the narrative, following the narrative flow and interpreting the subtext. This is similar to the Slice of Life story structure (in Part 3).

THE READER CREATES THE GOAL THROUGHLINE

Here the reader or audience must make decisions on where the story should go next. The reader takes the lead role in the piece and role-plays with the character. This is found most often in interactive fiction such as video games and novels that can be rearranged or restructured. The chapter on interactive fiction will explain this in detail.

This type of Dramatic Throughline has been around for centuries, way before modern technology, and has a very interesting and rich history all its own.

Combining Dramatic Throughlines

A story can have several Dramatic Throughlines if the main character's goal changes, though it is not a good idea to have more than one Dramatic Throughline at a time. Having a character abandon one goal and later pick up a new goal and succeed at it is perfectly fine. Think of the film *Wall Street* where Charlie Sheen abandons his goal of making money at all costs and then takes up the goal of saving the company he was ordered to liquidate.

Having a character that succeeds but is then defeated by circumstances is also fine. Think of the movies *City of Angels* and *Cold Mountain*. In both cases the two main characters are successfully reunited in the end, only to have one of them killed moments later.

So the next time you brainstorm an idea, make sure that if you are writing a happy ending it's because that's the best Dramatic Throughline for your story and not because you think it is the only way to write a story.

Questions to Consider
When Choosing a Dramatic Throughline:

- Do you want your character to succeed?
- Will you challenge traditional storytelling models or stick with what is known to work?
- Will you combine Dramatic Throughlines?
- Would changing the Dramatic Throughline add to the story at all? Or to the theme or subtext?
- Is there a story of yours you just couldn't finish? Do you have the wrong Dramatic Throughline for the piece? (You may want to take another look at it.)

The 6 Conflicts

"Conflict is the source of all growth and is an absolute necessity if one is to be alive."

–JEAN MILLER

Now that you know your Dramatic Throughline and whether or not you want your hero to succeed or fail, you are ready to select the types of Conflict you would like to use to make your story more dramatic and engaging.

Most writers have a lot of trouble keeping the second act of their story moving. Conflict can really help you with this as it is usually the hero's need to overcome the Conflict and the ways in which he goes about it that drive the story forward. And that is what the second act is all about!

On TakingITGlobal.org, Quacy Grant states:

> Conflict is an evitable and pervasive aspect of human life … It is sometimes physically violent, that is, expressed with fists, guns, or bombs. However, much of it exists within the mind and is expressed in words. It can erupt suddenly or it can smolder for years or even for generations.
>
> There are positive and negative effects of conflict. Although conflict is popularly associated with fighting and is generally viewed as destructive, unpleasant, and undesirable, conflict can also be something very good. It can promote new ideas, encourage better understanding, strengthen personal relationships, stimulate growth, and facilitate more effective solutions to problems.

The following are the six types of Conflict that can be used in stories.

Relational Conflict

This is a human vs. human Conflict. Two characters, usually the protagonist and antagonist, are competing or clashing with each other over mutually exclusive goals. Only one of them can achieve his goal because each goal requires the other to lose his goal. Some examples include:

- The hero wants to succeed and the villain's goal is to see the hero fail.
- The hero wants to buy a property but the villain wants to buy it as well.
- The hero and villain want to marry the same woman.
- The hero wants to change his life and get over his alcoholism and the villain doesn't want him to change.

Situational Conflict

This is a human vs. nature/environment Conflict. Characters disagree about how to deal with a natural or environmental situation. It is usually life threatening on some level and the hero must find inner strength to overcome it. Some examples include:

- The hero wants to go for help but the others want to wait for help.
- The others want to open the door to try to escape but the hero stops them because the door is hot and there may be a fire.
- A surfer is drowning and the characters are afraid to save him because there are sharks all around him.
- A tornado is coming and the characters argue about what to do. One selfish character may only be worried about his property.

Inner Conflict

This is a human vs. self Conflict. The hero is unsure of herself or her goal. She endures a mental struggle from internal opposing influences. Some examples include:

- She may have a perceived flaw of some sort that holds her back.
- She may have had a religious upbringing that makes her feel guilty about everything she does.
- She may not know what to do. She doesn't know what her true values and morals are.
- She may not be able to make an important decision until it is too late.

Paranormal Conflict

This is a human vs. technology/possibility Conflict. The hero has to look at the consequences of his actions when he pushes the limits of what is possible. Some examples include:

- Like Dr. Frankenstein, he may be playing with life and death.
- Like Neo in *The Matrix*, he may be taken over by technology, not knowing where the real world begins and ends.
- Like *2001: A Space Odyssey*, the computer may take over everything.

Cosmic Conflict

This is a human vs. fate/destiny/god Conflict. Dr. Linda Seger, noted script analyst and author, says:

> Cosmic conflict occurs between a character and a supernatural force. In order to watch the conflict unfold, we need to see the character project his problems with an invisible force onto a human being who just happens to be in the way.

Some examples include:

- The hero is upset with God for allowing her child to die.
- The hero is afraid to face the final battle, knowing it is her destiny to die in it.
- The hero is upset with the cards she has been dealt in life, and she plays the victim for a while.

Social Conflict

This is a human vs. group Conflict. The hero has problems with a group of people. They may be a religious group, an institution, a hospital, or a book club. Not every person in the group needs to be seen; you can have one person represent the whole group if needed. The hero may try to turn group members against each other, or he may learn something about himself through dealing with people who are different from him.

Wilf H. Ratzburg says of group Conflict:

> Destructive group conflict diverts energy from the real task, destroys morale, deepens differences, obstructs cooperative action, produces irresponsible behavior, creates suspicion and distrust, and decreases productivity. Constructive group conflict opens up an issue in a confronting manner, develops clarification of an issue, improves problem-solving quality, increases involvement, provides more spontaneity in communication, initiates growth, strengthens a relationship when creatively resolved, helps increase productivity.

Some examples include:

- The hero may need information and resources from a specific group he doesn't like too much.
- A group may not like the hero or what he stands for and therefore deliberately sets up obstacles in his path.
- The hero may be forced to deal with a group he previously judged in error.

Conflict

Conflict is essentially based on a character's perceptions rather than on reality and on a character's feelings rather than on facts. If a character has a calm, centered approach to the Conflict in her life, there will be no Conflict on the page. It is the character's interpretation of the Conflict-provoking event that creates the Conflict and gives it life.

Even if the potential for Conflict is provoked by a situation, such as being stuck in a sinking ship, it is how the character perceives the event that brings the Conflict to fruition.

If the character were to say, "Oh, look, the ship is sinking, but, I'm sure everything will be fine because it's not my time to go yet," and she meant it, there wouldn't be much Conflict in the story.

Now if she were stuck there all by herself and had an intense fear of water or of being alone, Internal Conflict would play itself out. Or she may be stuck there with a group of people she doesn't like very much, and Social Conflict would play itself out. Or if sharks came around and scared everyone, then Situational Conflict would play itself out.

Multiple Conflicts

As briefly stated in the How to Use This Book section on page four, many stories and scenes may have several types of Conflict at work all at once. This occurs, not because the writer has interjected more problems for the character, but because the main problem of the story or scene itself elicits several Conflicts at once.

The example given previously was of a young man moving out of his parents' home. His problem is that he wants to live with his girlfriend. This is the central problem of the scene and causes Relational Conflict between him and his family. Because the writer previously worked in a subplot regarding the young man's religious beliefs and how living together outside of marriage is considered a sin, Cosmic Conflict has also been created. Once his mother starts crying, telling him how much she needs him to help out around the house, Inner Conflict from guilt will also be present. One central problem has created three types of Conflict for the main character.

Of course, you can create several different problems for the character at the same time, each creating a different form of Conflict, but this can diffuse the intensity and drama in the scene. It is best to focus on all the Conflict regarding one problem at a time so as not to pull the reader in too many directions at once.

Questions to Consider
When Choosing Conflicts:

- What type of Conflict do you want to emphasize in your story? (You can have more than one.)

- Do you want to go back and change your Dramatic Throughline to suit a different type of Conflict?

- Will you have enough Conflict to sustain the second act?

- How many other characters will experience Conflict in the story? Will they have their own subplots?

- How will you show the character's need to overcome the Conflict?

- What is the character's main method for overcoming the Conflict? Does she have special skills? Contacts? Resources? Friends?

- Will a love interest be a Relational Conflict for the hero in a subplot? Can you put them at odds over something?

The 21 Genres

"There was never yet an uninteresting life. Such a thing is an impossibility. Inside of the dullest exterior there is a drama, a comedy, and a tragedy."

–MARK TWAIN

Since Lady Murasaki Shikibu wrote the first novel *The Tale of Genji*, around 1000 A.D., literature has been classified into Genres that have consistently changed with the times.

The number of ways in which to classify literature is still growing, so there are no set rules or even categories of Genre that everyone agrees upon. For some, Genre is merely Prose, Poetry, and Drama. For those in Shakespeare's day there was Tragedy, History, Comedy, Pastoral, Pastoral-Comical, Historical-Pastoral, Tragical-Historical, and Tragical-Comical-Historical-Pastoral.

Today, film has greatly influenced how we think about Genre, modifying and creating new genres according to this new medium. The mere mention of a "Western" story evokes images of John Wayne and men on horseback. It is likely that in the future there will be a new set of Genres according to the influence of video games, interactive fiction, and independent filmmakers.

Daniel Chandler in *Introduction to Genre Theory* states:

> How we define a genre depends on our purposes. For instance if we are studying the way in which genre frames the reader's interpretation of a text then we would do well to focus on how readers identify genres rather than on theoretical distinctions. Defining genres may be problematic, but even if theorists were to abandon the concept, in everyday life people would continue to categorize texts.

When selecting a Genre for your story, think about what it is you want to say or what it is you want your reader to feel. Also think about what you like to read yourself. Is there a specific Genre you love and know very well? Go with what you know if you are just starting out; otherwise, challenge yourself a little and try a new Genre.

Try your story idea in several different Genres and see if one gives you more excitement or more possibilities than another one does. After all, any of these Genres can be used with any of the structures. If you have experience writing Westerns, for example, you may want to try your hand at a mystery instead. In a typical Western, the hero's goal is to protect his land and family and seek revenge against those who take it away from him. What if the hero becomes a detective instead, searching for the whereabouts of his loved ones? The focus has switched from revenge to discovery.

If you want to combine Genres, by all means do so. Genre is subjective and open for revision and reclassification at any time. You could, in fact, create a mystery set in the West, combining the two Genres above. In this case, the hero above searches for his loved ones' whereabouts while also seeking revenge.

Now that you have selected a Dramatic Throughline and Conflict Type, you need to think about the type of Genre you want to work in.

The following are the main contemporary Genres:

ACTION. Action stories have a lot of activity, effects, and, well, action. They are fast paced and designed for pure audience escapism. They are primarily plot driven. Some subcategories are:

- SUPERHERO: The hero has exceptional power or prowess.
- UNDERDOG: The hero is misjudged and not thought to have power.
- REVENGE: The hero wants revenge against those who have wronged him.
- SAVIOR: The hero must save everyone.

ADVENTURE. Adventure stories are just that—adventurous, but they are also filled with risk and the unknown. When someone skydives, he is taking a chance, and that is what creates a thrill. Adventure stories are all about seeking something outside of ordinary experience that can be hazardous. Some subcategories are:

- EXPEDITIONS: The hero is venturing into the unknow.n
- TREASURE HUNTS: The hero is searching for something, usually fortune.
- DISCOVERY: The hero finds something thought impossible to find or something thought impossible to prove the existence of.

CHILDREN. Children's books are the same as adult books when it comes to Genre. For example, there are mystery children's stories ("What is that monster in the woods?"). And there are journey children's stories ("Will Billy find his way home?"). The difference is that you are writing for a specific audience at a specific reading and comprehension level. Children see the world much differently than adults. Some subcategories are:

- **SPECIAL BEINGS:** The hero meets a wolf, the tooth fairy, Santa Claus, or any other type of unusual character you can come up with.
- **LESSONS TO LEARN:** The hero learns a moral or other type of lesson.
- **ACCOMPLISHMENT:** The hero did something all by herself.
- **ANIMALS:** All the characters can be animals as in an animal fantasy story.

COMEDY. Comedies are subjective and as varied as *Who Framed Roger Rabbit* and *Seinfeld*. What one person thinks of as funny may be completely different from what another person thinks is funny. The writer of this Genre must be willing to take risks because, as most stand-up comics will attest, it is a tough business. The audience may not laugh at all. Comedies usually exaggerate situations, language, and characters for effect. Some subcategories are:

- **SATIRE:** Irony, sarcasm, or caustic wit used to attack or expose.
- **PARODY:** A mockery or work that imitates the style of another for comic effect or ridicule.
- **FARCE:** A work in which improbable plot situations and exaggerated characters are used for humorous effect.
- **DARK COMEDY:** A story with disturbing elements and morbid or grimly satiric humor.
- **SLAPSTICK:** Comedy of physical action; i.e., hero steps on the end of a rake and gets hit in the head.
- **SCREWBALL:** Impulsively whimsical or foolish or a totally unsound crazy scheme.

CREATIVE NONFICTION. This is a hybrid of literature and nonfiction that is based on true-life events. A true story is dramatized, especially when there are gaps in the story that need to be filled. The nonfiction elements are based on facts, and the fiction elements are based on setting, scene, place, and bringing out characterization. Some subcategories are:

- **TRUE CRIME:** Narrative follows the criminal's or the detective's perspective.
- **JOURNALISM:** Narrative reports the news through creatively telling the events as they happened rather than giving just the facts; a more personal look into the events.
- **AUTOBIOGRAPHY:** Narrative is the history of your life and accomplishments.
- **BIOGRAPHY:** Narrative is the history of another person's life or accomplishments.

CRIME. Crime stories are centered on characters that have done something wrong or are at least accused of doing so as the real criminal gets away. The criminals feel they operate outside the law and are entitled to what they have stolen or justified in what they have done.

DIARY/JOURNAL. These stories have first-person point of view accounts given in diary entries written by the main character. These accounts are presented as being the true thoughts of the main character. Think *Robinson Crusoe* and *Bridget Jones's Diary*. The main character talks to the reader firsthand through her diary. The diary can take up the entire story or just be small entries sprinkled throughout the story.

DRAMA. Dramas are serious stories that portray realistic characters in realistic settings. They can also be very over-the-top, exaggerating the seriousness of the problem and the character's reactions to those problems. Some subcategories are:

- REALISTIC: The drama is a very real and everyday type.
- OVER-THE-TOP: Exaggerated problems and reactions to them are presented; characters may be "drama queens."

FANTASY. Fantasies transcend the bounds of human possibility and physical laws. Magic, myth, and impossibilities abound. Other worlds are explored, characters can have supernatural powers, and the laws of physics are challenged. Anything is possible. Just be careful to define the laws of the world you are creating and stick to them. The reader will believe the hero can fly faster than a speeding bullet if you define why and how he does this. Never contradict that explanation or you will lose your reader.

HISTORICAL/EPIC. Historical fiction mixes detailed historical research with imagined characters. Think *Gone With the Wind*. This fiction may be turned upside down if the author wishes to imagine an alternate series of events that change history. Epics are often historical in nature and cover a large expanse of time set against a rich, vast setting.

HORROR. Horror stories are meant to frighten the audience. Challenging common fears works best here because everyone can relate to them, such as being left all alone in the dark, having a car break down in the middle of the night on a deserted street, or getting into an elevator with a scary-looking man. Some subcategories are:

- VIOLENCE: Many horror stories have violence or the threat of violence.
- DARK ASPECTS OF LIFE: Other types of horror expose the darker, more sinister aspects of human nature.
- PSYCHOLOGICAL: This type of horror plays with the reader's mind. Think *Dial M for Murder*. It is the helpless situation that evokes fear.

INSPIRATIONAL. Inspirational writing is meant to inspire readers into a new way of thinking, acting, or feeling. The goal is to teach the reader something positive about life and leave her feeling inspired by the end of the story. Some subcategories are:

- **RELIGIOUS:** This supports a particular faith and the teachings of that faith when inspiring others. Think *A Course in Miracles*.
- **SPIRITUAL:** This is a neutral support of a person's spirituality without the use of religious elements. Spirituality is an individual way of being and living without dogma. Think *Chicken Soup for the Soul*.
- **MOTIVATIONAL:** This motivates a reader without religious or spiritual elements; it just uses facts. Think *Personal Power* by Tony Robbins.

MUSICAL. Musicals are usually films and plays that use song and dance to convey significant parts of the story. This has yet to be explored by novelists but perhaps some metafictional authors will one day try this. (See section on Metafictional Structure in Part 2.)

Stuart Ostrow states, "The greatest question musical dramatists must answer is: Does the story I am telling sing? Is the subject sufficiently off the ground to compel the heightened emotion of bursting into song? Will a song add a deeper understanding of character or situation?"

MYSTERY. In a Mystery, a character needs to answer a question that solves something that is unknown—Where is the missing child? Who killed the CEO? Who stole the money? This Genre is heavy on the rewriting stage, as once the answer is found, you have to go back and make sure clues are planted. Some subcategories are:

- **HARD-BOILED:** These are gritty "noir" stories with grim details and tough, hard-nosed detectives.
- **COZY:** Country houses and villages, with peaceful and genteel exteriors, are usually the setting. There is minimal violence and everything is nicely wrapped up by the conclusion.
- **POLICE:** The protagonist is usually on the police force and the crime is solved by using the forces' resources and procedures.
- **DETECTIVE:** The protagonist is usually a licensed private investigator or ex-cop who works alone or with a larger agency.
- **AMATEUR DETECTIVE:** Nosy neighbors and inquisitive civilians get involved in an Amateur Detective story. Sometimes they are meddlers.

SUSPENSE/THRILLERS. Thrillers contain intense excitement and anticipation. The audience is left in the dark most of the time, figuring things out as the characters do. Who is just around the corner? Will the hero get caught? Who is lying? Will the car keep running long enough for the hero to make it home?

GOTHIC. These are stories of the macabre that invoke terror. Gothic stories feature terrifying experiences in ancient locations such as castles, crypts, and dungeons.

Gothic tales have tended to examine gender roles. In many Gothic stories there are very powerful male characters (such as Dracula) that "liberate" female characters, taking them out of the domestic sphere. In other Gothic tales the female lead has to deal with a very dangerous, alpha-male type of character. Contemporary Gothic tales place the female character in a more powerful role.

POLITICAL. Also considered social writing, political stories make a statement regarding social or political views or ways of being. The primary focus of the work supports a social or political view or critiques it. There is an element of exploration within them, as the writer is not trying to force-feed the reader an agenda. Herman Melville, Jack London, Norman Mailer, Ralph Ellison, Toni Morrison, and Margaret Atwood have grappled with this type of Genre, balancing radicalism and art.

PERSUASIVE. This type of story is aimed at converting the reader to a certain belief or idea. All that does not support the belief or idea is discarded. Often these works are one-sided and do not have any element of exploration within them. If a certain type of person is disliked, the characters that represent that type are stereotypical and undeveloped.

ROMANCE. Romances deal with love and affairs of the heart. The characters are often passionate, with unfulfilled desires and dreams. Two characters meet, fall in love, and try to form a bond against all odds. Some subcategories are:

- CONTEMPORARY: Stories are set in the present day.
- FANTASY: Stories deal with supernatural themes.
- HISTORICAL: Stories take place during a specific time period with all the clothing, mores, and events of that period.
- INSPIRATIONAL: Stories inspire the reader and evoke hope for love.
- REGENCY: Monarchs, rulers, and kings abound.
- ROMANTIC SUSPENSE: Elements of suspense drive the romance forward.
- TIME TRAVEL: One character travels across time to meet the other one.
- PARANORMAL: One character lives in regular reality while the other character has paranormal abilities of some sort.
- RELIGIOUS: The love story is governed by religious rules and customs.
- MULTICULTURAL: Characters of different cultures are brought together, or characters from a nondominant culture are explored in depth.

SCIENCE FICTION. Science Fiction stories are based on new or futuristic technological or biological advancements. Inventions abound, whether it's a new type of law, as in *Minority Report*, or a new way to travel through space. This Genre has the most fun with the "What if?" question writers love to ask. Anything is possible here. It just has to be made believable or at least probable. Set up the rules of the world you are creating and stick to them. Some subcategories are:

- **SUPERNATURAL:** Stories include gods/goddesses, ghosts, miracles, aliens, vampires, monsters, demons, psychics, angels, fairies, unusual powers and abilities.
- **REALISTIC:** Stories take normal everyday situations and twist them into a shocking conclusion.

WESTERN. Westerns come mainly from American writers and the American film industry. They involve settings in the Wild West, with a feeling of the open range. Westerns have themes of honor, redemption, revenge, and finding one's identity or place in life.

Questions to Consider When Choosing Genres:

- What Genres do you enjoy reading?
- Will you try writing in different Genres once you are familiar with one?
- Are there any Genres you don't like? Why?
- Are there other Genres not covered here that you would like to write about? (Look up information on the on the Internet at www.dogpile.com, a great resource for writers.)
- Will you combine Genres once you have a story or two under your belt?

Part 2

BUILDING
THE
STRUCTURE

How to Use the 11 Master Structures

> "A narrative is like a room on whose walls a number of false doors have been painted; while within the narrative, we have many apparent choices of exit, but when the author leads us to one particular door, we know it is the right one because it opens."
>
> –JOHN UPDIKE

Now that you know your Dramatic Throughline, Conflict, and Genre, you need to decide what type of Structure you want to use for your story.

In the following chapters the 11 Master Structures are outlined and explained with corresponding story development and examples as well as compared to Traditional Structure.

First I will outline the Traditional Structure model. Then as you read each of the corresponding chapters on Structure, you will see how they deviate from this traditional model. Once you understand how Traditional Structure works, you can then break that model to create any number of creative storylines that will help you stand out from the rest of the writers out there.

Traditional Structure

Traditional Structure has a clear beginning, middle, and end that happen in a clear three-act sequence. Act I is the Setup, Act II is the Development, and Act III is the Climax and Resolution. There is usually a Turning Point at the end of Act I and Act II to propel the story forward:

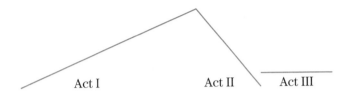

Act I   Act II   Act III

ACT I TRADITIONAL ELEMENTS

➤ **Setup:** The setup gives us the direction of the story. It gives all the information needed to get the story rolling as well as defining the story Genre and pacing. For example, if you are writing a comedy, try to work comedy into the Setup to set the stage for the rest of the story. (Mood and Hook below are part of the Setup in Traditional Structure but may not be in other types of Structure, which is why I have separated them.)

➤ **Mood or Tone:** According to Dr. Linda Seger of *Making a Good Script Great*, "In most great films the setup begins with an image. We see a visualization that gives us a strong sense of the place, mood, texture, and sometimes the theme. The first image could be a space battle (*Star Wars*), street gangs in New York (*West Side Story*), a woman singing in the mountains (*The Sound of Music*), or statues of lions that ominously guard a haunted library (*Ghostbusters*)."

Of course, this is easy enough for screenwriters, but what about novelists? Novelists can find a way to dramatize this in the Setup by paying close attention to setting, place, and character details. Take a look at the opening chapter of any Stephen King novel to see how he does this. If the story is a mystery about a young girl solving a murder case, can she be somewhere that signifies murder or death? Can we first meet her in a cemetery to set the mood?

➤ **Hook, Catalyst, or Inciting Incident:** This is a dynamic event that draws the reader into the story. The main goal or problem may not be stated just yet, but something happens that peaks interest. It can be an Action (someone is murdered), Dialogue (a character receives a mysterious phone call), or Situation (a character is thrust into a circumstance she may not be able to handle).

➤ **Serious Problem and/or Goal:** Why do we care? What is at stake? The problem or goal only has to be important to the main character. We may not think learning to drive is a big deal, for example, but if the main character is a paraplegic we will feel it is a big deal for him, especially if he has a strong reason to learn. Maybe he will lose custody of his children? Spend a lot of time on this because it is the element that will drive your whole story.

Don't be afraid to make things bad for your character, and always come up with several different Serious Problems and/or Goals to choose from. Ask yourself, "What is the worst thing that could happen to my character?" Maybe he will lose custody of his mother instead? Or he will be put into a home if he can't take care of himself properly. Or all of the above. Do a lot of research and you'll be amazed at how many ideas you come up with. After all, isn't there technology available to help a man like him drive?

➤ **Villain:** Who or what opposes the main character? Look over the chapter on Conflict for help. Somehow you need to introduce the Villain. You can show him in a brief scene that conveys his villainous behavior, you can have other characters talk about him foreshadowing his arrival, or you can infer that something bad is coming but is, as of yet, unknown.

➤ **Main Characters:** All of the Main Characters need to be introduced as soon as possible. It would be great to introduce all the supporting characters as well. Remember to keep your cast of characters to bare minimum. It's very difficult to follow more than four Main Characters at a time. And please don't have all their names start with the same letter—Danny, Donald, and Damon can get confusing. Combine several characters into one character when appropriate. Instead of having a lawyer and a chiropractor, have a lawyer/chiropractor. Or a lawyer who handles medical law.

➤ **Turning Point:** A Turning Point is like a cliffhanger—a moment where the story is taken in a new direction and we wonder what will happen next. A Turning Point may accomplish a variety of functions. Linda Seger says:

> It turns the actions around in a new direction, raises the central question/problem again, and makes us won-

der about the answer. It's often a moment of decision or commitment on the part of the main character.

ACT II TRADITIONAL ELEMENTS

➤ **Problem Intensifies:** The actions that drive the story forward are called Action Points, of which there are three types: Barrier, Complication, and Situation.

- Barriers occur when the character tries something and it doesn't work. The character must change directions or try another approach. Barriers stop the action for a moment as the character decides what to do. For example, the Main Character needs money but her mother won't lend it to her. What will she do? Maybe she'll accept the job as a bartender in a strip club even though her feminist sensibilities tell her not to.

- Complication is an action point that doesn't pay off immediately. It creates anticipation in the reader and builds suspense. For example, the hero is going about his business of catching a killer when all of a sudden the woman of his dreams walks into the room. His reaction to her tells us something will happen between them, but not just yet, and it may complicate things.

- Situation is when one of the Master Dramatic Situations (found in Part 3) happens to a character to move the story forward and add tension. It is usually brought on by another character that is integral to the Main Character's Serious Problem and/or Goal. The story may take a bit of a detour as the entire beginning, middle, and end of a Situation plays out all at once, or the Situation can be played out in pieces throughout the second act. For example, the Main Character finds out his sister was arrested for narcotics (Discovery of Dishonor of Loved One) and now his entire political campaign is in jeopardy.

➤ **Temporary Triumph:** The Main Character thinks she has achieved her goal (solved the crime, defeated the villain, or won the contest). But this Triumph is short-lived. A reversal is just around the corner. As we wait for it, the subplot may come in for a moment.

➤ **Reversal:** Now the Serious Problem and/or Goal worsens. The Triumph is no longer a true Triumph, and the Main Character's trials are not over by a long shot. In *Miss Congeniality* the FBI agents think they have captured the mad bomber so they leave, even though Sandra Bullock's character has her doubts. She finds out they caught the wrong guy and decides to stay behind alone.

The Reversal can happen several different ways. Some possibilities are:

- New information comes into play.
- A Dramatic Situation happens.
- Another character turns on the Main Character.
- Helpers and friends give up on the Main Character, leaving him alone.
- The meeting place or task the Main Character is going to achieve is changed at the last minute.
- What the Main Character thought was truth is now seen as lies.
- The Villain becomes the good guy and the good guy becomes the bad guy; perhaps your Main Character is after the wrong guy.

➤ **Dark Moment:** The Main Character fails or at least seems to. Think of action films where the hero has a confrontation with the Villain and barely gets out alive. The problem gets worse for the Main Character and his goal is pushed further out of reach. We wonder if he will ever succeed because it seems as if all is lost.

➤ **Turning Point:** This accomplishes the same things as the first Turning Point at the end of Act I. The one difference is that the Main Character is usually forced into making a decision that propels this Turning Point. This way he actively creates the events of the story. For example, in *The Wizard of Oz* Dorothy decides to pull back the curtain and in doing so exposes the Wizard as a fraud. Your Turning Point will be dependent on the type of Dramatic Throughline you are using in your story:

- If you are using the Character Succeeds Throughline, here is where the Main Character decides to keep going.
- If you are using the Character Is Defeated Throughline, here is where the Main Character's fate gets sealed. He makes the wrong decision.
- If you are using the Character Abandons Goal Throughline, here is where the Main Character gives up on the Goal—for better or for worse. Or she has been lied to and there is no Goal to chase after anymore, or so she thinks. Will she pick up a new Goal? In *The Wizard of Oz*, Dorothy's Goal was to meet the Wizard so she could go home. When she meets the Wizard she learns he is a fraud and her Goal seems destroyed, but her true Goal is not to just meet the Wizard; her true Goal is to go home. She can still find a way to do that if she picks herself up and decides to move forward.

ACT III TRADITIONAL ELEMENTS

➤ **Final Obstacle:** The Main Character is forced, through the momentum of the Turning Point, to face one last *huge* obstacle. This obstacle may test his faith, his resolve, his character, and his endurance. He is pushed to the limit not just physically (as is usually the case with comedy) but hopefully mentally and emotionally as well. Again, the final obstacle depends on the Throughline.

- If the Main Character is going to be successful, this is where he sets up the Villain to be destroyed. He may lie and lure the Villain out with deception. He may pretend to give up. He will do whatever it takes to ensure his future success.

- If the Main Character is going to be defeated, this is where he is set up for the Villain to come in and do away with him.

- If the Main Character is going to abandon his Goal, this is where he makes it known to everyone. Or this is where he tries to achieve a new Goal.

➤ **Climax:** The Main Character comes face-to-face with the Villain. The Problem is either resolved and the Goal is accomplished, or vice versa. This element is usually quick and fast paced.

➤ **Resolution:** All loose ends are tied up. All subplots are resolved and the Main Character reflects on the events of the story. Has he changed at all? How has the story affected him? What are his attitudes about the events he just went through? The theme can come out again here to show the moral to the story if applicable. Readers like to learn something even when they are being entertained.

The following eleven chapters each outline one of the Master Structures in depth, giving you alternatives to the Traditional Structure outlined in this chapter. Some of these eleven Structures challenge the Traditional Structure more than others, but all are presented in the context of how they deviate from the traditional model. Since most writers know Traditional Structure inside and out, it's best to use it as a reference point when working with other Structures.

The Roller Coaster Ride

FROM *INDEPENDENCE DAY*:

MARTY: A countdown ... wait, a countdown to what, David?

DAVID: Ah, it's like in chess ... first you strategically position your pieces, and then when the timing is right, you ... strike. See? They're positioning themselves all over the world, using this one signal to synchronize their efforts. In approximately six hours the signal's going to disappear and the countdown will be over.

MARTY: And then what?

DAVID: Checkmate!

MARTY: (Gasps in fear) Oh my God! Oh my God! I'd better call my brother! I'd better call my housekeeper! I've gotta call my lawyer! Ahh, forget my lawyer.

The Roller Coaster Ride is just that—a story that takes the audience on a ride of tension and suspense, never letting up on the gas.

Instead of having one major Climax at the end of the story, as with Traditional Structure, this structure has several Climaxes throughout the story. Each one builds upon the previous one, holding the reader in its thrall until the very end. Slowly the train climbs up the hill. It reaches the peak and then dives toward the ground where it starts uphill once again.

There is still a sense of a clear three-act beginning, middle, and end to it, but the acts themselves have their own mini acts:

Act I   Act II   Act III

This Structure is very plot driven. Just as a roller coaster moves people around the track—and not vice versa—the events of a Roller Coaster plot move the story forward—not the characters.

The characters are compelled to react to the events around them because failure to do so would mean disaster. They are at the mercy of the story events and have virtually no time to think things over. They can formulate plans of action but they are not able to stop the events from happening. They are only able to deal with events once they are already in motion. (They can't keep the Villain from planting a bomb, but they can try to stop it from going off.)

The Roller Coaster Ride Elements

ACT I TRADITIONAL ELEMENTS

- Setup
- Hook
- Serious Problem
- Main Characters
- Villain
- Turning Point

ACT I NEW ELEMENTS

➤ One of the major elements of the Roller Coaster Ride is what is known as the Ticking Clock. There is often a sense of urgency in this type of story structure to keep the story moving forward and the reader on the edge of her seat. For example, in one hour the bomb will go off, killing a lot of innocent children. Can the hero find the bomb before then?

➤ There is an Extremely Major Problem at Stake that is usually Life or Death. This story structure is very plot driven, with little time to explore the characters and their inner feelings when they are racing against the clock. So the problem has to be strong enough to carry the story forward and hold the reader's interest.

➤ Act I ends with a Mini Climax of its own and starts to build tension again.

➤ There is not much time for Mood and Theme to be presented, at least not in depth. Readers usually know going in that they are going to be taken on an action ride. Instead the Villain and his crazy way of thinking or acting can be shown to set up what he is capable of doing. Think of the movie *Speed*.

➤ All subplots are directly influenced by and connected to the main plot. Just as all supporting character stories are related to the main plot, all other subplots should also be related to the main plot. This is the best way to keep the tension moving. Think about *Jurassic Park*. Even the setup and introduction of characters relate to the events of the story. When we first meet the paleontologists they talk about the raptor's hunting strategies. This foreshadows the disaster to come when they meet a real raptor face-to-face.

➤ There may be several storylines going with different Supporting Characters. Again, these storylines all relate in some way to the main plot events. For example, if a bus filled with people is hijacked, the Supporting Characters will either have family and friends on the bus or they will be involved with rescuing those people somehow. We don't have time to learn about their hopes and dreams. To deviate from this by presenting a subplot entirely unrelated to the main plot would just slow the story down.

➤ All characters must be introduced in Act I so the plot can do its job and take off.

ACT I QUESTIONS

- How many Main Characters and Supporting Characters will you have in the story? Are they all introduced here?
- How will you introduce the Villain? What do you want the reader to know right away about the Villain? How will you show it?
- What does the Main Character want? How do the events of the plot cut short his true plans? (For example, in *Independence Day*, Will Smith just wants to be with his family and live a normal life. In fact, when he catches an alien, he yells that he should be "relaxing at a barbeque right now.")
- How soon will the time element come into play?
- How many Mini Climaxes will you have here? Are they all justified and organic to the story?

ACT II TRADITIONAL ELEMENTS

- Serious Problem Intensifies
- Temporary Triumph and Reversal (possibly)

- Dark Moment
- Turning Point (possibly)

ACT II NEW ELEMENTS

➤ There are several Mini Climaxes with beginnings, middles, and ends of their own. Perhaps the Main Character needs to rescue several people in different locations and each rescue is very dramatic on its own.

➤ The Villain may become larger than life, pulling out all his resources to stop the Main Character from ruining his plans—especially if he is desperate.

➤ If possible, the Stakes get bigger. The Main Character may think he is on the verge of reaching his goal only to find the goal has gotten farther away from him.

➤ Secondary Time Elements may come into play. If the bomb is going off in one hour, maybe the Main Character has five minutes to find the one woman who can disarm it before she gets on a plane to London.

ACT II QUESTIONS

- How many Mini Climaxes will you have? Are they too similar to Act I or Act III?
- How will the Stakes get higher?
- How can you use what the Main Character cares about against him?
- How far will the Villain need to be pushed to be villainous? Is there any redeeming quality about him? Why is he doing what he's doing?
- What kind of Secondary Time Element can you put in?

ACT III TRADITIONAL ELEMENTS

- Final Obstacle
- Climax
- Resolution

ACT III NEW ELEMENTS

➤ Another Mini Climax or two takes place, each with its own beginning, middle, and end. One or two Dark Moments can happen between each Climax, setting in motion the next Climax to follow.

➤ The Time Element intensifies. Perhaps the bomb diffuser made a mistake and now the bomb is going to go off in three minutes. Or the Villain got upset and changed the detonation time or some other rule of the game.

➤ Subplots resolve themselves quickly or get all tied up with the final Climax. As the Main Character reaches his goal, everything else falls into place.

ACT III QUESTIONS

- Will you have several Mini Climaxes here? Or just one big one? Why?
- Should the Time Element intensify? Will it enhance the plot? Will it make things harder on the Main Character?
- How has the Main Character's life changed from this story? Is his true Goal the same? Have his priorities changed in any way? (For example, in *Independence Day*, Will Smith decides to propose to his girlfriend because family has become the most important thing to him and he realizes life is too short to play around.)
- Will you leave any loose ends untied to foreshadow a sequel?

EXAMPLES

Jurassic Park, MICHAEL CRICHTON

Scientists clone dinosaurs to populate a theme park that suffers a major security breakdown, releasing the dinosaurs to wreak havoc.

Independence Day, ROLAND EMMERICH

Aliens come to Earth and their Goal is to invade and destroy. Fighting superior technology, a group of men try to figure out how to save Earth as the countdown to invasion begins.

Speed, JAN DE BONT

A young cop must save the passengers of a bus that has a bomb set to explode if the bus goes below fifty miles per hour.

The Replay

FROM *RASHOMON*:

PRIEST: If men don't trust each other, this earth might as well be hell.

COMMONER: Right. The world's a kind of hell.

PRIEST: No! I don't want to believe that!

COMMONER: No one will hear you, no matter how loud you shout. Just think. Which one of these stories do you believe?

WOODCUTTER: None makes any sense.

COMMONER: Don't worry about it. It isn't as if men were reasonable.

The Replay is defined as having two to three versions of events in one story. These versions may come from the point of view of one character over and over again as in *Run Lola Run* and *Groundhog Day*, where one character lives out the events in her life several times, or from several characters, one after the other as in *He Said, She Said* and *Rashomon* where there are two to three characters who relate their version of the same story.

The Character Is Defeated Throughline is hard to pull off here because it would call for the character being defeated in every version of the story that is shown. Of course it can be done, but the reader usually wants to see the character prevail at some point in this type of story, even if she abandons her Goal in the end. We would all love to be given a second chance to do things differently because we believe we would be successful at it the second (or third) time around.

Replay Structure

There is still a sense of a clear three-act beginning, middle, and end to the Replay:

Act I   Act II   Act III

Replay structure can be either plot driven or character driven. In the plot-driven type, the plot is the main focus of the story. In each version of the story the plot changes and the characters react to those changes. In *Rashomon* the three characters accused of a crime, and their accusers, all react to the different versions of the crime that are given as testimony by each of the accused.

In the character-driven type, the character is the main focus of the story. In each version, the story remains the same but the character changes his approach to the events. In *Groundhog Day*, Bill Murray relives the same day over and over again until he learns his lessons and changes his behavior. No one else knows the day repeated itself.

The Replay Elements

ACT I TRADITIONAL ELEMENTS

- Setup
- Mood or Tone
- Hook
- Problem
- Main Characters

ACT I NEW ELEMENTS

➤ The Time Merge is set up. Somehow the reader knows several different versions of a story are going to be presented. In film, this can be done by fading-out and fading-in, color washing, or other visual techniques. In novels, this can be done with any type of page break to show that a division in time has taken place. You can be as creative as needed to get the message across to the reader. If you are presenting versions of the events from different characters, then it is as if each character steps forward to tell her version of the story, one after the other. Either way, this breaking of linear time usually happens right away or at least by the end of the first representation of the story, which is usually at the end of Act I. It all depends at which point you want to clue the reader in as to what is going on.

➤ All characters must be introduced here to keep coherence. Since the story will be presented several times, the reader needs to know who the players are and why they are there. This way the reader can see how they change within each version presented.

➤ There must be a strong focus within the story being presented so it is easy to see where a character deviates from her previous actions. In a plot-driven story, show what makes the different version different. In a character-driven story, show why the character needs to change as he repeats the story over and over again.

➤ Act I should end with a Reversal: "We are now going to see the story again." In a plot-driven story, a new character comes forward to tell her version of the story. In a character-driven story, the character is taken back to the beginning of the story to relive the events

➤ There may or may not be a Villain in this type of story. If the Main Character is living the same events over and over again, he could be his own worst enemy, which is why he needs to learn some lessons and change his ways.

ACT I QUESTIONS

- Does the Main Character know right away that the events are repeating?
- Will this be plot or character driven? Why?
- Can you add anything to make the versions more dramatic or distinctive?
- Are there any characters you can't introduce right away?
- Will there be a Villain?

ACT II TRADITIONAL ELEMENTS

- Problem Intensifies: If the story is plot driven, the Problem Intensifies according to the reason it is important to find out which version of events is the truth. Is a criminal facing death row? If the story is character driven, the Problem Intensifies according to the reason why it is important for the character to get out of the replaying of events.

- Temporary Triumph: For a moment it seems as if the new story version is more successful or truthful than the first one seen.

- Reversal: We are going to see this story again because we still have doubts and questions.

ACT II NEW ELEMENTS

➤ The new story version raises questions. Is this version more successful or more truthful than the version just presented? What has changed? Which version should be believed? Has the Main Character's goal changed?

➤ Supporting Characters don't change or go through an arc in this structure as they may with Traditional Structure. If the story is plot driven, as in the case of *Rashomon*, they change only according to the opinions of whoever is telling the current version of the story. If the story is character driven, as in the case of *Run Lola Run*, we learn more about some of the Supporting Characters if the Main Character chooses to do things differently and gets a chance to see more of these characters' lives. For example, in one version Lola decides to wait longer at a bank, which leads to her learning about her father's adulterous affair. Her father hasn't changed; we have just seen more of his life.

ACT II QUESTIONS

- Will the Problem Intensify? Why does the Main Character need to get out of this Replay of events?

- Do we learn more about the Supporting Characters? Why? Does it enhance the story? Or set up the next version to come?

- Will you Replay the events more than once in this act? If so, what are you trying to show?

- What questions are being raised here that you will answer in the final version to come?

- Has the Main Character changed at all?

ACT III TRADITIONAL ELEMENTS

- Final Obstacle: This is the final version of the story. If it is plot driven, will the truth be revealed? If it is character driven, will the Main Character make the right decision this time?

- Climax

- Resolution: Loose ends are tied up, though possibly some have just been done away with as the final story version may omit them altogether.

ACT III NEW ELEMENTS

➤ For the first time the Main Character does something different or sees things differently. The cycle of repetition is broken.

➤ The Main Character may abandon the Goal easily here as is the case when searching for the truth, like *Rashomon*, because there just may be no definitive answer. In this case there is usually a larger question answered or explored, possibly about what truth itself is. This is where the theme will come out.

➤ The Resolution leaves the reader wondering about the previous events and where the character will go next.

➤ The Climax occurs as the Main Character decides to do something differently or change how she sees things. Things really heat up because the reader wants her to succeed this time. Perhaps the reader knows exactly what she must do to succeed and waits for her to figure it out.

ACT III QUESTIONS

- Is it clear that the Main Character is out of the Replay of events in the end? Or will you leave some question in the reader's mind?
- How will you make this version more dramatic than the previous ones?
- Will you show the reader what happens after the Main Character is out of the Replay? Does she continue with her life?
- What has the Main Character, or the reader for that matter, learned from seeing this story over and over again?

EXAMPLES

Rashomon, AKIRA KUROSAWA

A heinous crime and its aftermath are recalled from differing points of view.

Groundhog Day, HAROLD RAMIS

A weatherman is reluctantly sent to cover a story about a weather-forecasting groundhog. This is his fourth year on the story, and he makes no effort to hide his frustration. When he awakens the "following" day he discovers that it's the same day over and over again.

Run Lola Run, TOM TYKWER

Lola must run to save her boyfriend's life. Her first attempt ends in failure and she repeats the same events, making different decisions, two more times.

Fate

FROM MILDRED PIERCE

At a beach house at night a gun fires six times in rhythmic tempo, killing owner Monte Beragon.

The murderer is unseen.

The bullets shatter a mirror behind the victim. The victim lurches forward, slumps over, and falls to the floor in front of a flickering fire; the gun is tossed in front of the body. The dying man's only word: "Mildred!"

After being questioned by police, Mildred recalls the unfolding events that led to the breakup of her first marriage and to the murder in a flashback.

In the Fate structure, the Climax takes place at the beginning of the story as well as at the end. What follows from this Opening Climax is a flashback, or two, of events that led to the Climax just seen. Following the Final Climax is the Resolution, which is what the reader has been waiting for. "What happened to the character after the Climax?" is the real question that keeps the reader reading.

In this structure the hero cannot escape the climatic event—it is her Fate. There is nothing she can do differently and the events must be related as they exactly happened. The Resolution may have twists and turns or surprises for the audience, but the flashback must stick to the facts and events as they happened. Otherwise you are writing a Replay story where several characters tell their version of what happened. You can combine Replay and Fate in this way, but Replay will become the dominating structure. A twist in the Resolution may be that that the worst of the danger is averted. Perhaps the victim was wearing a bulletproof vest and survived the shooting in the Climax.

The Character Is Defeated Throughline works very well here. Think of the film noir type of stories—*The Postman Always Rings Twice* and *Double Indemnity*. A character is defeated in the opening scene and we see his panic and despair as he starts the flashback by relating how he got into this mess.

There can be a tragic/positive storyline such as "Look at what

happened to my friend who just died." Then there is a flashback
the Main Character's life with this friend where we learn in the R
olution that the Main Character is okay with his friend's death and
grateful for their time together.

As you can see, the Fate type of story can easily have first-person
narration as the hero tells us what has *already* happened to him.
For example, *Forrest Gump* opens with a feather wafting through
blue sky to land at Forrest's feet. He's sitting at a bus stop and proceeds to tell anyone who happens by about his remarkable life. This
story combines Fate structure with mini stories strung together like
a series of episodes.

Fate Structure

There is still a sense of a clear three-act beginning, middle, and end
to Fate, even though it opens with the Climax:

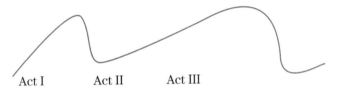

Act I   Act II   Act III

This structure is both plot and character driven. The plot pushes
the character into a harsh situation where the character in turn has
to make choices. Both work together to propel the story forward. The
Main Character reacts to events within the story but she also acts to
create events of her own.

Fate Elements

ACT I TRADITIONAL ELEMENTS

- Setup: This comes from the Final Climax being presented, setting up
  what will happen in the flashback.
- Mood or Tone
- Hook, Catalyst, or Inciting Incident: This comes from wondering how
  the Main Character got to the point of the Climax or from wondering
  what will happen to the him after the Climax.
- Serious Problem and/or Goal
- Villain: This may be the hero, or antihero. This is common in this struc-
  ture, as the hero has often done something wrong in the opening Climax.
- Main Characters: All of them should be introduced here.
- Turning Point

ACT I NEW ELEMENTS

➤ The story opens with the Final Climax. The Main Character may be defeated, killed, or arrested, or he may barely get away from danger by the skin of his teeth. He may be nostalgic and just have the desire within him to tell his story even if it isn't tragic. There needs to be some sort of psychological component here to make it interesting.

  After all, Fate wouldn't work very well if it were an action film where Sylvester Stallone kills some meaningless bad guy in the opening climatic scene. Who would sit and watch the entire movie after the fact? Now if the man he kills was his father or he was sitting on death row for murder because of it, then it would be interesting.

➤ Once the Final Climax is shown, the story begins with introducing all Main Characters.

➤ Besides plot and character to drive the story forward, there is always the sense of Fate driving the story and Main Character to a specific ending. We know the Main Character should make different choices along the way, but we also know there is no way she can.

➤ The Final Climax may set up the hero as an antihero if we know he has done something terribly wrong but we want to root for him anyway. Perhaps he robbed a bank or stole from his family.

➤ Sometimes the tragedy of the situation is magnified if we see the hero or other characters within the main story getting a chance, however small, to make a different choice or accept help from someone who is available and willing.

ACT I QUESTIONS

• Will this be an antihero story? If so, how bad will the hero be?

• Will you have first-person narration? Or tell the story in third person after the beginning Climax?

• How many characters are involved?

• What is your purpose in telling this story? Is there a theme you are examining if writing about unscrupulous characters? (Unscrupulous characters, if used, usually stand for society as a whole or for what society does to an individual to drive him to such behavior. Of course these characters could have dealt with things in a more positive way, so don't forget to state why they didn't.)

ACT II TRADITIONAL ELEMENTS

- Problem Intensifies
- Temporary Triumph: This is optional but used to keep the character going down the road she is going. If she is destructive, she thinks she'll get away with it, so why not keep forging ahead?
- Reversal: This is used if there was a Temporary Triumph.

ACT II NEW ELEMENTS

➤ The Main Character moves along, getting herself in deeper and deeper. If she's destructive, she may trust the wrong people and make bad decisions. If she isn't destructive, she may find herself more emotional about the events in the story she is telling, or she may see the story in a new light as she recounts it.

➤ Things happen to make us like the Main Character a little. No character is ever totally evil; there should always be at least one endearing quality about her.

➤ Act II is all about getting to the end and showing the reader how it all came to be. Don't be afraid to make it interesting.

ACT II QUESTIONS

- Will you have a Temporary Triumph? Why? Make the Reversal believable?
- Will you explore the psyche of the Main Character? Show us more about her and how she got into this mess?
- How do other characters feel about the Main Character?
- What motivates the Main Character to keep going? Is he greedy? Does she want to pay respects to someone who has passed on through telling their story?

ACT III TRADITIONAL ELEMENTS

- Final Obstacle: This is the moment the reader has been waiting for. What is the Final Obstacle that leads to the Opening Climax?
- Climax
- Resolution

ACT III NEW ELEMENTS

➤ The Main Character is thrust into a Final Obstacle. This is the big scene that leads to the Opening Climax. Everything is explained and all loose ends are tied up here instead of being tied up in the Resolution. We know who, what, when, where, why, and how. Now we wait to see the Climax again so we can see what the Resolution will bring.

➤ The driving force behind the Main Character is revealed. She spills the beans and may try to defend herself against the "law." She may even try to charm her way out of punishment.

➤ The Resolution is our first moment in real time since the film began. The narration is over and the Climax is completed. What will happen to the Main Character now if she is still alive? Many noir films show the hero being driven off in a police car.

ACT III QUESTIONS

- How will you show the Final Obstacle? How many characters will be involved?
- Do unscrupulous characters get away with it in the end?
- Do sympathetic characters find the closure they may be looking for? (Think *Forrest Gump*.)
- If destructive, is the Main Character sorry for her actions? Or still trying to get away with it? (Think film noir.)
- How did the story affect the other characters? Does anyone feel vindicated?
- What is the theme or message here if you have one?

EXAMPLES

Double Indemnity, JAMES M. CAIN

The story opens as Walter arrives at his office in the middle of the night to deliver his confession for killing a man "for money and for a woman" into a dictating machine.

Mildred Pierce, JAMES M. CAIN

A mother feels guilty for raising a destructive daughter and tries to protect her at all costs. The opening scene shows a murder where the mother is implicated. The present-day voiceover tells us she is being held by the police.

Forrest Gump, ROBERT ZEMECKIS

Forrest sits at a bus stop, talking to strangers who pass by about the events of his life and his love, Jenny. He starts at the beginning and when he reaches the present moment of him sitting on the bench, the story proceeds in real time towards his ultimate goal.

The Parallel

FROM *THE LORD OF THE RINGS*:

GANDALF: The veiling shadow that glowers in the East takes shape. Sauron will suffer no rival. From the summit of Barad-dur his eye watches ceaselessly. But he is not so mighty yet that he is above fear. Doubt ever gnaws at him. The rumor has reached him. The heir of Numenor still lives. Sauron fears you, Aragorn. He fears what you may become. And so he will strike hard and fast at the world of Men. He will use his puppet Saruman to destroy Rohan.

War is coming. Rohan must defend itself, and therein lies our first challenge, for Rohan is weak and ready to fall. The King's mind is enslaved, it's an old device of Saruman's. His hold over King Theoden is now very strong. Sauron and Saruman are tightening the noose. But, for all their cunning, we have one advantage. The Ring remains hidden. And that we should seek to destroy it has not yet entered their darkest dreams.

And so the weapon of the Enemy is moving towards Mordor in the hands of a Hobbit. Each day brings it closer to the fires of Mount Doom. We must trust now in Frodo. Everything depends now upon speed and upon the secrecy of his quest. Do not regret your decision to leave him. Frodo must finish this task alone.

ARAGORN: He's not alone. Sam went with him.

GANDALF: Did he? Did he indeed? Good. Yes, very good.

The Parallel plot structure is defined as having two or more stories going on at the same point in time. They are not flashbacks or subplots but two distinctly different plots with a complete beginning, middle, and end all their own. The Parallel plot is a simultaneous multi-plotted story that eventually intersects all plots presented.

Parallel Structure

There is still a sense of a clear three-act beginning, middle, and end to the Parallel structure:

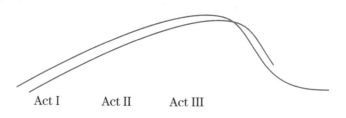

Act I   Act II   Act III

This structure can be either plot driven or character driven. With character-driven pieces, the Main Character can even be living two lives at the same time, as is the case with the film *Sliding Doors*. The Main Character is at the point of making a decision as she gets off a train, and the film splits into two stories showing us how her life would have been different if she stays with her current boyfriend (plot one) or if she leaves him (plot two).

Plot-driven pieces can do the same thing if a character's actions or decisions are influenced by whether or not a taxicab is on time, for example. In any case, with this type of Parallel plot, the character may wind up in the same place regardless of choices or of external circumstances—as if the ending is fated no matter what decisions the character makes. Or one decision can be shown to be the better one depending on your theme and the point you want to make to your reader.

You may also present one whole story in one plot and an entirely different story in another. Toward the end they will intersect somehow, each affecting the other. The characters may even know each other. They may be fighting for the same Goal. Think of *The Lord of the Rings: The Two Towers*. While Tolkien wrote the two storylines presented in the film as two separate volumes, they were still two parallel storylines. There were several intersecting events, such as weather problems and battles taking place, and in the large gaps of time when the stories didn't intersect, characters from one storyline wondered about the characters in another storyline.

Think of Kramer in *Seinfeld* buying a strongbox for his valuables in one plotline and Jerry trying to impress Jerry Lewis in another plotline by wearing special cufflinks to a big dinner event. Toward the end of this episode Jerry can't find his cufflinks for his big evening. Kramer tells him he put the cufflinks into his strongbox for safekeeping. Kramer then says he has lost the key to the strongbox, which he hid in a bird's cage. It turns out the bird ate the key and died, and now they have to go dig up the dead bird to get the key. Jerry's evening is ruined to say the least. It seemed as if the two plots were in no way related, but in the end things all came full circle.

The Parallel Elements

ACT I TRADITIONAL ELEMENTS

- Setup: The setup here needs to set up two stories instead of one.
- Mood or Tone
- Hook, Catalyst, or Inciting Incident
- Serious Problem and/or Goal
- Villain
- Main Characters: all of them introduced here
- Turning Point

ACT I NEW ELEMENTS

➤ All of the traditional elements must work for two stories. Both storylines need to be set up and given a Hook or Inciting Incident. All Main Characters for both stories need to be introduced. You can do this by coming up with an Inciting Incident that involves all the characters for plot-driven stories or through asking a dramatic question in character-driven stories.

➤ It's easiest for the reader to follow both storylines if all the Main Characters are introduced right away and if there are few of them to follow.

➤ Both storylines may intersect in the very beginning, but by the end of the Hook or Inciting Incident they are completely separated.

➤ It is best to have separate storylines that are traditional in nature. You risk confusing your reader if you try to use the Fate or Replay structures, for example. There already are two plots to follow, after all.

➤ The Turning Points can happen at the same time, with the same Inciting Incident affecting both storylines, or they can happen spread apart, showing one Turning Point in its entirety and then later showing the other one.

ACT I QUESTIONS

- Will you use the same Main Character in both storylines showing the different decisions she could make?

- Will both storylines start out intersected in the beginning?
- If you are not using the same Main Character in both storylines, what ties the two storylines together? What is the common element?
- Can you limit your number of characters?

ACT II TRADITIONAL ELEMENTS

- Problem Intensifies
- Temporary Triumph
- Reversal
- Dark Moment
- Turning Point

ACT II NEW ELEMENTS

➤ Act II is all about each storyline moving along separately. They may intersect for a moment during the Temporary Triumph, or perhaps both storylines are just very similar at the moment each seems successful. But they do separate again. In *Sliding Doors* the Main Character is successful in both storylines for a brief period.

➤ The Turning Points can happen at the same time, with the same Inciting Incident affecting both storylines, or not. Or they can happen spread apart, showing one Turning Point in its entirety and later showing the second Turning Point.

ACT II QUESTIONS

- Will you have the storylines intersect at all in Act II? Why? How will they separate again?
- Will you use a Temporary Triumph and Reversal?
- Are both storylines equally dramatic, or does one slow down a bit to give the reader a break in tension?
- Will any characters cross over from one storyline into the other?
- Do the characters in one storyline know about the characters in the other storyline? Are they adversaries?
- Does one storyline take place in another world?
- What do both storylines have in common? Do they share a common theme?

ACT III TRADITIONAL ELEMENTS

- Final Obstacle
- Climax
- Resolution

ACT III NEW ELEMENTS

➤ In Act III both storylines have a separate Final Obstacle that relates to each storyline. Following that is the Climax, where both storylines intersect and move toward the Resolution.

➤ Both storylines should have had something in common all along. It is this common element that brings them together now. Otherwise, why write a parallel story at all? Just write two different stories if these have nothing to do with one another.

➤ Two endings may be needed. In *Sliding Doors*, the Main Character is brought to a hospital in both storylines: In one she dies, and in the other she lives a happy life.

ACT III QUESTIONS

- How will you intersect the two storylines? Do you need to go back and flesh out the common element more?

- What do the characters learn from the intersection?

- Do you still feel this structure is the best way to tell the story?

- Should you have the two stories intersect in Act II if you did not? Will this help you set up the intersection here?

- Is there a character or two who knows both storylines? Can they help bridge the two together in the end? (This is not appropriate with character-decision stories like *Sliding Doors* because we are seeing two sides to one decision with the same characters in each storyline.)

EXAMPLES

Sliding Doors, PETER HOWITT

A London woman's love life and career both hinge on whether or not she catches a train. We see what happens if she catches the train and what happens if she misses it, in parallel.

The Best Years of Our Lives, WILLIAM WYLER

Three World War II veterans share a cab while returning home to small-town America. They each get dropped off at their houses and we follow their individual life stories as they discover their family lives have been irreparably changed.

The Lord of the Rings: The Two Towers,
PETER JACKSON (novel by J.R.R. Tolkien)

Frodo and Sam continue on to Mordor in their mission to destroy the Ring while their companions launch an assault on Isengard. Both plotlines support each other and all the characters know about each other.

The Episodic

FROM *ORLANDO*:

QUEEN ELIZABETH I:[conferring the family estate upon Orlando] For you and for your heirs, Orlando—the house.

ORLANDO: Your Majesty, I am forever …

QUEEN ELIZABETH I: But on one condition. Do not fade. Do not wither. Do not grow old.

***

NARRATOR: She's lived for 400 years and hardly aged a day but, because this is England, everyone pretends not to notice.

The Episodic plot structure is made up of a series of chapters or stories linked together by the same character, place, or theme but held apart by their individual plot, purpose, and subtext. In fact, the chapters or stories could be shuffled around and placed in a different order if desired because there is no overall beginning, middle, and end to the book or story as a whole.

In some cases there may be a sense of time passing throughout the episodes, as if the character is growing or changing through each successive chapter or story. Or perhaps the years are passing by for a character or place and we see the "seasons of change" in the background of the main plot.

The book also could be like the *Chicken Soup for the Soul* series. These books have an overall theme to them, yet each chapter has a different story to illustrate that theme.

Episodic Structure

There is only a clear three-act beginning, middle, and end in each of the individual chapters or stories of an Episodic piece:

This structure can be either plot driven or character driven. Keep in mind that a "place" can be considered a character if it is the central figure in each episode.

If the story is character driven, you will most likely have at least one character showing up in every episode, using this character as the driving force in each story.

If the story is plot driven, you will see a similar character, place, or theme in each chapter or story, but the driving force will be the events within each.

TELEVISION AND COMICS

Television sitcoms have an Episodic structure, and although they are comedic and may lack a coherent theme or message, each sitcom episode stands on its own. Some of the jokes require you to know a lot about the characters from previous episodes and the Main Character's goal is often developed over time, but overall each episode can stand alone as an individual story.

Comic books fall into this category. Think of the *Wonder Woman* and *Spider-Man* comics. There are numerous episodes for each that stand on their own as individual stories.

The Episodic Elements

ACT I TRADITIONAL ELEMENTS PER EPISODE

- Setup
- Mood or Tone
- Hook, Catalyst, or Inciting Incident
- Main Characters: all of them introduced here

ACT I NEW ELEMENTS PER EPISODE

➤ While each episode is a mini story of its own, it is usually shorter in length than most stories or novels. For this reason several traditional steps may be missing: Serious Problem and/or Goal, Villain, and Turning Point. You can have all of these if you wish, but decide beforehand how long you want each episode to be. All together the episodes should make up the page count of one traditional novel.

➤ The Villain can also be more abstract here due to the shorter length of story. For example, society as a whole can be the Villain, and the sexist or racist problem the hero faces is his obstacle.

- In the case of writing a comic book, the Villain can also be carried over from episode to episode.
- The theme can drive the story forward as in an exploration or observational story.

ACT I QUESTIONS

- Why have you chosen this structure?
- Will your stories be character or plot driven? Will place or theme take a significant role?
- Will you have a Turning Point in each episode?
- Will you spend time building a Villain?
- How serious will the Main Problem and/or Goal be? Is it universal?

ACT II TRADITIONAL ELEMENTS PER EPISODE

- Problem Intensifies
- Dark Moment
- Turning Point

ACT II NEW ELEMENTS PER EPISODE

- Just as there may not be room for the Serious Problem and/or Goal, the Villain, and Turning Point in Act I, there may not be room for a Temporary Triumph and Reversal in Act II. The story itself should be so interesting on its own that these steps won't enhance it much and may even come across as being contrived if there is not enough page space to set them up properly.
- Subplots are not typically explored in this structure, but there may be a scene sequence which is a series of scenes, one right after the other, with their own mini beginning, middle, and end. For example, *Spider-Man* goes home to talk to his family and faces tragedy. We don't cut back and forth between his family tragedy and the main storyline; instead, we see the tragic mini storyline in its entirety.

ACT II QUESTIONS

- Will you use a scene sequence to possibly develop the Main Character's backstory or advance the plot?
- Will the Villain be prominent in this Act?
- Will any new characters be introduced?
- What theme will you develop?

- How will you set things up for the Climax?
- Will you use a Turning Point at the end of Act II?

ACT III TRADITIONAL ELEMENTS PER EPISODE

- Final Obstacle
- Climax
- Resolution

ACT III NEW ELEMENTS PER EPISODE

➤ Many times with dramatic episodic pieces, the Resolution is open-ended. The story may continue on, a question is left unanswered for the reader to ponder, or the theme requires it, as is the case with a theme that deals with racism. There is just no way to completely resolve such a huge problem or societal conflict.

➤ Act III may be quick, requiring the least amount of page space. For example, in sitcoms the audience isn't as concerned with how the Main Character will fix things after he is caught doing something wrong or after he messes everything up. The audience wants to see how far the Main Character will go to cover his tracks or how the other characters will react to what he has done when they find out.

When Jerry Seinfeld is caught digging up his neighbor's dead bird to find the key to Kramer's strongbox, that's all we need to see and the episode ends with a one-page resolution that really doesn't resolve anything. Jerry says he'll have to use the fire escape to get in and out of the building to avoid the neighbor, and that's it. We don't care if he makes up with his neighbor or if he feels bad about what happened. We just want to see Jerry get into trouble and then get caught red-handed.

➤ In comics or short horror trilogies (see *Trilogy of Terror*), there may be a false ending where the reader thinks everything is over but the Villain comes back for one more confrontation.

ACT III QUESTIONS

- How will you get your theme across to the reader in the end?
- How strong will the Villain be?
- Will things tie up neatly or be left open-ended?
- How does this story fit with the remaining stories?

EXAMPLES

Orlando, VIRGINIA WOOLF

Young nobleman Orlando is commanded by Queen Elizabeth I to stay forever young. Miraculously, he does just that. The story follows him as he moves through several centuries of British history, experiencing different ways of living and even changing sex.

Any Small Goodness: A Novel of the Barrio, TONY JOHNSTON

Set in East Los Angeles, this novel shows the daily life of an extended Mexican-American family in a series of vignettes.

Buffy the Vampire Slayer, JOSS WHEDON

This television series has Episodic plots that show character development throughout the seasons. Buffy grows and changes as the overall Episodic story continues each week.

The Melodrama

FROM *REBEL WITHOUT A CAUSE*:

JIM STARK: If I had one day when I didn't have to be all confused and I didn't have to feel that I was ashamed of everything. If I felt that I belonged someplace.

JUDY: All my life, I've been—I've been waiting for someone to love me, and now I love someone. And it's so easy. Why is it so easy now?

JIM: I don't know; it is for me, too.

JUDY: I love you, Jim. I really mean it.

JIM: Well, I mean it …

The Melodrama plot structure is sometimes referred to as "women's fiction," as soap operas and television movies fall into this category, but this is not entirely accurate.

While both women's fiction and Melodrama primarily focus on women's lives, relationships, family, and the female point of view and are emotionally engaging, they differ in that women's fiction also encompasses books such as *Bridget Jones's Diary*, which is not considered Melodrama at all and has a fairly traditional plot structure to it.

Melodrama is at its core just that—melodramatic. In fact there are two types of Melodrama—the Female Melodrama and the Male Melodrama. This is why Melodrama is not just considered women's fiction.

The Two Types

Female Melodrama differs from women's fiction in that it is always centered on tragedy, usually involving family relationships; it is sometimes open-ended and goes over-the-top in emotionality and sentiment as it primarily focuses on a Victim.

The male characters are brought into the female domestic space where they must learn to value domestic life. The Female Melodrama is left unresolved in the end. It is the process of and behavior within the narrative that brings pleasure to the reader or viewer, as the female character will usually lose out in the end. Patriarchal culture usually has no place for her outside of the standard female role and domestic sphere.

Of course many new writers are doing away with this type of tragic ending for the female melodramatic character, which is fine because Melodrama is centuries old and is constantly changing with the times. Melodrama first appeared in medieval morality plays and has since been in a state of revision according to the social structure of the time period.

The Male Melodrama encompasses many science fiction stories such as Dune and Westerns that deal with issues revolving around family. Susan Hayward, author of *Key Concepts in Cinema Studies*, says,

> The characters played by James Dean in his films of the 1950s certainly reflect an unwillingness to fulfill society's expectation of male adulthood. … In male weepies, through a portrayal of masculinity in crisis, melodrama exposes masculinity's contradictions. … The male either suffers from the inadequacies of his father, is in danger of extinction from his murderous father, or he fails his own family.

Unlike the Female Melodrama, the Male Melodrama is reconciled in the end, but the character must find a compromise between his family life and his "other" life outside the domestic sphere. The main focus of the Male Melodrama is on family relationships.

The Melodrama Structure

There is a sense of a clear three-act beginning, middle, and end to Melodrama, but the ending in the Female Melodrama is open-ended or ambiguous and follows a Final Obstacle. Like a soap opera, the Female Melodrama reader is left knowing the story will continue.

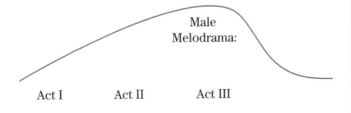

Male Melodrama:

Act I   Act II   Act III

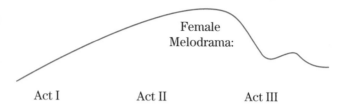

Female
Melodrama:

Act I   Act II   Act III

Both types of Melodrama are primarily character driven as the emotions, decisions, and dreams of the characters drive the story forward.

The Melodrama Elements

ACT I TRADITIONAL ELEMENTS

- Setup
- Mood or Tone: This is very important in Melodramas. Happy, colorful sunsets are not the best choice for a story such as this. Depressive, dark, oppressive, and mournful are great adjectives to think about here.
- Hook, Catalyst, or Inciting Incident
- Serious Problem and/or Goal: This is an internal problem for both the Male and Female Melodramas.
- Villain
- Main Characters: All of them should be introduced here.
- Turning Point

ACT I NEW ELEMENTS

➤ The Turning Point in Traditional Structure calls for a cliffhanger. In Melodrama it calls for things to get seriously worse for the Main Character at a personal level. It's not just that he's stuck on the side of a cliff, but that his father put him there.

➤ Melodrama involves family and relationships so the Villain, if there is one, will not be a stranger.

➤ In Melodrama, the Villain can easily be the Main Character herself, as she makes one bad choice after another, usually never learning from her mistakes. Of course, some of these choices may be fun and liberating at the time, which is why women like these stories.

➤ The Male Melodrama will have more scenes and locations outside the home than the Female Melodrama. He is at odds with the demands of family and relationship.

➤ You may want to set the Mood or Tone several times in Act I.

➤ Conflict comes between characters that are related in some way, not between characters and the environment, for example. If the Main Character drives into a river, it is not the fault of the curvy road or the rainfall—it's because he was upset about an argument he had with his father.

ACT I QUESTIONS

• What makes you feel uncomfortable? Can you use that to set the Tone in the opening scenes?

• Who or what will the Villain be? If it is the Main Character hurting herself, how will you show this?

• Can you come up with different characters to use in the Turning Point? Is one more traumatic than another? Is the Main Character closer to one over the other? Will this add betrayal to the Turning Point?

• Can you spice up a supporting character so he really rubs the Main Character the wrong way?

ACT II TRADITIONAL ELEMENTS

• Problem Intensifies
• Temporary Triumph
• Reversal
• Dark Moment
• Turning Point

ACT II NEW ELEMENTS

➤ The Temporary Triumph is very short-lived, if there is a Triumph at all. The Main Character finally receives roses, and only a moment or so later she learns they were meant for her neighbor. Or the Main Character will finally have some time with his father, only to find out his father's business partners will be there and he's being used to impress them.

➤ Fill this act with psychological tragedies. Don't be afraid to make things hard on your character.

➤ The Turning Point will definitely be heavy with angst and longing just below the surface. When a character is angry at his father's absence or her husband's indifference, deep down that character just wants love but can't seem to obtain it.

ACT II QUESTIONS

- What types of psychological issues does your Main Character have? Does she seek help at all? Is she even aware of it?

- How much Conflict will you have in this act? (There is never too much in Melodrama; make sure it is organic to the story and don't throw in extra characters just to make it work.)

- Will you have more than one Temporary Triumph? (In Melodramas you can. Using the previous example, the Main Character receives roses—but they're for the neighbor. Then the phone rings and she's all excited as she goes to answer it—but it's the wrong number. Finally she hears a car horn outside and rushes to the window as happy as ever—only to find an angry cabdriver yelling at a man in the street.)

- Will a theme start to emerge in this Act?

ACT III TRADITIONAL ELEMENTS

- Final Obstacle
- Male Melodrama: Climax and Resolution

ACT III NEW ELEMENTS

➤ Traditionally, the Female Melodrama has a Final Obstacle but then stagnates. She can't find completion in a patriarchal society. Again some writers are changing this, allowing the hero to succeed at her Goal. Though the "rules" are being broken, this happy ending usually has many sad elements, and the hero's life is not seen as perfect anymore.

➤ The Male Melodrama has a Climax and Resolution, but that does not mean it has to have a happy ending. It could still be very tragic, but there is a feeling of the main story being resolved for the main character.

➤ The Final Obstacle is also psychological in nature and usually involves family or other close relationships.

ACT III QUESTIONS

- If using Female Melodrama, will the hero be successful in the end? If so, in what ways is her life still unsuccessful?

- If using Female Melodrama, will the story continue on after this ending? (Think of soap operas that continue on indefinitely.)

- If using Male Melodrama, will the hero find peace in the end?

- What happens to other characters in the story? Do they change at all? Do they resist change and therefore extend the story beyond the ending?

- Will the Main Character have to separate from the family to grow?

EXAMPLES

All That Heaven Allows, DOUGLAS SIRK

A wealthy widow falls in love with a much younger gardener. This gives the country club set something to gossip about, and her children are ashamed that she plans to remarry below her station.

The First Time, JOY FIELDING

Art dealer Mattie Hart seems to be enjoying a perfect life. But ever since her hasty marriage, her husband has been sleeping around and he now plans on leaving her. Just as he is about to tell her he's leaving, she is diagnosed with a life-threatening illness.

Rebel Without a Cause, NICHOLAS RAY

A rebellious young man with a troubled past comes to a new town, finding friends and making enemies. He hopes to fill the emptiness inside him, where his family's love should be.

Romance

FROM *EVER AFTER*:

DANIELLE: You, sir, are supposed to be charming.

PRINCE HENRY: And we, princess, are supposed to live happily ever after.

DANIELLE: Says who?

PRINCE HENRY: You know, I don't know.

NARRATOR: My great-great-grandmother's portrait hung in the monastery up until the Revolution. By then, the truth of the rumors had dissolved into a simple fairy tale. And, while Cinderella and her prince did live happily ever after, the point, gentlemen, is that they lived.

The Romance plot structure is defined as having a structure around two Main Characters who are falling in love. This structure focuses on the content of the structure rather than on structure design.

Make no mistake about it—romantic fiction is the hottest thing around, accounting for over 56 percent of all paperback fiction sold. While some may look down on this type of storytelling, it is by far the most lucrative market out there. In fact, many men write these novels under a female pen name.

Even action stories contain a romantic theme, so don't hesitate to take the structures presented here and use them as a subplot. Analyzing the top three romantic fairy tales—*Cinderella, Beauty and the Beast*, and *Sleeping Beauty*—will teach you firsthand how to structure the Romance plot. Fairy tales are universal, just as archetypes are.

The Cinderella Structure

In the *Cinderella* Romance structure, the heroine falls in love with the hero first and is left at his mercy, so to speak, even if she is an independent woman at heart. Her actions are centered on the one she loves and whether or not he will love her back. Very often these stories focus on the hero and how he's feeling. Hamlet and Ophelia come to mind.

Romantic themes that can be explored are:

- **RAGS TO RICHES:** The character gets her due against all obstacles. She goes from a place of longing and dissatisfaction to a place of abundance and happiness. She's earned it.
- **ROMANTIC RESCUE:** The character saves his partner from self-destruction, or he needs to be saved or nursed back to health himself.

ACT I

- We meet the hero and learn about his unhappiness or about his cynical look at life.
- We meet the heroine and see how desperate her life situation is. We also learn how exceptional she is as compared to other women.
- They meet each other and she falls in love with him.

ACT II

- A task or situation forces them to be together.
- He is skeptical and unsure of their relationship. He may try to send her away.
- He realizes he loves her, too, but obstacles and uncertainty keep them apart.

ACT III

- He finally goes out and gets her. He saves her with his love.
- He teaches her a little about love and life. She's had it tough until now.
- They live happily ever after.

The Beauty and the Beast Structure

In the *Beauty and the Beast* Romance structure, the hero falls in love with the heroine first and is left at her mercy. The story often focuses on how the heroine is feeling. The hero is usually an extremely powerful man in every area of his life except where she is concerned. Very often his whole life depends on her decision to love him back and save him from his meek existence. *The Phantom of the Opera* comes to mind.

Romantic themes that can be explored are:

- **INDEPENDENCE:** The character desires someone different than the people she has previously dated or desires someone completely different from herself. She wants a life change and needs someone who is already where she wants to go.

- **LOVE VS. HONOR:** This theme concerns what the character wants to do vs. what she feels she should do while considering others' needs and her duty to her family. There is a major obstacle in her relationship and she needs to learn to value her own needs. This fits well with paranormal stories, as the hero is usually otherworldly and "normal" people and family members may not accept her relationship with him.

ACT I

- We meet the heroine and see how stable her life is, good or bad.
- An obstacle or chance meeting brings her in contact with the hero. He seems rough around the edges and is often a loner.
- The hero immediately falls in love with her for who she is, not just her looks.

ACT II

- A task or situation forces them to be together.
- She is hesitant about their relationship.
- He does something so wonderful, thoughtful, or protective that she starts to fall in love with him.
- Obstacles keep them from expressing their love.

ACT III

- The hero is in trouble and she saves him with her love.
- They live happily ever after.

The Sleeping Beauty Structure

In the *Sleeping Beauty* romance structure, both the heroine and hero fall in love at the same time, which puts them on equal footing. They save each other through their mutual love. *Romeo and Juliet* comes to mind, though the ending is tragic.

Romantic themes that can be explored are:

- **LOVE CONQUERS ALL:** The character needs someone to help him gain the courage to face himself and his inner demons so he can heal (for example, the hero has a drug addiction). There's a tug between desire for the love of his life and a fear of commitment. Other things try to take precedence over the relationship.
- **SECOND CHANCES:** The character tries to recapture his lost love and wants to go back to a specific time in his life when things were better. This love is a chance to recapture what he is missing in his life.

ACT I

- The innocent heroine is a victim of fate. There's a stain on her perfect world.
- She either feels lost and alone, with no hope for anything better, or she doesn't even know there is a problem yet, but she still feels sad.
- Others come along and try to help her, but it doesn't work.
- The wandering hero, who feels like something is missing, goes about his life.

ACT II

- Something catches the hero's eye and he decides to go after it, taking a big risk.
- Through this risk he finds the heroine and they both feel true happiness.
- Both of their lives are completely changed by this love. They are two completely different people than they were in the beginning of the story.
- Obstacles keep them apart.

ACT III

- They fall deeper in love and make their plans, regardless of what others think.
- They are determined to be together regardless of the cost. And they live happily ever after.

Romance Structure

There is still a sense of a clear three-act beginning, middle, and end to Romance Structure because it is the content that is specific here:

Act I   Act II   Act III

This Structure is character driven, as it is the love and relationship between the two Main Characters that drives the story forward.

Romance Elements

ACT I TRADITIONAL ELEMENTS

- Setup
- Mood or Tone

- Hook, Catalyst, or Inciting Incident
- Serious Problem and/or Goal
- Villain
- Main Characters: all of them introduced here
- Turning Point

ACT I NEW ELEMENTS

➤ The reader wants to meet the lovers as soon as possible, even if it takes a while for the hero and heroine to meet each other.

➤ The hero or heroine needs to have a serious problem or goal that has the capacity to involve the other one in it. For example, he's a fireman and someone keeps setting her shop on fire.

➤ If the lovers fall in love right away, there must be a great feasible obstacle to keep them apart from either each other or from being happy together.

➤ If the lovers don't fall in love right away, they can be their own obstacles to love. For example, he's afraid to commit right now.

➤ Keep other characters to a minimum so the focus stays on the lovers.

ACT I QUESTIONS

- Who holds the power and main focus of your story?
- Who falls in love first? Or do they fall in love at the same time?
- Do they go from falling in love at first sight to a series of chaste dates and then marriage?
- Do they hate each other at first?
- Is the heroine aggressive?
- What are the moral standards you live by? Do you want to write sex scenes that border on erotica? (When writing Romance you need to decide what your philosophy is. Think about it, make a decision, and then you will feel more comfortable as you write.)

ACT II TRADITIONAL ELEMENTS

- Problem Intensifies
- Temporary Triumph
- Reversal

- Dark Moment
- Turning Point

ACT II NEW ELEMENTS

➤ A Task or Situation may force them to be together, especially if one party is not interested in the other. It is the glue that keeps them together when they may not have chosen to stay together. For example, they sit on a committee together, they work for the same company, or they have both been robbed by the same person.

➤ If the lovers are not sure about each other, many of the obstacles will come from the lovers themselves. For example, she's unsure so she lets her family talk her out of seeing him.

➤ If the lovers want to be together but can't, the obstacles will come from the lovers themselves and other characters. Why can't they be together? Make it believable. Unless they are in jail or something like that, they can make the choice to be together regardless of what is going on in their lives. For example, he can quit his job if it interferes with the relationship. She can leave her family if they are stopping her from being with him. So tell us why they won't.

➤ If the lovers are together but can't find peace, the obstacles will come from the plot. For example, someone is chasing after them and they are on the run. Or they are of different races and the racist neighbors won't leave them alone.

ACT II QUESTIONS

- What will keep the lovers apart and the story moving?
- Do the obstacles come from the plot? Or from the characters?
- Why should they be together?
- Have they kissed yet?
- Will the reader like both lovers? Are they larger than life or real, everyday people?

ACT III TRADITIONAL ELEMENTS

- Final Obstacle
- Climax
- Resolution

ACT III NEW ELEMENTS

➤ In romantic fiction the lovers are always together in the end "living happily ever after." If not, you are writing a more melodramatic piece.

➤ Many of these stories involve traditional family values where the heroine desires children in the end. But this is changing as more people are deciding to either not have children at all or to wait until they are much older to have them. Different cultures hold different family values as well as different ideas of what love is, so do research here.

➤ It is very important for the heroine to be at least somewhat heroic in the end, even if she is rescued. The audience for this type of fiction demands it.

ACT III QUESTIONS

- What role does the heroine play in the Climax?
- Why do we care if these two get together or not? Have you made it personal? Did you tell us why they should be together?
- How will their lives be different now that the story is over?

EXAMPLES

Ever After, ANDY TENNANT (*Cinderella* type)

The story of Cinderella, a girl who finds her Prince Charming.

Queen of the Damned,
ANNE RICE (*Beauty and the Beast type*)

After many years of sleeping in his coffin, the vampire Lestat awakens to find that the world has changed and he wants to be a part of it. He gathers a following and becomes a rock star. Yet he is still lonely and depressed with his life—until he meets Jesse.

The Last of the Mohicans,
JAMES FENNIMORE COOPER (*Sleeping Beauty* type)

During the French and Indian War in colonial America, a white scout and two of his Indian brothers help escort two women through dangerous territory. The white scout falls in love with one of the women, and their first kiss is electrifying.

The Journey

FROM *TITANIC*:

JACK: Wait, just let me try and get this out. Rose you're … [pause] I'm not an idiot. I know how the world works. I've got ten bucks in my pocket, I have nothing to offer you and I know that. But I'm too involved now. You jump, I jump, remember? I can't turn away without knowing you'll be alright.

ROSE: Well, I'm fine. I'll be fine. Really.

JACK: Really? I don't think so. They've got you trapped Rose and you're gonna die if you don't break free. Maybe not right away because you're strong, but soon, that fire that I love so much about you Rose, that fire's going to burn out.

ROSE: It's not up to you to save me Jack.

JACK: I know, only you can do that.

The Journey plot structure is defined as having one Main Character either go it alone through a major internal growth experience—as with the Feminine and Masculine Journeys (discussed in Part 3)—or go it alone through a major series of events that test courage and resolve—as in the Joseph Campbell model. This structure focuses on the content of the structure rather than on structure design.

In case you are unfamiliar with it, the Joseph Campbell model is a story model developed by Chris Vogler as he interpreted Joseph Campbell's book *The Hero With a Thousand Faces*. Campbell's book explores mythic heroes throughout numerous cultures, and Vogler compiled the structure of these myths into twelve steps in his book *The Writer's Journey*. This Journey model became so popular at one point that many feel it has now been overdone.

The Feminine and Masculine Journeys are character driven even though they may be full of action or suspense. The decisions the Main Character makes drive the story forward. At any point the Main Character may face the temptation to give up altogether, and the story itself would be over because the Main Character has stopped acting and creating new events and problems.

The Joseph Campbell Journey is plot driven even though the Main Character may go through changes and realizations throughout the Journey. The events drive the story and the Main Character forward.

For example, it is the call to adventure from an outside force that sparks the beginning of the Journey. In the Feminine and Masculine Journeys the Main Character sparks the beginning of the Journey herself.

Also you may wonder what the differences are between the Feminine and Masculine Journeys. The biggest difference is that, traditionally, the male hero is supported in his quest to leave the "tribe" and seek his goal, and the female hero usually is not. (Male heroes can embody the Feminine Journey model and vice versa, especially when they are venturing somewhere they shouldn't. Think of the film *Three Kings*.)

Also, men and women live in very different worlds most of the time. For example, leaving work alone at night may not be a big deal at all for a man, but a woman has to put up her guard and hope things will be okay as she quickly walks to her car. Women need to build their ego strength; in many cases, they often sacrifice themselves for others and don't really know who they are. They need to find their power. Men, on the other hand, are taught to be powerful early on, and they need to lose part of their ego strength and power on their journey.

While this chapter contains all you need to get started with using the Journey structures, you can see *45 Master Characters: Mythic Models for Creating Original Characters* for very in-depth information on the Feminine and Masculine Journeys and *The Writer's Journey* for more information on the Joseph Campbell Journey.

Combining Other Structures

These Journeys are a unique addition to this book because they can be combined with the other structure types very easily. For example, in Act II of the Feminine Journey, the hero may experience an event or a certain lesson several times to get it right. It's as if she thought she had all the answers and accomplished the goal, but she really hasn't found the core issue yet.

While this typically happens in real time, with the hero trying over and over again to conquer her fears, you could play with it and combine it with the Replay structure so the hero literally re-experiences the event over and over again. But the main thrust of the story will be the Journey itself.

Journey Structures

With all three models there is still a sense of a clear three-act beginning, middle, and end. The following is an outline of the three main Journey models.

THE FEMININE JOURNEY

The Feminine Journey is a Journey in which the hero gathers the courage to face death, even if only symbolic, and endure the transformation toward being reborn as a complete being in charge of her own life.

The Journey starts with the Main Character questioning authority, then gaining the courage to stand up for herself and finally embodying the willingness to go it alone and face her own symbolic death. This Journey is based on *The Descent of Inanna*, one of the oldest recorded myths in history. Think *The Wizard of Oz*.

The Feminine Journey as a structure is cyclical in that, in the end, there is a sense that the Journey may continue or that the Main Character will return home to help someone else embark on the Journey she has just taken. This hero has gone through an inner process of change that can only be experienced directly, not shared. The other characters must experience it themselves to fully understand what the hero went through. In this way, everyone has the potential to be the hero. The Feminine Journey is available to all, not just the rich, strong, or admired.

In Act II the hero may face the same event or internal conflict a few times to get it right or learn the lesson she needs to learn. In Act III the hero goes through a rebirth of sorts and comes full circle, establishing a strong character arc.

Act I   Act II   Act III

THE MASCULINE JOURNEY

In the Masculine Journey, the hero is living in his version of a perfect world with friends and enemies alike. He is thrust into a situation and must make a decision based on how he will react to this situation—will he go inward or remain outwardly focused? The Masculine Journey branches out in two directions, and the Main Character must choose which path to take because they both lead to different conclusions. One choice will lead him to a mini Feminine Journey where he will face the same event or internal conflict a few times to get it right or learn the lesson. He will also face a symbolic death and attain inner growth. This Journey is based on *The Epic of Gilgamesh*. Otherwise he will choose the outwardly directed path, which usually brings destruction. Think *Moby-Dick*.

Act I   Act II   Act III

THE JOSEPH CAMPBELL JOURNEY

The Joseph Campbell Journey keeps in line with the traditional storytelling model because it is based on the same myths and stories used to develop traditional Aristotelian structure.

In the end, the Main Character returns to the tribe in this Journey, but it is not cyclical as there is no sense that the Journey will continue after the hero returns. He has accomplished all that needed to be accomplished by himself and has helped the "tribe." Think *Lethal Weapon*.

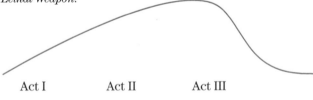

Act I   Act II   Act III

The Journey Elements

(Parts of the following are from *45 Master Characters* and *The Writer's Journey*.)

ACT I TRADITIONAL ELEMENTS FOR ALL THREE JOURNEYS

- Setup
- Mood or Tone
- Hook, Catalyst, or Inciting Incident

- Serious Problem and/or Goal
- Turning Point

ACT I NEW ELEMENTS FOR ALL THREE JOURNEYS

The Feminine Journey has:

➤ The Illusion of the Perfect World Stage: The Main Character has a false sense of security and is trapped in a negative world that stops her growth. She avoids the reality of her situation by using a coping strategy.

➤ The Betrayal or Realization Stage: Everything important to her is taken away and she is pushed to a fork in the road.

➤ The Awakening Stage: She actively prepares for her Journey and wants to reclaim her "power."

The Masculine Journey has:

➤ The Perfect World Stage: The world seems full of opportunities for him, but he doesn't know what he wants deep down inside.

➤ The Friends and Enemies Stage: Friends help push him toward a challenge.

➤ The Preparing for the Journey Stage: Unsure of what he wants deep down inside, he goes for an outwardly focused goal.

The Joseph Campbell Journey has:

➤ The Ordinary World Stage: This is the mundane world to contrast the world to come.

➤ The Call to Adventure Stage: The hero is presented with a problem, challenge, or adventure to undertake.

➤ The Refusal of the Call Stage: Fear may be the driving force behind the refusal to go on the Journey.

➤ The Meeting with the Mentor Stage: The mentor prepares the hero to face the unknown.

➤ The Crossing the First Threshold Stage: The hero commits to the adventure and enters the world of the story.

ACT I QUESTIONS

- What is it that propels the hero to go on an inner or outer Journey?
- Why does the hero need to go on a Journey? Has he started to question what life is all about?

- Is preparation needed to embark on a Journey?
- Has the hero journeyed before? Or known someone else who has?
- Does the hero have a mentor or someone to talk to? (The Feminine Journey hero may not.)
- How will the Villain make his first appearance?

ACT II TRADITIONAL ELEMENTS

- Problem Intensifies
- Temporary Triumph
- Reversal
- Dark Moment
- Turning Point

ACT II NEW ELEMENTS FOR ALL THREE JOURNEYS

The Feminine Journey has:

➤ The Descent Stage: Also known as passing the Gates of Judgment. She faces one of the fears or obstacles and may want to turn back but can't. Her weapons won't work; they are useless here.

➤ The Eye of the Storm Stage: She comes to terms with the ordeal she just faced and thinks her Journey is over; Supporting Characters may want her to come back, but it is not over yet.

➤ The Death Stage: All is lost. A total Reversal happens. She faces her own death, or a symbolic one, and learns more about herself.

The Masculine Journey has:

➤ The Small Success Stage: A small taste of success gives him the desire to reach higher.

➤ The Invitations and Preparations Stage: He's invited to embark on the Feminine Journey toward awakening. If he says "no" he is on the path of Rebellion and gathers his weapons together. He won't give up his "power." Is his current goal what he truly wants? If he says "yes" he is on the path of Awakening.

➤ The Trials Stage: He faces obstacles. If he is Rebelling he has a false sense of superiority. If he is Awakening things seem to be falling apart for him. Either way, warnings and prophecies may surround him.

The Joseph Campbell Journey has:

➤ The Test, Allies, and Enemies Stage: The hero encounters new challenges and learns the rules of the road.

➤ The Approach to the Inmost Cave Stage: The hero is at the edge of a dangerous place, perhaps the Villain's headquarters.

➤ The Supreme Ordeal Stage: The hero's fortunes hit bottom. Will he survive?

➤ The Reward Stage: The hero takes possession of a "treasure."

ACT II QUESTIONS

• Why does the hero keep going forward? What is important to him?
• What tools does the hero have at his disposal?
• Does the hero have any helpers?
• How does the Villain play into this act?
• Why did you pick the Journey model you did? Is it working for this story? Would changing Journeys make it better? More challenging?

ACT III TRADITIONAL ELEMENTS

• Final Obstacle
• Climax
• Resolution

ACT III NEW ELEMENTS FOR ALL THREE JOURNEYS

The Feminine Journey has:

➤ The Support Stage: She accepts her connection to the larger whole. Hopefully someone or something supports her now or she may not make it. Many feminist novels stop at this stage. The hero can't fit into society in the way she wants so death may be her only answer. (Think *The Awakening* by Kate Chopin and how the hero walks into the water at the end of the story. There is just no place for an independent woman in the world she lives in.)

➤ The Moment of Truth Stage: She has found her strength and goes for her goal with gusto. She has awakened and sees the whole world differently. She faces her worst fear and still remains compassionate and complete.

➤ The Full Circle Stage: She returns to the perfect world to see how far she's come. She may pick the next person to go on the descent now so this person can grow as the hero has.

The Masculine Journey has:

➤ The Death Stage: All is lost. If he is Rebelling, he rages against death and fights his own transformation and change. If he is Awakening, he faces death and is humbled by it; all his tools are useless.

➤ The Awaken or Rebel Stage: If he is Rebelling, he won't face his flaws or face change (think *Moby-Dick*). He has little character arc because nothing has changed for him. If he is Awakening he, faces himself and knows what he truly wants. He gives up some of his perceived "power" in order to be successful. He is willing to help others (think *Three Kings*).

➤ The Victory or Failure Stage: Rebellion brings him down the path of failure. Awakening brings him victory and reward, if only internal. He does the right thing.

The Joseph Campbell Journey has:

➤ The Road Back Stage: The hero deals with the consequences of confronting dark forces.

➤ The Resurrection Stage: Death and darkness get one last attempt at the hero before being defeated.

➤ The Return With Elixir Stage: The hero returns with a treasure or lesson.

ACT III QUESTIONS

• Did the hero fail or succeed? Does the Feminine Journey hero find support?

• Do you need to go back and flesh out more character history to make character choices believable?

• Why do we care if the hero is successful or not? (Would *Moby-Dick* have been as great if he caught the whale? Probably not! Would *Three Kings* be as good if they didn't stop to help the people escape? No! Would *Thelma and Louise* have been as wonderful if Thelma and Louise gave up and went to jail? No! So the choices made by these characters are very integral to the story. There is only one choice these characters can make at the end of their stories.)

EXAMPLES

Titanic, JAMES CAMERON (Feminine Journey)

A rich girl and poor boy meet on the ill-fated voyage of the "unsinkable" ship. The heroine is betrayed by her own mother, who forces her to marry a man she doesn't love. The hero helps her to face her situation, become independent, learn about love, and change her life.

Three Kings, DAVID O. RUSSELL (Masculine Journey Awakening)

In the aftermath of the Gulf War, four soldiers set out to steal gold that was stolen from Kuwait, but their plans change when they discover people who need their help.

Moby-Dick, HERMAN MELVILLE (Masculine Journey Rebelling)

The sole survivor of a lost whaling ship relates the tale of his captain's self-destructive obsession to hunt the white whale, Moby-Dick.

48 Hrs., WALTER HILL (Joseph Campbell Journey)

A hard-nosed cop (Nick Nolte) reluctantly teams up with a wisecracking criminal temporarily paroled to him in order to track down a killer. Nick Nolte doesn't want a partner. He rejects helpers and allies. He wants to go it alone. He takes risks and places both of them in great danger until he can return with the killer he is seeking.

Interactive

FROM MYSTREALM.COM
REGARDING THE GAME *MYST*

You begin on the dock. As you walk to the stairs, note the marker switch. Flip it and all other marker switches on the island. There are eight in total, but you cannot reach the marker by the clock tower just yet. The remaining seven are accessible.

Their locations are: the Dock, Gear, Planetarium, Spaceship, Sunken Ship Model, Log Cabin, Brick Building.

Read Atrus's letter to his wife that is conveniently lying on the grass.

Go back to the dock. You will see a door panel set into the hillside. Press it. Go inside …

The Interactive plot structure is one of the most unique plotting structures to date. Because of its infancy, it is hard to say exactly how far this type of writing will go, especially since it is so intimately tied into technology. If you are interested at all in narratology this is the structure to explore. (New York University has classes on this subject.)

While Interactive Fiction is most notably a part of video games, DVD edutainment, and role-playing games, it is also a part of the written novel. The following two novels are early examples:

- Marc Saporta's *Composition No. 1* is a fictional narrative consisting of about 150 unnumbered, loose sheets of paper. Readers are required to create a narrative themselves by shuffling the pages prior to reading them.

- In *Hopscotch*, Julio Cortazar creates two variations for reading his work. Readers must explore and work out possible connections between chapters.

As Espen Aarseth in *Cybertext* states, "The variety and ingenuity of devices used in these texts demonstrate that paper can hold its own against the computer."

Print encourages us to see narrative events in a linear fashion. Words seem locked into changeless and closed lines. Interactive Fiction challenges this by forcing the reader to leave open the possibilities of narrative flow. Each event can have several meanings and several courses of action may result.

In *Hypertext 2.0*, George Landow says Aristotle pointed out that:

> Successful plots require a probable or necessary sequence of events. But removing a single probable or necessary sequence of events does not do away with all linearity. Linearity, however, then becomes a quality of the individual reader's experience within a single text and his or her experience follows a reading path even if that path curves back upon itself or heads in strange directions.

Interactive stories are multidimensional, infinite, inclusive, and untamed, which is a more open-ended matriarchal type of storytelling, completely beyond Aristotle's time of pure patriarchal storytelling. There is never just one way of creating a work of art.

Interactive Fiction challenges traditional literary structure and forces the writer, as well as the reader, to question accepted storytelling rules. Again, in *Hypertext 2.0* Landow says, "Looking at *Poetics* by Aristotle, a discussion of (Interactive Fiction) means one of two things: Either one can simply not write Interactive Fiction (and *Poetics* shows us why) or else Aristotelian definitions and descriptions of plot do not apply." Indeed they do not. Interactive Fiction is, by its very nature, poly-sequential and in a completely different category. There are sequences, but none are necessary!

Michael Joyce, professor at Vassar College and award-winning novelist, say:

> [Interactive Fiction] replaces the Aristotelian curve (of beginning, middle, and end) with a series of successive, transitory closures. ... The core of [Interactive Fiction] is not to get to some secret ending. It's more about successive understanding of kaleidoscopic perceptions that I think characterizes any art and makes our lives worthwhile.

Interactive Structure

The best way to teach Interactive Structure is to look at the way video game designers approach the subject, which is what I will do here. Most of you will probably want to combine Interactive Fiction with technology anyway.

Video game writers call this type of writing Branching. It is like creating a flowchart instead of an outline for your narrative. Each branch is a different path for a character to follow.

For wonderful in-depth information on all of the following, see

Writing for Interactive Media: The Complete Guide by Jon Samsel and Darryl Wimberley. Eastgate Systems publishes highly regarded Interactive Fiction and *Storyspace* software to design them. Also read James Joyce's *Finnegans Wake* for a wonderful example, and play the computer game *Myst*.

Bear in mind that Branching at its best is motivated by inner urges. It should be a path or area for a character to explore, not just one standard choice among many. Joyce says, "[Interactive Fiction] is about the inner possibilities of the story. … We choose our lives by inclination, by urges, by happenstance or seductions."

For example, many of us would rather swim a hundred feet in a calm lake than run five miles uphill, but someone who almost drowned as a child would make the opposite choice. That, then, is an inner-directed choice or "branch path."

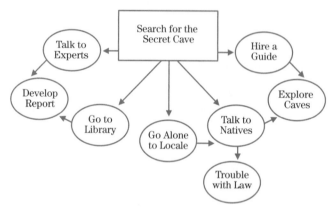

The Interactive Structure is driven by the reader. The reader decides where to go and what to read or do next according to his own preferences. Since there is usually no clear three-act beginning, middle, and end with an Interactive Structure, I will not even use Act I, Act II, and Act III as reference points. It would only confuse the explanation. As you will see, the move away from narrative structure requires much more work from the writer. This is why it is a good idea to know a lot about Traditional Structure before you go breaking all the rules.

Interactive Elements

TRADITIONAL ELEMENTS

All the traditional elements can be found in an Interactive Structure, though instead of two Turning Points you have many Decision Points. It's all up to your imagination, preference, and goal as a writer.

- Setup
- Mood or Tone
- Hook, Catalyst, or Inciting Incident
- Serious Problem and/or Goal
- Villain
- Main Characters:all of them introduced here
- Problem Intensifies
- Temporary Triumph
- Reversal
- Dark Moment
- Final Obstacle
- Climax
- Resolution

NEW ELEMENTS

➤ According to *Writing for Interactive Media*, there are "ten geometric design structures within Interactive Fiction." They are:

1. SEQUENTIAL WITH CUL-DE-SACS: The entrance to the branch or decision point is also its exit.

2. BRANCHING: This consists of traditional branching where the user is presented with several choices at predesignated "forks in the road" and extended branching where the story line has forks in the road, after forks in the road, indefinitely.

3. CONDITIONAL BRANCHING WITH BARRIERS: The reader is forced to solve a puzzle, for example, before she can move on.

4. CONDITIONAL BRANCHING WITH FORCED PATHS: For example, a user is supposed to find a crystal; she has two choices, but no matter which choice she makes she will find the crystal. Both choices have the same forced outcome.

5. CONDITIONAL BOTTLENECK BRANCHING: Branches of the story are brought back into the spine of the story to rein everything in.

6. CONDITIONAL BRANCHING WITH OPTIONAL SCENES: This is an edutainment where one can click on a link to gain information but must return to move forward.

7. EXPLORATORIUM: This allows the reader to stop the main story and explore another world.

8. PARALLEL STREAMING: This occurs when various states or paths exist simultaneously at various levels.

9. **WORLDS:** This is when two or more environments are interconnected by a common thread and have a series of predefined events.

10. **MULTILINEAR OR HYPERMEDIA:** This encompasses every type of user path imaginable or no path at all (think of the World Wide Web).

➤ Temporary Triumph and Reversal, as well as other elements, may only be used in one sequence of the story depending on the decisions made by the reader. In other words, you will most likely not need to use them in every sequence or Decision Point that branches out on its own path.

➤ Instead of two Turning Points you will have many Decision Points. Depending on your goal you may:

- have the reader decide where to go next based on the options you give (for example, go after a specific character's goal)
- have the reader decide where to go next based on the options she gives herself (for example, shuffling scenes around and putting them back together)
- have the reader decide if he wants to select a link to learn something new (for example, click a link to read a character's bio)
- have the reader perform some task (for example, edutainment pieces that teach; add up numbers to find the next page to turn to or solve a riddle to move on)

➤ If you are writing an Interactive story for the Web, you would highlight selected text that a reader can choose to click on. Once clicked, any of the above can happen.

➤ Keep the choices as personal as possible. Think about all the different types of people out there; maybe even read a bit about psychology. Use this to develop your characters. Perhaps each one of your characters has a different psychological makeup and the reader can select which character to follow.

➤ Interactive Fiction is limited only by your imagination. You can do whatever you want, but keep in mind if it seems too easy you are probably doing something wrong! In many ways this structure takes the most planning of all structures.

QUESTIONS

- What type of Interactive Fiction will you write (video game, role-playing, edutainment, print, Web, or something new)?
- Will you use Branching? How many branches leading to alternate stories or situations will you have?

- Will you use Decision Points?
- Will you do an experimental piece, similar to Saporta's *Composition No. 1*?
- How many characters will you have? Will they be drastically different? Approaching situations differently?
- Most importantly, who is your audience? (Interactive Fiction games are equally made for all age groups from kids to teens to adults.)

EXAMPLES

Myst, UBISOFT ENTERTAINMENT

Myst is the number-one selling CD-ROM title of all time. *Myst* sends you to fantasy worlds where you must solve puzzles as you seek to unlock the secret of ages past.

Composition No. 1, MARK SAPORTA

This book is a 150-page story consisting of loose sheets of paper to be shuffled around to create a narrative.

Finnegans Wake, JAMES JOYCE

This experimental novel is the story of a man, his wife, and their three children. The novel presents history as cyclic, and the book begins with the end of a sentence left unfinished on the last page.

Metafiction

FROM *FERRIS BUELLER'S DAY OFF*:

SLOANE: What are we going to do?

FERRIS: The question isn't "what are we going to do," the question is "what aren't we going to do?"

CAMERON: Please don't say we're not going to take the car home. Please don't say we're not going to take the car home. Please don't say we're not going to take the car home.

FERRIS: [to the camera] If you had access to a car like this, would you take it back right away?

[beat]

Neither would I.

The Metafiction plot structure is defined as fictional writing that consciously draws attention to itself. It is self-reflexive and introverted, posing questions about the relationship between fiction and reality. In other words, Metafiction will often contain elements that draw the reader out of the story in order to examine the subject of story itself.

Patricia Waugh, author of *Metafiction: The Theory and Practice of Self-Conscious Fiction*, says, "Metafictional works are those which explore the theory of writing fiction through the practice of writing fiction." It is, therefore, not a genre but a type of structural technique that calls attention to itself. Think of *Ferris Bueller's Day Off* and how the character Ferris speaks into the camera, addressing the audience and breaking down that wall between reality and fiction.

Waugh also says, "Contemporary metafictional writing is both a response and a contribution to an even more thoroughgoing sense that reality or history is provisional: no longer a world of external verities (truths) but a series of constructions, artifices, impermanent structures."

Some argue that Metafiction has been around since the fifteenth century, starting with Miguel de Cervantes' *Don Quixote*. And that

Shakespeare's *Hamlet* shows metafictional tendencies when Hamlet talks about acting.

Metafiction is sometimes seen as a mature version of the novel, which at its best can challenge the authority of histories. Victoria Orlowski of Emory University explains:

> Some works are dubbed "historiographic metafictions" because of their conscious self-reflexivity and concern with history. Their earliest histories contain fictional elements. They are implicit amalgamations of fact and myth. The composition of the "history" itself contains the word "story." Yet, as realism took root, history came to represent "objective" fact and the novel came to represent "subjective" fiction. ... Through its play upon "known truth," historiographic metafiction questions the absolute knowability of the past ... (and can) rediscover the histories of suppressed people such as women or colonized natives.

Metafiction has also been used extensively in film and can be used with great effect in comedies. Think of Mel Brooks' *Spaceballs*, *Forrest Gump*, and *Ferris Bueller's Day Off*.

As I write this chapter, there are two new films out titled *What the Bleep Do We Know!?* and *Empathy*. Both films combine a fictional narrative story with nonfictional documentary style interviews to further explore the theme and subject.

Metafiction Structure

There may still be a sense of a clear three-act beginning, middle, and end to Metafiction, but it is almost impossible to graph due to its lack of organized structure and form.

According to Patricia Waugh, "To show that reality is no longer understandable or that history is just fiction," there may be:

- severe over-plotting, as in the use of too many coincidences and miracles (*Forrest Gump*)
- severe under-plotting to make a statement about language

To show that language is an arbitrary system, there may be:

- blank pages
- pictures (like Kurt Vonnegut's illustrations in *Slaughterhouse-Five*)

To show the paradoxical status of author (power vs. no power of author), there may be:

- the appearance of the author, as in the *The French Lieutenant's Woman*, or the director, as in *The Icicle Thief*

• conflict between reader and author
• a character that is out of the author's control

To show the foregrounding of the fiction and reality there may be:

• juxtaposition of fictional characters and historical figures (*Forrest Gump*)
• discussion of writing or film techniques such as the preface, author, reviewers, and advertisements (Think of Mel Brooks' *Spaceballs* and how they stop the film to talk about *Spaceballs* the movie and how to buy *Spaceballs* products.)

This structure can be plot driven, character driven, or possibly narrator driven. There really are no hard and fast rules. I present the following as Act I, Act II, and Act III to keep things consistent with the rest of the book and to give you a frame of reference only. Any of the elements listed can be deleted at whim, as long as the majority of them are in place.

Metafiction Elements

ACT I TRADITIONAL ELEMENTS

• Setup
• Mood or Tone
• Hook, Catalyst, or Inciting Incident
• Serious Problem and/or Goal
• Villain
• Main Characters: all of them introduced here
• Turning Point

ACT I NEW ELEMENTS

➤ The Setup and Hook are great places to lull your reader into the story so you can shock her later. If you really want to call attention to the structure and expectations of story, first bring the reader into a story and get her involved. Then, when you deviate from it later, she will be shocked out of the story and forced to examine what happened.

➤ The characters may have a Serious Problem and/or Goal stated, but that does not mean it has to be the purpose of the story. The Problem and/or Goal can take a back seat for a while if needed or the narrator or other element can step in and out of the story to address it. If the character is sick, you could even include a medical report outlining what the disease is.

ACT I QUESTIONS

- What is your overall purpose for writing this story? What do you want to say?
- Will you wait for the really big moments in the story to break the structure? Or use the more quiet moments?
- How do you want the reader to feel? Do you want to just shock her? Or do you want to make her think?
- Will you use Traditional Structure at all?

ACT II TRADITIONAL ELEMENTS

- Problem Intensifies
- Temporary Triumph
- Reversal
- Dark Moment
- Turning Point

ACT II NEW ELEMENTS

➤ The traditional elements here are usually played with in Metafiction and are often overexaggerated or blown all out of proportion. They almost seem silly to have at all. They can be presented in such a formulaic way as to make them seem absurd.

➤ Think about how often you want to show metafictional techniques in this section.

➤ Think about the rules of genre and characterization as well as plot.

ACT II QUESTIONS

- Will you keep lulling your reader back into the story for a while? Or will you constantly call attention to the medium?
- Will you put in any historical elements? Or comedy?
- Do you have a new point to get across in this section? Do you want to say something different?

ACT III TRADITIONAL ELEMENTS

- Final Obstacle
- Climax
- Resolution

ACT III NEW ELEMENTS:

➤ Unlike other types of structure, in Metafiction new characters can come out of nowhere to help the characters out. This is called the "hand of God" technique where things seem contrived, as if God just stepped in and saved everyone.

➤ Again, you can play with traditional elements here.

➤ You can call attention to the ending through imitation—of something from reality (a current event) or another popular piece of fiction.

ACT III QUESTIONS

- Will there be any type of Resolution? Perhaps the story will resolve itself but the questions the reader has will not.
- Have you challenged your reader?
- Did you use any comedy at all?
- Have you considered all of your creative options? (Remember, you can combine historical and fictional characters, run things backward, stop the story to talk to the reader, or even create new words.)

EXAMPLES

Ferris Bueller's Day Off, JOHN HUGHES

A high-school wise guy is determined to have a day off from school, despite what the principal says. He constantly talks into the camera addressing the audience.

Slaughterhouse-Five, KURT VONNEGUT

Billy Pilgrim is a man who becomes unstuck in time after he is abducted by aliens from the planet Tralfamadore. There is a plot-scrambling aspect to the piece as we follow Pilgrim simultaneously through all phases of his life.

The Things They Carried, TIM O'BRIEN

This is a fictional study of war. O'Brien examines the process of writing itself by using so many layers of writing techniques in one book. He also plays with point of view and discusses within the story what the best way is to *tell* the story.

The Slice of Life

CEREMONY BY LESLIE MARMON SILKO

I will tell you something about stories

(he said)

They aren't just entertainment.

Don't be fooled.

They are all we have, you see,

All we have to fight off

illness and death.

You don't have anything

if you don't have the stories

Their evil is mighty

but it can't stand up to our stories.

So they try to destroy the stories

let the stories be confused or forgotten.

They would like that

They would be happy

Because we would be defenseless then.

He rubbed his belly.

I keep them here

(he said)

Here, put your hand on it

See. It is moving.

There is life here

for the people.

And in the belly of this story

the rituals and the ceremony

are still growing.

The Slice of Life plot structure can be defined as a momentary glimpse of reality rather than a carefully composed, formal imitation of it. By its very nature it rejects the traditional three-act structure and is therefore more open to multicultural types of storytelling.

Since the eighteenth century, the French have had what is called the anti-novel, where novelists free fiction from the expectations of conventional ideas about plot and characterization.

Slice of Life Structure

Again, there is no sense of a clear three-act beginning, middle, and end to a Slice of Life piece, but there is an incident of some sort in the beginning that gets things rolling:

This structure is definitely character oriented but not necessarily character driven. There is usually an Inciting Incident, in the form of a circumstance, in the beginning of the story, but its use is to give a reason for telling the story and not drive the story toward a definite Goal and Climax. In fact, some of the writers of these stories feel they are an exploration into the human condition and relationships, that a day in the life of a character, without a Climax and Resolution, is just as valid a storytelling model. We have just become conditioned to seek out the Problem, Goal, and Climax in our entertainment and devalue stories that don't provide it.

Slice of Life stories are very stream of consciousness. Some Slice of Life writers set out to challenge our expectations regarding literature and entertainment, and other Slice of Life writers are writing from a cultural perspective that is not influenced at all by traditional Aristotelian structure. (Many Native American stories, for example, do not draw a distinction between prose and poetry.)

This is not to say that those who write without plotting are writing a Slice of Life piece. On the contrary, many who write this way still have the traditional plot structure in their work because it has become so ingrained into westernized culture. It is almost impossible for most Westerners to write without Traditional Structure unless one has never seen a television show, watched a movie, or read a book.

Many people judge Slice of Life stories as bad, wrong, boring career killers and try to force students into the traditional three-act structure. In many ways, this is a shame, as they are not honoring the differences in writers and in storytelling as they should. There is an audience for every mode of expression.

Some successful Slice of Life stories include the following:

- The film *Before Sunrise* did so well they have released a sequel to it titled *Before Sunset*.

- Spike Lee protégé Lee Davis has created a Slice of Life piece titled *3 AM* where he takes the viewer into the world of taxi drivers.

- *Daughters of the Dust* is a fairly famous Slice of Life film used in many Western universities.

- English director Jamie Thraves created *The Low Down*, which follows a twenty-something Londoner through that difficult time in life when you realize your youth is ending and you're not ready to grow up.

- Anton Chekhov's *An Upheaval* is a great example for a novelist. It is an observation of life within an upper-class household where the reader is left without a resolution. It is a sort of right-of-passage story.

So how do you write a Slice of Life piece? You select a moment in time, or a character that interests you, and you just start writing, paying attention to the details of everyday life. In a traditional story your character may not stop to smell the roses, but in a Slice of Life piece he may. He could sit and ponder an anthill or meet a girl and just walk around the city (*Before Sunrise*).

The key is to have interesting characters for the reader to watch and to have a rich setting to work with. It's like a voyeuristic look into a character's daily life. Read the reviews of *Daughters of the Dust* on Amazon.com, where it is referred to as a visual miracle.

I use the terms Act I, Act II, and Act III just to keep things consistent with the rest of the book. They are only frames of reference.

Slice of Life Elements

ACT I TRADITIONAL ELEMENTS

- Setup

ACT I NEW ELEMENTS

➤ While there is a Setup, it is not one that presents a great problem to be solved. The character may have a sense of wanting to go on an inner journey or nothing at all. Something may take him by surprise, like the meeting of a pretty woman or the loss of a job, to show the reader why you have chosen this moment to write about. But like in real life where things don't clean up quickly and easily, this character won't be resolving this Setup quickly and easily.

➤ Act I may end with a decision by the character to go somewhere or do something, but his goal is just to see what will
happen—to go with the flow.

➤ Make sure you have spent a lot of time on developing your
setting and visual elements, even if you are writing a novel.

ACT I QUESTIONS

• Why do you want to write this type of story?

• Is there a theme you would like to explore?

• How many characters will you have?

• What different settings can you use to make it more interesting?

• If writing a movie script, how can you make this visually pleasing?

• Is there a feeling or mood you want to invoke in your audience?

ACT II TRADITIONAL ELEMENTS

• Turning Point: There may be a small Turning Point that is more like a new
Setup that does not state a Serious Problem or Goal. It is more like an observation or a chance happening that the character had little to do with.

ACT II NEW ELEMENTS

➤ The observation or exploration continues. Time moves
forward, setting, people, places, and objects change.

➤ The character may discover new things, see things differently, or ponder deep questions that relate to the theme.
In *Before Sunrise*, two characters spend the night wandering the city together—eating, playing, and talking.

➤ A new area of the character's life can be explored. If you
were primarily in the Main Character's work environment
you can switch to his home environment, for example, or
from his family life to his work life.

➤ This is where more of the character's psychological make-
up can be shown.

➤ Other characters can be brought in with problems and
goals of their own but they don't become the main focus
of the story or of the Main Character's attention.

ACT II QUESTIONS

• Will you reinforce a theme here?

• Can you change locations or spice things up to show how the Main
Character behaves in different places?

- Will you bring in some new characters?
- Is there anything that will shock your reader?
- Why would you read this story? What does the reader take away from it?

ACT III TRADITIONAL ELEMENTS

- Not applicable

ACT III NEW ELEMENTS:

➤ The setting, time, place, etc. may change to show the Main Character, in a new way, with a new stimulus.

➤ Other characters can come and go or stick around.

ACT III QUESTIONS

- How will you show that the story is over? Is it the end of the Main Character's day so we see him walk into his house and shut the door? Or do we get a sense that the story is never over but continues on and on?
- Will you reinforce the theme again?
- Are there any other interesting characters you can bring in?

EXAMPLES

Before Sunrise, RICHARD LINKLATER

A French graduate student meets an American boy on the Budapest-Vienna train. They get off the train in Vienna and hang out for a while.

Daughters of the Dust, JULIE DASH

A languid look at the Gullah culture of the Sea Islands off the coast of South Carolina and Georgia where African folkways were maintained well into the twentieth century.

The Low Down, JAMIE THRAVES

Frank, in his late twenties, becomes restless as he realizes that his life is at a standstill. He is aware of a need to move on with his life, but while he knows something must change, he is not sure what or how.

Part 3

ADDING STORIES

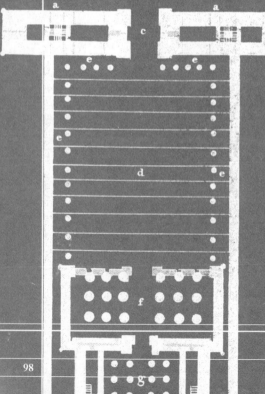

Introducing the 55 Dramatic Situations

> "Gozzi maintained that there can be but thirty-six dramatic situations. Schiller took great pains to find more, but he was unable to find even so many as Gozzi."
>
> —GOETHE

In 1945 Georges Polti wrote a book titled *Thirty-Six Dramatic Situations*. It contained brief outlines of thirty-six situations found in literature that created conflict within stories. Since Polti allowed only approximately two pages for each situation, including long lists of plays, he left much to the imagination of the reader. Likewise, he did not include any concrete writing steps to implement these situations. It seems his focus was to categorize the situations, giving us a wonderful way to analyze stories already written.

While we are indebted to Polti for his work, there is a great void in it, for the writer, that needs to be filled. Hopefully this book will do just that, while also updating the examples for modern times. Polti opens his book with the above quote by Goethe, and for the last sixty years writers and professors have taken this quote as fact, as no one has been able to find any more situations to add to his work.

Are there only thirty-six situations? Today the answer is "Yes" and "No."

How did I find more situations to add? Let's start at the beginning. As I have stated in my previous book, *45 Master Characters*, it has been a passion of mine to find and dissect the Feminine and Masculine Journeys. As a woman I wanted to write heroic female stories but found no model I could work with (the Joseph Campbell/Chris

Vogler models are really for the Masculine Journey—which I know women can go on). There had to be another journey out there, a feminine one, that would emulate the female experience.

I then realized I would have to create a feminine model myself, or better yet uncover one that had been overlooked. Luckily I was successful and I outlined the Feminine and new Masculine Journeys in my book *45 Master Characters*. (Note: Men can partake of the Feminine Journey and vice versa, so I don't use the term feminine to mean only women.)

Through this experience I learned to look at literature, film, and creativity from a feminine as well as a masculine perspective, and a whole new world was opened up for me. There was a different side to everything—a yin to each yang—even in the world of writing.

So back to the question—are there only thirty-six dramatic situations? "Yes" and "No." These thirty-six dramatic situations created by Polti may be the only *tragic* dramatic situations, but like everything else, these situations each have an opposite—two sides sharing the same common experience.

With my newfound perspective, I was able to see that the original thirty-six situations were very masculine and somewhat violent in nature as well as very plot driven. This isn't bad or good, it's just an observation.

With this in mind I decided to put on my "feminine glasses" and take another look at these situations. It became clear to me that there was a feminine, nonviolent, more character-driven side to each situation that hadn't been explored.

For example, Madness—killing something—could very easily become Genius—creating something, and Flight—fleeing from punishment—could very easily become Pursuit—pursuing a reward. (Although Polti calls this situation Pursuit in his text, I felt Flight conveyed his description more closely so I switched the name here.)

The opportunities for Drama and Conflict are the same for both types of situations, even though one is not based on true tragedy. After all, it has always been the writer's responsibility to find the Conflict in every scene whether it's a happy scene or a tragic one.

Let's strive not to use the words tragic and dramatic interchangeably as Goethe himself did when he referred to these situations.

The question is whether or not the writer can find the Conflict and Drama in a more uplifting story or not. This is a fun challenge, as we have become conditioned to believe that Conflict is all about tragedy, pain, and suffering. It is much easier to create Conflict in that way—but great literature does not just take the easy way out.

Conflict is defined as a state of disharmony between incompatible or antithetical persons, ideas, or interests. Conflict may be a war, but it may also be a psychic struggle. It is the opposition between characters or forces in a work of fiction, and this opposition does not have to come from tragedy.

This definition of Conflict does not imply that there must be tragedy or violence in the narrative to have Conflict. Though it is fine to use them. I am not making a judgment here about tragedy; I'm just trying to expand the definition of the word to allow for different types of stories.

Western culture has defined literature a certain way, but once you move outside of western culture you will see there are many ways of writing. Aristotle's *Poetics* is not the one and only writer's bible—as great as it is. I realized this when I read the section on how women do not make great characters and shouldn't be heroes. I read this while in the UCLA screenwriting thesis class; needless to say it didn't help my confidence level as I was writing a heroic female lead!

Let's keep our minds open to new ideas and new ways of writing—otherwise we will accomplish nothing but a rehash of what has already been done. And why not allow male heroes to explore their inner selves, too?

For those of you who adore Polti I would like to list the situations of his that I have combined in order to make the list as a whole much stronger. I could not ignore the numbers of Polti fans out there who insisted some of Polti's situations overlapped way too much. (If you are unfamiliar with Polti's work, don't worry—you'll be up to speed in a few chapters.) So I have chosen to combine:

- Abduction with Recovery of a Lost One, which is actually the positive side of Abduction—Reunion!

- Rivalry of Kinsman, Rivalry of Superior and Inferior, and Ambition into the situation titled Competition

- Murderous Adultery and Adultery into the situation titled Adultery

- Involuntary Crimes of Love and Crimes of Love into the situation titled Crimes of Love

- Slaying of a Kinsman Unrecognized and Necessity of Sacrificing a Loved One into the situation titled Slaying of Loved One

- Self Sacrifice for an Ideal, for Kindred, and for a Passion into a situation titled Self Sacrifice

- Obstacles to Love and Enemy Loved into a situation titled Obstacles to Love

- Mistaken Jealousy and Erroneous Judgment into a situation titled Mistaken Judgment

This leaves us with fifty-five situations. I have combined ten of Polti's situations with his remaining twenty-six situations and added an additional twenty-eight situations of my own, which gives us a total of fifty-four situations. Then, to encourage creativity and honor cultural differences, I have added a fifty-fifth situation as a blank template for you to design your own situations.

As Georges Polti stated in 1945, "Since we now hold this thread (of thirty-six situations), let us unwind it."

I would add, nearly sixty years after him, "Let us unwind this thread a little more, though not all the way, as someone in the distant future may have more to say in the matter …"

Situations 1 & 2

SUPPLICATION AND BENEFACTION

"The more you depend on forces outside yourself, the more you are dominated by them."

–HAROLD SHERMAN

Supplication

Supplication means to appeal, request, beg, call, plea, ask, invite, invoke, pray, petition, worship, or honor something or someone for help or assistance.

While Supplication in real life is the act of asking for help, in drama it requires a Persecutor, a Petitioner (the suppliant), and a Power in Authority to make it interesting and to add Conflict.

The Persecutor acts as the obstacle to the Petitioner's goal, which is receiving help. He is in direct opposition to the Petitioner's needs.

The Power in Authority adds Conflict by either forcing the Persecutor to give help (for the time being) or allowing the Persecutor to refuse to help.

As a writing device, Supplication presents a wonderful opportunity to explore character as well as notions of power and authority.

First of all, the character is placed in a very dire situation where she needs outside help. How she responds to her situation and whether or not help is offered to her will show us a lot about her and what is important to her. In every moment of life a person has the choice to be happy or angry no matter what is occurring around him.

Second, the character that has the power to help her can choose to wield that power in many ways. This is a great opportunity to develop a strong theme or message about the abuses of power, control, and authority.

THE PETITIONER

There are three general types of Petitioners according to their situation—Need or Desperation, Superstition or Fear, and Laziness or Inertia.

Need or Desperation means a Petitioner is in need of help from an outside source and can not possibly fix her situation on her own. This can be due to social factors such as women in certain circles not being allowed to go to work or school. They won't have the education they need to help themselves. Think of the character Ada Monroe in *Cold Mountain*. She lived on a farm yet nearly starved to death because she never learned how to plant a crop or run a farm.

Superstition or Fear means the Petitioner strongly believes that if he does not ask for help or a blessing he will surely fail. An example of this would be a character out of mythology invoking the gods for help before going off to battle. To overlook such an act would surely mean defeat in his eyes.

Laziness or Inertia comes into play when a character probably could help herself but chooses not to. She possibly fears change or sees her options as beneath her. An example would be a character going to her parents for money when she is capable of working but doesn't like the jobs that are available.

THE PERSECUTOR

The Persecutor usually uses power to instill fear in the Petitioner. Otherwise, asking the Persecutor for help would be an easy thing to do.

There are generally five types of power available for the Persecutor, according to Dr. Christopher L. Heffner in *AllPsych*:

> Coercive power is the power to punish. Parents are said to have coercive power because they can place their child in time-out, for example; bosses have coercive power because they can fire an employee or assign an employee a less pleasing job.
>
> Reward power is almost the opposite; it is the power to reward. In that sense parents and bosses have this type of power as well, as do many others in our lives.
>
> Legitimate power refers to the power granted by some authority, such as the power a police officer has due to the local or state government or the power a professor has due to the rules of a college or university.
>
> Expert power results from experience or education. Those individuals with more knowledge tend to have more power in situations where that knowledge is important. For instance, the physician will have more power in a medical emergency than the plumber. But, when the pipes explode and the house is being flooded, the physician is not the person to call.
>
> Referent power refers to admiration or respect. When we look

up to people because of their accomplishments, their attitude, or any other personal attribute, we tend to give them more power over us. Imagine being asked to do something by your hero or your favorite movie star; we are very likely to comply out of admiration or respect.

There is one more type of power I'd like to mention, and that is the power of forgiveness. This can fall under Reward Power. The Petitioner may be asking for forgiveness, which gives the Persecutor power over the Petitioner's inner feelings at a very deep level.

The Persecutor can have one or all of these types of power at his disposal to use against the Petitioner.

POWER IN AUTHORITY

The Power in Authority is usually someone who has power and the will to use it. Whether he helps or harms is purely up to him. Power is this character's identity and he lives to exercise it. He may be a judge, policeman, parent, teacher, boss, or anyone who is "above" another person.

The Power in Authority can also be a group of people. These people all have an agenda and often get together to make rules or discuss their beliefs. They then judge others according to their standards. In some cases the group has become so large that it encompasses almost all of society. In this case the Power in Authority is a more abstract social mores that must be adhered to.

As an elder friend of mine once said, "We had to dress for dinner and there was no such thing as women wearing slacks. It was just not allowed." (You'd be amazed at the type of characters and stories you can create from just talking to your elder family members!)

Whether Supplication is used as plot, subplot, or incident, the elements of the beginning, middle, and end are the same:

BEGINNING: A Petitioner, who has had a tough time of it, asks a Persecutor for help.

- Is she humiliated by asking?
- Does she feel entitled to the request?
- Was she pushed by someone else into asking?
- Does she really need help?
- How dire is her situation?
- Is she asking for help to assist someone else?
- Have the Persecutor and Power in Authority been introduced?

MIDDLE: The Petitioner receives or is denied help and responds accordingly.

- If help is given, will she play the victim and not join in helping to change her situation? Or will she become active and learn how to help herself as she works with her rescuer?

- Does help come from someone other than the Persecutor? (This gives the Persecutor two characters to deal with now.)

- If help is not given, will the Petitioner play the victim and wind up in a worse situation? Or will she pull her resources and help herself? (Usually, if help is refused, the situation ends tragically for the Petitioner.)

- Does the Petitioner have a positive outlook about her situation? This would enable her to press on no matter what happens. Or is she negative about her situation?

- Where does her strength come from? A character biography may help to flesh out where she gets her determination.

- Will the Power in Authority take an interest in what transpires here? Or does he feel his job is done?

END: The Petitioner seals her own fate by her response to the events.

- Since the Petitioner depends so strongly on outside forces for help, she is at their mercy. If she managed to fend for herself a bit, she may be able to turn the coming tragedy around. The one thing in life a person has control over is her response to events.

- Is the Petitioner better off for her supplication? How did she grow?

- Did the Persecutor learn anything?

- Does the Power in Authority care about what happened to the Petitioner?

- What point did the story make?

> "Let him that desires to see others happy, make haste to give while his gift can be enjoyed, and remember that every moment of delay takes away something from the value of his benefaction."
>
> –SAMUEL JOHNSON

Benefaction

Benefaction is the act of conferring aid of some sort, a charitable gift or deed, an act of goodwill, or a contribution.

Benefaction can also be used as a dramatic device to reveal character and explore notions of power and authority, just like Supplication. Perhaps Benefaction can show the positive side to power when power is justly used or show the importance of helping our fellow man.

Maybe the act of Benefaction empowers a character before Supplication becomes necessary. Or Benefaction can be used alongside Supplication, only to come halfway through the story and change the power structure between all the characters completely. The Benefaction can get in the way of the Persecutor's plans, for example.

The Petitioner becomes the Benefactor in this situation, and like Supplication, you must also have a Persecutor and a Power of Authority to make this situation work.

Whether Benefaction is used as plot, subplot, or incident, the elements of the beginning, middle, and end are the same:

BEGINNING: The Benefactor sees a chance to help a person or a cause. She decides to help but a Persecutor tries to stop her, possibly confusing her. A Power in Authority gets involved.

- Why does the Benefactor want to help? Is she being selfless or selfish?
- What is the Power in Authority?
- Why does the Persecutor want to stop the Benefactor? What is the Persecutor's motivation beyond just being nasty?
- How strong is the Benefactor's motivation to help? Will she take risks?
- Does the Persecutor hate the Benefactor or the one who needs help?

MIDDLE: If the Benefactor offered her help to someone in need, the Persecutor is trying to cause the Benefactor trouble. If the Benefactor didn't offer to help someone in need, she is at odds with herself.

- If she offers help, what kind of trouble will the Persecutor cause?
- If she didn't offer help yet, does the Persecutor hold any power over the Benefactor?
- Has the Power in Authority gotten involved yet?
- Are there any other characters that can help or harm the situation?
- Can another character push or guilt the Benefactor into doing the right thing? Or the wrong thing?

END: The Benefactor responds to the Persecutor and tries to do what she feels is right. The Power in Authority will either support her or cause her downfall.

- Does the Benefactor face the Persecutor herself? Or does she sneak around?

- Does she think the Power in Authority will help her? Is she counting on it?
- How important is it for the Benefactor to confer help? What is at stake here?
- What does the reader want the Benefactor to do?

EXAMPLES

The Iliad, HOMER

SUPPLICATION USED AS INCIDENT—King Priam asks Achilles to return his son's body to be buried properly.

The Ninth Gate, ROMAN POLANSKI

SUPPLICATION USED AS SUBPLOT—A rich book collector hires Johnny Depp to find a book that will allow him to piece together a Supplication to the devil to obtain immortality.

Planes, Trains and Automobiles, JOHN HUGHES

BENEFACTION AS INCIDENT—All Neal Page wants to do is to get home for Thanksgiving. When his flight is cancelled due to bad weather, he has no choice but to merge resources with another stranded traveler, the shower curtain ring salesman Del Griffith. After several mishaps and arguments, Neal invites Dell home for Thanksgiving dinner when he learns Dell has nowhere to go.

The Corn Is Green, IRVING RAPPER

BENEFACTION USED AS PLOT—Schoolteacher Lilly Moffat is dismayed by conditions in a Welsh mining town. She sets up a school to teach fundamental education to the villagers. Her housekeeper and daughter oppose the project, as does the local Squire, who will not rent her space. Using part of her own home, she goes ahead with Miss Moffat's School. One of her students, Morgan Evans, turns from bully to brilliant student.

Situations 3 & 4

DELIVERANCE AND SOJOURN

> "I don't know what your destiny will be, but one
> thing I know—the only ones among you who will
> be really happy are those who have sought and
> found how to serve [others]."
>
> –ALBERT SCHWEITZER

Deliverance

*Deliverance is the act of delivering or freeing from restraint,
captivity, and peril—to rescue someone from bondage or danger. It can be a chivalrous act.*

Deliverance is similar to Supplication in that a character receives
help, but it differs in that the character didn't go out and ask for
help. An unexpected protector comes of his own will to rescue the
distressed. This usually occurs between two strangers.

This situation requires an Unfortunate, a Threatener, and a
Rescuer.

The Threatener not only acts as the obstacle to the Rescuer's
goal, which is to protect the Unfortunate, but also acts as the catalyst to bring forth the Rescuer.

Without the Threatener, the Rescuer cannot exist. Therefore, on
some level, the Rescuer depends on the Threatener to give him an
opportunity to be heroic. After all, what would a fireman be without
a fire? The two go together. Their destinies are intertwined.

There is also the possibility that the Rescuer won't be able to
rescue the Unfortunate. This is a great opportunity to reveal character and delve into the mind of the Rescuer more deeply to see
how not being able to rescue someone affects him. This may also motivate him to take more chances later on in the story.

THE UNFORTUNATE
The Unfortunate can play a large or small role in the story. He can
just be a catalyst to get the Rescuer and Threatener together. Or

several characters throughout the story can take the role of the Unfortunate.

He can also be in the act of trying to rescue someone else when he finds himself in trouble. In this case he won't be too happy about having to be rescued himself.

The Unfortunate can also contribute to the conflict in several ways:

- He may attempt to save himself, ignoring the Rescuer, and wind up in more trouble.
- He could keep getting himself deeper and deeper into trouble. In this case, the Rescuer may have to save him over and over again.
- He could mistake the Rescuer for a Threatener and fight her off.
- He could be angry with the Rescuer for rescuing him (wounded pride).
- He could critique the Rescuer's plan or technique and drive her crazy.
- He can antagonize the Threatener, making him more forceful than ever toward the Rescuer.
- He could misjudge the Threatener and think he is perfectly safe.
- He could be completely oblivious of the Threatener and think the Rescuer is crazy to warn him of danger.

THE THREATENER

The Threatener can take many forms. He can be a person, a place, an animal, an institution (the law), or a natural force (tornado). As such, he has a lot of power behind him whether it's the power of nature, the power given to him "by the people," or the power he gives to himself because he feels entitled to it.

If the Threatener is a person, he knows right from wrong; he just works it out so that in his head he is in the right. In his strange little world he is acting as he should.

The Threatener can be a seen or unseen influence of the story events. He is unseen in many Deliverance-types of films where a falsely accused character is running from the law. The presence of the law is always there, driving the story forward through the Unfortunate's psyche and fear of getting caught.

THE RESCUER

There are three types of Rescuers: the Savior, the Samaritan, and the Opportunist.

The Savior is one who needs to save and help others. He is a person who has talents, abilities, or morals that allow him to be a Rescuer without question. When the time comes for him to stand up and help a stranger, he doesn't hesitate or think about his ability to help—he just helps.

Rescuing gives him an identity and a reason to get up in the morning. He genuinely wants to help others and feels great when he helps someone else. Whenever he sees someone in trouble he thinks, "That could be my mother or brother in trouble, and I would want someone to help them." This Rescuer usually has some training (fireman, martial artist, soldier, doctor) and makes a point to be physically fit so he can rise to any challenge that may come his way.

The Samaritan is someone who isn't looking to help others, per se, but will step in and help someone if it's at all possible to do so. He is a little bit concerned for himself but can't bear to watch someone else in pain, especially if that person didn't do anything wrong. So he may not help a heroin addict who is being beat up, but he will definitely help someone who was in a car accident.

The Opportunist will help someone if he has something to gain from helping (think of Dustin Hoffman in the film *Hero*). His ego and self-preservation system is so strong he won't risk his safety for anyone unless it helps his image, career, finances, or dating situation. It would have to help fulfill one of the basic human drives toward pleasure—fame, money, and sex. As in the film *Hero*, the opportunist may not even help at all, but he won't correct others if they give him credit for it.

Whether Deliverance is used as plot, subplot, or incident, the elements of the beginning, middle, and end are the same:

BEGINNING: An Unfortunate is in trouble.

- Is the source of trouble a person, place, animal, institution, or natural force?
- Will the trouble start out small and escalate over time?
- How serious is the Threatener at this point? Is he just toying with the Unfortunate?
- Does the Unfortunate feel capable of rescuing himself? How can you show this?
- Was he trying to rescue someone else and got himself into trouble?
- What events got him into this predicament?
- Will he welcome help from the Rescuer?

MIDDLE: The Rescuer knows someone is in trouble and rushes to help.

- What type of Rescuer is he? Savior, Samaritan, or Opportunist?
- Will he get there before any real damage is done?
- Will he understand and see the threat right away?
- Where does the incident take place? Can location add to the Conflict?

- How quickly will he rescue the Unfortunate?
- Will he be able to rescue the Unfortunate?
- Does he know the Threatener? Has he fought similar battles before? Or is he out of his league?

END: The Rescuer stops the Threatener and may or may not have saved the Unfortunate.

- Will the Rescuer save the Unfortunate? If not, why? What goes wrong?
- How is the Threatener stopped? (Make sure you have foreshadowed any devices or tricks the Rescuer may use.)
- If the Unfortunate is saved, what does he think of the Rescuer? Is he grateful? (If the Threatener was a fire and he was saved but his house is gone, he may be upset with the Rescuer for not allowing him to try and save his home.)
- If the Unfortunate is not saved, how does this affect the Rescuer?
- How does the ending tie in with the theme?
- Is there a special location that can be used to add more conflict?

Depending on the type of Threatener chosen, many different themes can be woven using the Deliverance situation. For example, if the Threatener is a tornado, a theme about respecting nature and valuing life over material possessions can be explored. If the Threatener is the law, a theme about the legal system and the cracks and injustices therein can be explored.

Since the Unfortunate is facing such a vital survival threat that may literally be life and death, you have a wonderful opportunity to develop a universal theme. Everyone is concerned with survival and can therefore relate to this situation.

> "How strange is the lot of us mortals! Each of us is here for a brief sojourn; for what purpose he knows not, though he senses it. But without deeper reflection one knows from daily life that one exists for other people."
>
> –ALBERT EINSTEIN

Sojourn

Sojourn is a temporary residence—to spend a certain length of time somewhere as a visitor.

Whereas Deliverance is about a stranger coming to the rescue, Sojourn is about a stranger coming to visit. He may lend a hand and help out, but usually there is not a life-or-death situation involved.

There could be a festival or celebration going on that draws the Sojourner to the area, or the Sojourner could be a distant family member that no one in the family has met before.

His visit will enrich the lives of those around him, though some may feel as if he is destroying their lives because they are resistant to change. Perhaps a father doesn't like him being near his daughter and filling her head with all sorts of independent thoughts or a small town doesn't like his big-city ways.

Like Deliverance, there must also be an Unfortunate and a Threatener. But the Unfortunate is not in any real danger; the Threatener will be more focused on the Sojourner than the Unfortunate.

Whether Sojourn is used as plot, subplot, or incident, the elements of the beginning, middle, and end are the same:

BEGINNING: An Unfortunate is unhappy. A visitor decides to take a brief Sojourn.

- Why is the Unfortunate unhappy? What happened to him?
- Why is the visitor taking a brief Sojourn? Does she need to recuperate?
- Do they know the same people? Or place?
- Have they met a long time ago and forgotten about each other?
- Are there a lot of unfortunate types of people around the Unfortunate? (They may not want to see the Unfortunate change.)

MIDDLE: The Unfortunate and Sojourner meet. Those who know the Unfortunate may not be happy about it. (Perhaps there are many unfortunate women around who are enamored with the handsome Sojourner.)

- What do the Unfortunate and Sojourner have in common to keep them together? Or is it their differences that attract them?
- What does the Unfortunate have to lose by spending time with the Sojourner, or vice versa?
- Are they the same sex? How is it different if you change the genders around?
- Do they meet in front of others or at a secret place each thought no one else knew about?
- Does one see the other first and pursue a meeting?

END: The Sojourner changes people's lives for the better, though some may not realize it, and then he either moves on or decides to stay.

- How does the Sojourner change people's lives? Why?
- If he seemed to destroy some lives in the beginning, how has that turned out to be a blessing in disguise? For example, did a loveless marriage break up because of him in the beginning and now both parties are happier for it?
- Do the people think their lives are better or worse?
- As well as having her life changed, does the Unfortunate change internally?
- Is the Sojourner changed from this experience?
- Why does he stay? Or leave?

EXAMPLES

The Count of Monte Cristo, ALEXANDER DUMAS

DELIVERANCE AS SUBPLOT—The Count is rescued by a Samaritan who happens to be in the jail cell next to him.

King Kong, MERIAN C. COOPER AND ERNEST B. SHOEDSACK

DELIVERANCE AS PLOT—A young woman is held captive by a large gorilla and a party of men come to rescue her. Then the gorilla becomes the captive who is not rescued.

The Spitfire Grill, LEE DAVID ZLOTOFF

SOJOURN AS PLOT—Percy, upon being released from prison, goes to the small town of Gilead to find a place where she can start over again. She is taken in by Hannah to help out at her place, the Spitfire Grill. Percy brings change to the small town, stirring resentment and fear in some and growth in others.

There's Something About Mary, FARRELLY BROTHERS

SOJOURN AS SUBPLOT AND INCIDENT—A man gets a chance to get together with his dream girl from high school, even though the last time they saw each other he made a fool of himself. While the main character takes a Sojourn to find Mary, Mary also flows in and out of the story (and the frame) as an unwitting Sojourner in the hearts of all men who see her.

VENGEANCE FOR A CRIME AND REHABILITATION

> "Men are disturbed not by things that happen but
> by their opinion of the things that happen."
>
> –EPICTETUS

Vengeance for a Crime

*Vengeance is infliction of punishment in return for a wrong com-
mitted; it is retribution with great violence or force to an extreme degree.*

Vengeance for a Crime has always been considered a noble act,
however illegal it may be. An Avenger who feels sympathy for or
duty to a Victim seeks to punish a Criminal.

This situation requires an Avenger and a Criminal. The Victim
does not play a major role and may even be killed in the opening
chapters.

While this situation has been used by many writers throughout
time, there are still many themes to be explored.

- What ties the Avenger and the Victim together?
- What ties the Criminal and the Victim together?
- Does the criminal act make a comment about society or the legal sys-
  tem in some way? How was the Criminal able to get away with it? (Think
  of the Wild West when the law couldn't be counted on in times of need.)
- What keeps the Avenger from giving up?
- Does the Criminal think he was right to do what he did? Did the Victim
  hurt him in some way first?
- What sparks the Criminal's actions?
    - A disagreement?
    - An insult?
    - A misunderstanding?
    - A desire for power, money, or prestige?
    - Self-defense?

◦ A mistake?

  ◦ Does the Criminal think of himself as the Victim?

The list of criminal acts committed by the Criminal and the list of punishments wielded by the Avenger are infinite.

Sampling of acts by the Criminal:

- physical acts against property
- physical acts against the Victim or people close to him
- acts against a person's character or societal standing
- acts against that which the victim holds dear—a favorite dance hall burned down, a park closed
- getting the Victim or someone close to him hooked on drugs
- getting the Victim fired or thrown out onto the street
- messing up plans the Victim has been looking forward to

Sampling of punishments by the Avenger:

- deciding to delay punishment and torture the Criminal for a while
- terrorizing the Criminal into a confession
- performing the exact same fate on the Criminal as the Criminal did onto the Victim
- forgiving the Criminal and allowing the authorities to take over
- devising an intricate plan that makes the Criminal punish himself

THE AVENGER

The Avenger is someone who has close ties to the Victim or the Victim's family. He has a strong sense of duty about him and a touch of the Rescuer within him. He sees himself as the only one fit to get justice, especially if the local law enforcement doesn't have enough evidence to pursue the Criminal.

He is judge and jury as far as he is concerned and no one can convince him otherwise. He doesn't care if he breaks the law because the law has let him and the Victim down.

He has a tough streak in him that will allow him to endure any hardship to catch the Criminal. Depending on his personality, his vengeance can be swift and predictable or slow and incalculable. He will use any means available to him and will put himself in jeopardy to accomplish his objective.

His reputation may also be on the line. If he is a mobster or a "work for hire" he must not fail to get revenge or he'll never be hired again. If he is an otherwise upstanding citizen seeking revenge, other characters may want the police to handle the situation, so he may lose his reputation if he succeeds in getting revenge.

THE CRIMINAL

In this situation the Criminal is not related to the Avenger as he is in the next situation, "Vengeance taken for kindred upon kindred."

There are two types of criminals: The Justified who thinks he is right about his actions and the Remorseful who knows he was wrong but can't change things.

The Justified thinks he was right to harm the Victim as he did. Perhaps he felt like the Victim himself, especially if the Victim did something to spark his attack as far as he's concerned. He will then also feel like a Victim when the Avenger comes after him: "Why is everyone picking on me?"

The Remorseful knows he acted hastily and possibly wishes he could undo what he has done, but that's impossible now. He would like to explain things to the Avenger, but that never works out. Every word he says comes out wrong, and he gets himself in deeper trouble with the Avenger. Midway through the story he changes events around in his head so much that he turns into a Justified Criminal in order to have the willpower to fight the Avenger. He will commit another act of violence at this point so the Avenger is in the right at the end of the story for wielding justice upon him.

Whether Vengeance for a Crime is used as plot, subplot, or incident, the elements of the beginning, middle, and end are the same:

BEGINNING: A victim is harmed.

- In what way is the Victim harmed?
- Does it happen before the story starts?
- How many characters are involved?
- Does the Victim survive? If so, will he play a large role in the story?
- What theme are you working on and how does that play into the crime?
- Does the Avenger witness the crime? If not, where is the Avenger?
- Does the Criminal act alone?
- How does the Criminal feel after his crime?
- Does the Avenger know the Criminal?

MIDDLE: The Avenger seeks the Criminal to wield vengeance.

- Will this be a physical/action story or will you explore the psychologies of the Avenger and Criminal?
- Do the Avenger and Criminal meet several times throughout the story or only at the end?

- What settings can you use to "up the stakes" and add Conflict?
- Does the Victim play a role at all?
- What keeps the Avenger going? How much does he have to endure?
- Has the Criminal gotten worse? Has he hurt any other people or their property?
- Will the Avenger work with law enforcement at all?
- Will the Avenger almost catch up to the Criminal?
- How will you foreshadow the ending?

ENDING: The Avenger wields justice upon the Criminal.

- What brings the Avenger and Criminal together? How does the Avenger catch him?
- Will justice be swift or torturous?
- Is there anyone else the Avenger has to fight before getting to the Criminal?
- What last-ditch effort does the Criminal make to save himself?
- Can the setting play a role in how creative the Avenger gets in serving justice?
- Will the Victim witness the justice?
- Will the Victim forgive the Criminal and try to stop the Avenger?
- How will you tie up the theme here?

> "It is only with the heart that one can see rightly,
> what is essential is invisible to the eye."
>
> —ANTOINE DE SAINT-EXUPÉRY

Rehabilitation

Rehabilitation means to restore someone to a useful place in society through therapy and education.

In this opposite situation, the Avenger becomes the Rehabilitator who tries to change the Criminal for the better rather than punish him. This may come at the request of the Victim, who has found a way to forgive the Criminal and does not believe in an "eye-for-an-eye" mentality. This is a great change for the Avenger to go through during the story and creates a wonderful character arc for him. This type of situation focuses more on characterization than on plot as all the major characters will transform. The main characteristics are:

- The Victim puts her ideals of nonviolence to the test.
- The Avenger has to let go of his anger and need for justice.
- The Criminal feels weak and insignificant in the face of people who would forgive him and treat him like a human being who made a mistake.

Whether Rehabilitation is used as plot, subplot, or incident, the elements of the beginning, middle, and end are the same:

BEGINNING: A Victim is harmed.

- Does the Victim survive the ordeal?
- Why is the Victim harmed?
- Does the Victim know the Criminal?
- Will the Victim request leniency for the Criminal?
- Does the Criminal feel justified?
- When does the Rehabilitator come into the story and why?
- Why does the Rehabilitator want to help the Criminal? Why doesn't she want revenge? Is it her morals?

MIDDLE: A Rehabilitator goes after the Criminal in the hopes of catching and possibly helping to change the Criminal. Either the Rehabilitator or the Victim does not believe in vengeance. If the Victim is dead it won't bring him back.

- Why does the Rehabilitator get involved? What does he hope to gain out of the situation? A sense of pride in helping?
- How does the Rehabilitator attempt to save the Criminal? What tools will he use?
- Does the Criminal care at all? Or has he built walls around himself emotionally?
- Will the Criminal play along with the Rehabilitator only because he thinks it will keep him out of jail?
- Will the Rehabilitator ever feel like giving up?

END: The Criminal is caught and steps are taken to see if he can be saved.

- Is the Criminal truly remorseful? Or will he self-destruct?
- What has the Rehabilitator risked during this process? Will he lose whatever this is now?
- How has the Victim dealt with the Criminal's capture?
- Has the Rehabilitator developed a relationship with the Criminal?
- Will the Criminal survive in the end? If so, has he changed?

EXAMPLES

The Godfather, FRANCIS FORD COPPOLA

VENGEANCE USED AS SUBPLOT AND INCIDENT—A Mafia boss' innocent son gets involved in the bloody family business when his father is critically wounded in a mob hit.

The Princess Bride, ROB REINER

VENGEANCE USED AS SUBPLOT—Inigo Montoya spends his life trying to avenge his father's murder.

Dead Man Walking, TIM ROBBINS

REHABILITATION USED AS PLOT—A nun, while comforting a convicted killer on death row, empathizes with both the killer and his victim's families.

Good Will Hunting, GUS VAN SANT

REHABILITATION USED AS PLOT—Will Hunting, a janitor at MIT, has a gift for mathematics. A psychiatrist tries to help him with this gift and the rest of his life. His crime is in wasting away his genius.

Situations 7 & 8

VENGEANCE TAKEN FOR KINDRED UPON KINDRED AND APPEARANCE OF A NEW KINSMAN

"The tragedy of a man's life is what dies inside of him while he lives."

—HENRY DAVID THOREAU

Vengeance Taken for Kindred Upon Kindred

Vengeance is infliction of punishment in return for a wrong committed, retribution with great violence or force to an extreme degree. When it involves family members it is even more earth-shattering.

Vengeance Taken for Kindred Upon Kindred is similar to Vengeance for a Crime, but in this situation the Avenging Kinsman, Guilty Kinsman, and Victim are all related on some level. They do not have to be blood relatives but can be one of three types of Kinsman:

1. a relative through marriage only

2. a hierarchal relationship such as a mentor and his protégé or a teacher and his student or a mob boss and right-hand man; two people interact on an intimate level

3. friends who have gone through something very intense, intimate, and personal together such as being attacked, going off to war, or saving each other in some way

A very interesting twist in this situation could be a *Dr. Jekyll and Mr. Hyde* type of story where the Avenging Kinsman and the Guilty Kinsman are the same.

This situation requires an Avenging Kinsman, a Guilty Kinsman, and Remembrance of the Victim that may come in the form of a Relative of the Victim and/or Avenging and Guilty Kinsman. More often than not the Victim in this situation is killed rather than harmed because a very strong motivating force is needed to propel two kinsmen against each other. It's much easier to seek vengeance upon a stranger than it is to seek vengeance upon a kinsman.

THE AVENGING KINSMAN

The Avenging Kinsman will always face a moment of disbelief, where he doesn't want to believe the Guilty Kinsman is guilty. At the same time he is also dealing with his grief over the Victim's misfortune. He is intimately tied to both of these people and cannot separate himself from this unfortunate triangle. He may be reluctant and try to wish away the whole event, but sooner or later his grief will turn into anger and his disbelief will turn into a realization of the truth.

The Avenging Kinsman sees it as his duty to keep things "in the family" and seek vengeance himself. Perhaps another kinsman asks him to take care of things or the dying Victim begs him to seek revenge in his name.

His sense of duty and right vs. wrong is very strong and nothing can sway him from his task.

THE GUILTY KINSMAN

The Guilty Kinsman may or may not know he did something wrong. Perhaps he was out partying with the Victim and didn't realize she overdosed, or he felt like the Victim needed to learn a lesson of some sort only things went too far.

This type of character is rarely remorseful, as is the case with the Criminal in Vengeance for a Crime. Family situations such as this are very emotional and personal. It takes a lot of anger, resentment, or jealously to hurt a kindred as opposed to a stranger.

He is like the wife-beating husband who hurts his wife one day, apologizes to her the next, and then repeats the offense again. This is not a remorseful person. He is locked in a pattern of behavior and may not think there is anything wrong with him at all.

He may even have one of two types of psychological disorders:

> 1. PARANOID PERSONALITY DISORDER: an unwarranted tendency to interpret the actions of other people as deliberately threatening or demeaning. He suspects, without sufficient basis, that others are exploiting, harming, or deceiving him. He bears grudges. Symptoms include suspicion, inability to relax, poor self-image, being argumentative and easily slighted. This type would probably think the Victim was out to get him in some way.

> 2. BORDERLINE PERSONALITY DISORDER: an individual trait that reflects ingrained, inflexible, and maladaptive patterns of behavior characterized by impulsive and unpredictable actions, mood instability, and unstable interpersonal relationships. He has inappropriate, intense anger

or difficulty controlling his temper. He sees things in extremes. Symptoms include unstable interpersonal relationships, frequent displays of temper, and often being impulsive and bored. This type would probably think the Victim was going to leave him or he just couldn't contain his anger during an argument. This type is usually remorseful.

For more information on these disorder, see http://my.webmd.com or www.mentalhealth.com.

REMEMBRANCE OF THE VICTIM

As stated earlier, usually in this situation the Victim is killed. Therefore, Remembrance of the Victim is present throughout the story. This can come in the form of a Relative of the Victim and/or Avenging and Guilty Kinsman.

In Vengeance for a Crime, the personal relationship between the characters is not as intense as it is with kindred. The Criminal in that situation may even have several Victims, never giving any one Victim much of a role in the story. But here the Victim is present like a ghost haunting the characters until vengeance is served.

A relative of both the Avenging Kinsman and the Guilty Kinsman is present to speak up for the Victim, motivate the Avenging Kinsman, and condemn the Guilty Kinsman. He is a symbol that lets everyone know the Avenging Kinsman is right for seeking vengeance. The family is behind him.

Whether Vengeance Taken for Kindred Upon Kindred is used as plot, subplot, or incident, the beginning, middle, and end are the same:

BEGINNING: A Victim is slain by the Guilty Kinsman and the Avenging Kinsman grieves.

- Does the Guilty Kinsman have a psychological disorder of some type? How will you show this?

- How is the Victim slain? Does anyone witness it?

- Was the act impulsive or thought out ahead of time? How long have they been at odds with each other?

- Does the Guilty Kinsman kill for power? (Think of the *Godfather* movies.) Does he stand to gain anything?

- How closely related are the Guilty Kinsman and the Victim?

- What does the Guilty Kinsman do after the "act"?

- Is the Victim alive long enough to ask for vengeance? Does he make the Avenging Kinsman promise him he will do it?

MIDDLE: The Avenging Kinsman has accepted the situation and vows to hunt down the Guilty Kinsman for vengeance. The Guilty Kinsman reacts.

- Does the Guilty Kinsman run away or stand his ground? Does he have a group of people on his side?
- Does the relative of both play a significant role? (He could pretend to be on the side of the Guilty Kinsman, only to double-cross him later.)
- What are the Avenging Kinsman's plans for the Guilty Kinsman? What tools does he have at his disposal?
- Does the Avenging Kinsman have any special skills or resources to help him?
- Will they have one big confrontation at the end of the story or meet several times in the middle—each meeting more intense than the last one?
- Will law enforcement get involved?
- How will you foreshadow the ending?

END: The Avenging Kinsman defeats the Guilty Kinsman.

- How will vengeance be served?
- Will this be physical punishment? Humiliation? Financial ruin? (Be creative.)
- How does the Guilty Kinsman react to his downfall? Does he repent? Ask forgiveness? Does he curse his family?
- How do the family members feel after it is all over? How does the Avenging Kinsman feel?
- What will the Avenging Kinsman do now?
- Do they formally remember the Victim after it's over?

> "There is not enough magic in a bloodline to forge an instant, irrevocable bond."
>
> –JAMES EARL JONES

Appearance of a New Kinsman

Appearance here refers to the act of appearing in a particular place, company, or proceeding.

In this opposite situation, the Avenging Kinsman becomes the Protecting Kinsman, helping to bring a new member into the clan or to look at an existing member in a new way. This can be through:

- the birth of a child (especially an heir to a throne)
- a friend or ally who wishes to join the clan
- a long-lost, New Kinsman who is returning home
- a New Kinsman who has developed a talent and wishes to advance in the clan
- a clan member who wishes to break with accepted roles

In each of these types a New Kinsman comes into the clan, and there are those who do not want to allow him entrance, especially if this new member has or will have power. Think of stories that have been about:

- one King ordering the death of another King's heir
- a father who should not have fathered a child because he is married to someone else or the mother is too young for him, creating an illegitimate child, which could possibly split the clan apart
- a man returning home to take over his father's business, taking it away from an uncle
- a child who will be born with a handicap and the family isn't sure he should be brought to term

The Protecting Kinsman would be focused on the child and keeping him safe, no matter how old the child is during the story. His duty is still to the family as it was in the opposite situation as an Avenging Kinsman, but here it is to keep the New Kinsman alive rather than to avenge a kinsman's death.

If the story is about a New Kinsman trying to challenge stereotypes held within the clan, the Protecting Kinsman will take more of a mentor role, serving to give him confidence to keep going.

Whether Appearance of a New Kinsman is used as plot, subplot, or incident, the elements of the beginning, middle, and end are the same:

BEGINNING: A New Kinsman joins the clan.

- Are others suspicious of him right away?
- Is his parentage in question?
- What type of power does the New Kinsman have?
- Why do some of the kinsmen want to get rid of him?
- Does the New Kinsman have allies in the clan?
- What will the New Kinsman potentially do for the clan? What benefit is he?
- Will some want to use him as a pawn? Making false alliances with him?

MIDDLE: A Protecting Kinsman decides to guard the New Kinsman at all costs.

- Why does the Protecting Kinsman guard him? What's at stake for him?
- Why does the New Kinsman stay when the situation gets tough? Does he feel a need to serve the clan? To help others as if it is his duty?
- What obstacles are thrown in front of him? Does he know who is against him?
- Is the New Kinsman trusting the wrong people?
- Who speaks for the New Kinsman if he is a child?
- What motivates the Guilty Kinsman?

END: The Protecting Kinsman defeats the Guilty Kinsman, and the New Kinsman contributes to the clan in a positive way.

- What does the Guilty Kinsman do to try to defeat the New Kinsman? Does he get others to help him?
- How does the Protecting Kinsman make everyone see what has happened? Why didn't they want to see the truth before?
- How does the New Kinsman learn more about his power, duty, or perhaps his true lineage?
- How is the whole tribe strengthened by the New Kinsman? And how is the Guilty Kinsman punished?
- How does the New Kinsman contribute to the clan? (He could be an inventor, scientist, doctor, royalty, or guru, someone who has secret knowledge or skills.)

EXAMPLES

Richard III, WILLIAM SHAKESPEARE

VENGEANCE TAKEN FOR KINDRED UPON KINDRED AS PLOT—Richard seeks to gain the throne from his elder brother, Edward, by any means within his grasp including murder, marriage, and fratricide.

The Bacchae, EURIPIDES

VENGEANCE TAKEN FOR KINDRED UPON KINDRED AS PLOT—*The Bacchae* is a classic myth in which Dionysus, son of Zeus, seeks vengeance on Thebes, the city of his birth and site of his mortal mother Semele's cruel and horrible death.

The Golden Child, MICHAEL RITCHIE

APPEARANCE OF KINSMAN (TO HUMANITY) AS SUBPLOT—Eddie Murphy plays a detective with a specialty of finding lost chil-

dren. He is told he is the "chosen one" who will find and protect the Golden Child, a Buddhist mystic who was kidnapped
by an evil sorcerer.

Whale Rider, NIKI CARO (based on the novella)

APPEARANCE OF KINSMAN AS PLOT—The story begins with a
girl's birth and the simultaneous death of her mother and
twin brother. Her grieving father Porourangi gives her a
boy's name, Paikea, after the legendary warrior who rode
in from the sea on a whale's beak to found the Maori people.
Years later, little Pai is being raised by her grandfather Koro,
the tribal chief descended from a centuries-old line of chiefs,
who remains disappointed that his granddaughter lived
while his grandson died. Only a firstborn son can inherit the
title. His belief in tradition blinds him to the fact that Pai is
the best choice for the title.

FLIGHT AND PURSUIT

> "Fate leads him who will, him who won't they drag."
>
> –LUCIUS ANNAEUS SENECA

Flight

Flight is the act of running away. It is to flee, to escape, or to make a hasty departure.

As I stated previously, I have renamed Polti's Pursuit as Flight because I feel this better describes what he wrote. Polti was speaking of the person who was running away as being the Main Character, not the pursuer. Therefore, the focus is on Flight, not Pursuit. The opposite situation is better served by being called Pursuit.

Flight is similar to the previous vengeance situations in that you have someone who is accused of doing something wrong (he may or may not be innocent) who is being pursued. Flight differs from the previous vengeance situations in that the Avenger doesn't play a role here.

The interest is in the Fugitive alone. He seems to be a victim of fate, and the audience sympathizes with him to some degree because we are all afraid of being in the wrong place at the wrong time. If he is guilty of his crime, there is a valid reason he committed the crime, so the audience can sympathize with him—he is the Main Character, after all.

This situation requires a Punishment and a Fugitive. The police may be after him but they are not personally out to get him as an Avenger would. They are just doing their job and may even grow to respect the Fugitive—think of Leonardo DiCaprio and Tom Hanks in *Catch Me If You Can*.

There are three types of Punishments: Just, Injust, and Unjust.

Just Punishment occurs when the Fugitive has done something wrong. It is the upholding of what is just and due in accordance with the law. In this case, the Fugitive has committed an illegal act or crime and should be punished, but his actions are excusable. Again the audience must be able to identify with this character.

In *Catch Me If You Can*, Leonardo DiCaprio's character commits the crimes Tom Hanks' character is chasing him for, but we come to realize it was Leonardo's father who caused him to become a criminal. In scene after scene, we see that this is really a good kid who didn't receive the parental love and support he needed to become an upstanding citizen. He barely had a chance. His desire to "get out" of his life of crime and live somewhere out of the country also tells us that he is sorry and is trying to change—albeit too late.

In *Thelma and Louise*, the Main Characters just want to get away and start new lives somewhere after they commit a crime. We know how hard their lives have been and that Thelma killed a man, but it was in self-defense. This makes them sympathetic characters even though they are guilty.

Injust Punishment occurs when the Fugitive has not done anything wrong but is still punished. An injustice is in violation of another's rights or of what is right. In this case, the audience identifies with the Fugitive right away because he's innocent. As long as he doesn't commit a major crime while he flees punishment, he will be a likable character. Think of Harrison Ford's character in the film *The Fugitive*.

This type of Punishment brings out two types of Fugitives—one who wants to set things right and one who wants to just escape and save himself. If he wants to set things right he is determined to save his name, avoid capture, and find those who are guilty. If he just wants to escape he won't care at all who committed the crime he's accused of. He just wants to get away and leave it all behind him.

Unjust Punishment occurs when the Fugitive is fleeing a power in authority. It is a want of justice not received. In this case it is the Punisher who commits a crime against the Fugitive.

Perhaps the Fugitive didn't agree with the Power in Authority and was going to:

- expose their illegal practices
- publish his negative opinion about their products
- show people how to get by without this power figure taking care of them

Or the Fugitive was just in the wrong place at the wrong time:

- She couldn't care less about this power in authority but for some reason they think she's a threat and want her out of the way.
- The power in authority could be after one of the Fugitive's friends and come after her to find the friend.
- Maybe the Fugitive saw something she shouldn't have seen and is now considered a threat.

THE PUNISHMENT

The Punishment literally is what's at stake in the story. It motivates the Fugitive to flee in the beginning and then pushes her to endure any obstacle set in her way. Her goal is to be free from Punishment.

Punishment is a loss. It can be the loss of time as in jail, the loss of dignity as in a scandal, the loss of physical health as in torture, the loss of mental health as in scare tactics being used, or the loss of emotional health as in family and friends being harmed.

Whatever the Punishment, it is strong and compelling enough to make the hero flee. Show how important time and freedom are to the hero and then threaten her with jail. Show how important family is to her and then take away her child. If we first see who the hero is and what is important to her, we will be able to sympathize with her when Punishment is wielded.

THE FUGITIVE

The Fugitive has something to lose by not running. She is a resourceful person who has enough self-confidence to flee and think she will be successful. She knows the law cannot help her and that doing things through traditional channels won't get her anywhere. She has to take things into her own hands and is willing to risk everything to try. She feels she doesn't have much more to lose.

She may become so wrapped up in what she is doing that her whole personality changes, and she won't be the same person by the end as she was in the beginning. She gains self-esteem, learns a lot about survival, and delves into a new "underworld" while she's on the run.

She may meet people from a social class she considered to be much lower than hers. This will make it harder for her to go back to life as normal with her old friends. Her ordeal may force her to look at what she has been doing wrong in her life. Is there someone, or a whole group of people, she punishes on a daily basis for being different?

Whether Flight is used as a plot, subplot, or incident, the elements of the beginning, middle, and end are the same:

BEGINNING: A crime or injustice occurs and the potential Fugitive is present. She is either guilty or innocent of the act and may just be in the wrong place at the wrong time.

- Which type of Punishment is she fleeing—Just, Injust, or Unjust?
- Is she upset by what happens? Is it personal for her?
- Is anyone there to witness it?
- How will you foreshadow things to keep the second act of your story

interesting? (Add some intrigue; throw a couple of other characters into the mix who can cause some trouble for the Fugitive.)

- Is there anyone on the Fugitive's side?

- Will the Fugitive get a taste of Punishment? (Think of *The Fugitive*— the character was already in prison for a while when he escaped.)

MIDDLE: The Fugitive is on the run. Punishment follows right behind her.

- What type of Punishment will she suffer if she is caught?

- Will she seek aid from someone?

- What resources does she have?

- Will she face a few major obstacles or many small ones? How fast is the story pace? (This is a chase, so keep it moving!)

- Will there be any detours on her path? Is there any unfinished business she has to take care of? (Perhaps a friend passes away and she wants to attend the funeral.)

- Has her personality started to change? (Stress can have that effect.)

- How often will you show the Punishing Force?

- How many times will this Force get close to capturing the Fugitive?

END: The Fugitive faces the Punishing Force and gets away.

- Is the Fugitive guilty? Will she get away with it by dying (think *Thelma and Louise*) or by giving up something like citizenship as she moves out of the country?

- If the Fugitive is not guilty, is the Punishing Force proven to be wrong and exposed? (Think about Russell Crowe's character in *The Insider*.)

- How dramatic will the ending be?

- How much has the Fugitive changed? Will she be able to go back to her former life?

- Will the Fugitive die in the end? Will justice be served?

"When your dreams tire, they go underground; and out of kindness that's where they stay."

–LIBBY HOUSTON

Pursuit

Pursuit has three meanings—the act or an instance of chasing or pursuing, the act of striving for something, or an activity (such as a hobby) engaged in regularly.

is situation, the Fugitive becomes the Pursuer. She is striving toward something whether it's a person, an activity, or her own education. She has a goal to better her life by bringing something into it. The antagonist in this case is anything that stands in her way of achieving this goal, whether it's a lack of education that prevents her from getting a good job or a parent who doesn't want her to change. Many "chick lit" stories fit in this category where the heroine is up against her own shortcomings.

She is the hero who chases her ex-boyfriend all across the country, trying to win him back because she realizes she made a mistake in leaving him. Think *My Best Friend's Wedding* with Julia Roberts.

She is the hero who wants to make a better life for her family so she works two jobs to pay for a college education.

Whether Pursuit is used as plot, subplot, or incident, the elements of the beginning, middle, and end are the same:

BEGINNING: This type of situation focuses on the hero and her noble goal of bettering herself.

- What is it she wants to change? (Let's see the bad habit or situation at work here.)
- Why does she want to better herself?
- What is she pursuing?
- Does someone want to stop her? Why?
- What is at stake for her if she changes?
- What is at stake for her if she doesn't change?
- Is there a time period in which she must reach her goal?

MIDDLE: The second act is about how she handles obstacle after obstacle toward this goal.

- What types of obstacles will she face? Physical, emotional, mental, or spiritual?
- Will the obstacles get worse, testing her resolve?
- How will the obstacles change her? By overcoming them, does she feel stronger?
- Is she pursuing someone? If so, why does he keep running?
- Has her goal changed at all? (It usually changes for the better because rarely do we go for the gold and then change our minds half way to go for the bronze instead.)

END: In the end she may or may not attain her goal, but it is the Pursuit that makes it all worthwhile.

- Will she attain her goal? Why?
- What does she learn from her Pursuit? How did she grow? How will you show this?
- Would she do it again?
- How do other characters feel about her now? Are they jealous?
- Is there a concrete ending or a sense that she will continue to pursue her passion and continue to learn?

EXAMPLES

The Fugitive, ANDREW DAVIS

FLIGHT AS PLOT—Wrongly convicted of murdering his wife, Dr. Richard Kimble escapes from a prison bus and tries to find out why she was killed and who the murderer really was. He is fleeing a U.S. marshal while pursuing the truth.

Thelma and Louise, RIDLEY SCOTT

FLIGHT AS PLOT, PURSUIT AS SUBPLOT—Thelma and Louise decide to break out of their normal routine and take a road trip. Their journey turns into a flight when Louise kills a man who threatens to rape Thelma. They decide to go to Mexico, but soon they are hunted by American police.

My Best Friend's Wedding, P.J. HOGAN

PURSUIT AS PLOT—When Julianne's long-time friend says he's getting married, she realizes she loves him and sets out to get him.

The Bachelor, GARY SINYOR

PURSUIT AS SUBPLOT AND INCIDENT, FLIGHT AS INCIDENT—A commitment-phobic man has to get married in one day in order to inherit his grandfather's 100-million-dollar estate. When he botches up a proposal to his girlfriend, she flees to Greece and he pursues many women in an effort to find a bride.

Situations 11 & 12

DISASTER AND MIRACLE

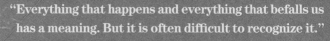

> "Everything that happens and everything that befalls us
> has a meaning. But it is often difficult to recognize it."
>
> –NIZAMI

Disaster

*Disaster is an occurrence that causes widespread destruction.
It is a catastrophe or a grave misfortune.*

This situation requires a Vanquished Power and a Victorious Enemy,
a Messenger, or a Victim.

Disaster plays on a basic human fear of the unknown for dramatic effect. At any moment in time, a catastrophe could occur. We never know exactly what will happen each day when we leave the house. The news is full of stories about people who are victims of one kind of disaster or another, and all the victims are completely shocked by what occurred.

There are four stages toward healing that a Victim of Disaster will go through: Disbelief/Shock, Fear, Anger, and Acceptance.

- **DISBELIEF/SHOCK:** If the Victim has some time before the Disaster occurs, such as being forewarned of a tornado, he may be in Disbelief for a period. Otherwise he moves straight into Shock as the Disaster occurs.

- **FEAR:** The Victim may wonder if another Disaster is coming or if this Disaster has really ended. He may become over-sensitive and emotionally paralyzed. Or he may try to disguise his fear with fake laughter or by taking risks—he's not acting rationally.

- **ANGER:** The Victim feels a little more secure that the Disaster is over and he now looks at the mess it created. He's angry at being so helpless in the face of Disaster: Is life really that fragile? If he acted in a way that was embarrassing for him, he may feel some shame, which would exacerbate his Anger.

- **ACCEPTANCE:** Usually with the help of friends or other victims, the Victim realizes that he shouldn't expect himself to be able to take care of everything that happens in life. He's still alive and that's all that matters. Maybe someone else didn't fare as well as he did and he should look on the bright side of things and be thankful. If he has lost someone, it will take a while for him to reach this stage. His support system is a big factor in how long it takes him to reach Acceptance. The more friends and resources one has, the stronger one seems to be in the face of disaster.

The stories that bother us the most are those where the Victim was going about her normal everyday routine and something unexpected just happens. There is a very strong identification with the Victim here, which is rare in storytelling because people usually want to identify with a hero. It's interesting to note that very few classical works (and modern for that matter) have been written about societal defeat, as in the losing of a war, for example. The Greeks were some of the only ones to do this, with the fall of Troy as an example.

THE VANQUISHED POWER
The Vanquished Power is the cause of a Disaster. A tornado, or a ruling king for that matter, is not a disaster in and of itself but causes a catastrophe by its very presence or nature.

The Vanquished Power can be a natural force, a ruling king, a parental figure, or an entire group of people. Whatever is seen to be powerful in the story by other characters can take this role. Perhaps an object that is said to be cursed—like a mummy's tomb—can be considered very powerful by characters on an archeological dig site.

The Vanquished Power should be introduced right away because it is the source of Conflict for the story and will keep the momentum going. In the film *Independence Day*, we see the Vanquished Power right away when dark shadows fill the sky as the alien spaceships approach. We then see reactions to such an event from the point of view of everyday people as they go about their lives. This personalizes the Disaster for the audience.

A VICTORIOUS ENEMY, A MESSENGER, OR A VICTIM
This character can be one of three types: a Victorious Enemy, a Messenger, or a Victim, depending upon the type of Disaster you are writing. As a rule, Victorious Enemies require offensive situations and Messengers require defensive situations. Victims are just in the wrong place at the wrong time.

If you are writing about war or any manner of personal type of disaster, a Victorious Enemy should be used. War does not require a Messenger heralding doom before the Disaster strikes, and personal catastrophes usually don't involve enough people to warrant a Messenger. In these situations, the characters know who their enemies are and are aware of impending disaster. A Victorious Enemy charges ahead and attacks, leaving Disaster in his wake. All the other characters must deal with this Disaster.

Think of the invasion of Troy and how all the people who lived there had to deal with the fall of the city. This type of story would start with the fall of Troy and go from there.

If you are writing about natural or supernatural disasters, the Messenger is usually used. Something that is outside of the realm of normal experience (sadly, war is somewhat normal in civilization), such as aliens attacking Earth, requires someone who can prove what is going to happen or at least explain it, as Jeff Goldblum's character does in *Independence Day*.

Likewise, there will always be a Messenger to announce the coming of a tornado. There is always a scientist or some kind of warning device heralding these Disasters. Aliens and tornados do not have Victorious Enemies. They may be defeated in the end, but the characters defeating them are in a defensive position, not an offensive one, as the Victorious Enemy is.

If there is a Victim, he is usually a normal, everyday person who is thrust into an event or situation that requires him to reach deep down inside to overcome it and survive. He usually does not think of himself as a hero or a great person.

Whether Disaster is used as plot, subplot, or incident, the elements of the beginning, middle, and end are the same:

BEGINNING: A Disaster is about to happen.

- How soon will the characters realize this?
- What type of Disaster will this be?
- Will they try to save themselves or help others?
- Do some of the people want the Vanquished Power to win?
- When will the Messenger or Victorious Enemy be introduced?
- Can you change the setting to make it more interesting?
- Will you explore one character more deeply to build audience identification?
- Will you add animals and children in jeopardy to add tension?

MIDDLE: The Disaster happens.

- How tragic will the Disaster be?
- Will the event take up the entire second act? Or more?

- Will you show the effect of the Disaster on several different people? Or just one?

- If you use a Victim, how will he deal with the Disaster? Will his true colors shine?

- Will the Disaster be one event or several events—one after the other?

- Will new characters with new tools show up to help?

END: The Vanquished Power is vanquished or endured (in the case of a natural power).

- How will the Vanquished Power be defeated?

- Are there any last-minute battles?

- Will everyone survive the ordeal?

- Will you check back in with everyone you introduced in the beginning to show what happened to them as a result of the story?

- Do the characters have new skills to help vanquish powers like this in the future? (Think of the film *Tornado!* and the new information they received about tornados in the end.)

- Have you made sure the Vanquished Power loses with a strong fight. (Let his downfall be due to something it took the characters a long time to figure out. It shouldn't be too easy for him to fall.)

> "There are only two ways to live your life. One is as though nothing is a miracle. The other is as though everything is a miracle."
>
> –ALBERT EINSTEIN

Miracle

A Miracle is an event that appears unexplainable. Miracles, like disasters, are spontaneous and come of themselves.

In this situation, the Vanquished Power becomes the reason for the Miracle. For example:

- Cancer can be a Vanquished Power that a Miracle drug cures.

- A hero miraculously finds the shelter needed to save a group of people from an earthquake.

- A woman finds her long-lost child just in the nick of time.

In this situation, the Miracle is the center of the story around which everything else revolves. The characters are very much focused on it—waiting for it in the beginning, witnessing it in the middle, and questioning it in the end.

Whether Miracle is used as plot, subplot, or incident, the elements of the beginning, middle, and end are the same:

BEGINNING: A tragedy happens.

- How harsh is the tragedy?
- Is there any hope of reversing the tragedy? (There must be room for a Miracle to happen.)
- Do all characters believe in and request a Miracle, or only one? (Or perhaps no one does.)
- What type of tragedy will you use? Why? Is there a theme you want to explore?

MIDDLE: A Miracle cures or conquers the tragedy.

- How does the Miracle come about? Does a new character come to facilitate it?
- Does anyone try to stop the Miracle?
- What is at stake if the Miracle doesn't happen? What is at stake if it does? Are they afraid of persecution? (Some may brand the Miracle as the work of the devil.)
- How does the Miracle change the characters' lives?

END: The characters examine the Miracle and question what happened.

- Do they try to keep the Miracle a secret?
- How are the belief systems of the characters tested, if at all?
- Do the characters try to rationalize the Miracle away?
- Do they feel unworthy of the Miracle?
- Does the Miracle scare them on some level? (It can be a very powerful experience.)

EXAMPLES

Titanic, JAMES CAMERON

DISASTER AS PLOT—On the ill-fated voyage of the "unsinkable" ship, a rich girl and poor boy find love.

Twister, JAN DE BONT

DISASTER AS SUBPLOT—A research couple on the point of divorce keeps bumping into each other as they both chase tornadoes.

The Third Miracle, AGNIESZKA HOLLAND

MIRACLE AS PLOT—A skeptical Bishop sends a broken priest to investigate the possible beatification of a simple, devout woman whose death caused a statue of the Virgin Mary to bleed upon and cure a girl with lupus.

The Wizard of Oz. L. FRANK BAUM

MIRACLE AS SUBPLOT—Dorothy Gale is swept away to a magical land in a tornado and embarks on a quest to see the Wizard, who can tell her how to find her way home. Many miracles happen along her journey, keeping her safe.

Situations 13 & 14

FALLING PREY TO CRUELTY OR MISFORTUNE AND BECOMING FORTUNATE

"Be willing to have it so; acceptance of what has happened is the first step to overcoming the consequences of any misfortune."

–WILLIAM JAMES

Falling Prey to Cruelty or Misfortune

Cruelty is a cruel act or remark that causes pain, suffering, or the infliction of physical or mental distress.

Misfortune is unnecessary and unforeseen trouble, an unfortunate state resulting from unfavorable outcomes.

This situation requires an Unfortunate and a Master or a Misfortune.

Falling Prey to Cruelty or Misfortune is a pessimistic situation. Just when a character doesn't think things could get worse, they do. This has usually been considered a type of melodrama or "woman's story." Soap operas are based on this type of situation happening over and over again, but true melodrama is very bleak.

This is a hard situation to write because it demands a deliberate dissection of the heart of a character. Most writers tend not to broach the more serious and heavy-handed subjects such as the Holocaust, "witch" burnings, and other mass tragedies. It is very draining on the writer to immerse himself in these situations for a few years while writing the story, day after day reliving the story with the characters.

This is why this type of situation tends to focus more on one individual character than a whole group (as in the next similar situation, Revolt). It makes it a little easier to grasp. Very often you will see one character stand for the whole group, but this can take away from the story's potential.

Another way to really understand this type of situation is to watch a European or foreign film of its type, not an American one. American cinema tends to show characters living above their means. They are always glamorous and heroic. Foreign cinema tends to show the harshness of reality. No pretty lighting, make-up, or fancy clothes for the Unfortunate here! The ending may not be all that neatly tied up, either.

THE UNFORTUNATE

The Unfortunate in this situation is someone who has already had a tough life. She may be doing okay in one or two areas of her life right now, but overall she's had it pretty tough. This doesn't mean she is jaded or cynical; on the contrary, she may be a somewhat positive person (making the audience love her even more), but she knows things don't always go her way. She may be trying to better herself by:

- finding a husband
- trying a new hobby
- getting a new job
- moving to a different city

But obstacles keep jumping in front of her. She picks herself up and tries again. It takes a lot to break her.

A MASTER OR A MISFORTUNE

A Master is used for situations with Cruelty. He is someone who has some sort of control over the Unfortunate, whether it's a boss, a family member, or a personal ideal. The Master won't let her change her life or help herself. Perhaps the Unfortunate could leave the Master or the situation, but she doesn't seem strong enough to do it. She may also have several friends around her who are plugging away just as she is—"Who is she to change and leave them behind?"

A Misfortune can be any number of variables that don't work in her favor. It's not necessarily personal:

- She may miss a train, wind up lost in a big city late at night, and get robbed of every penny she has.
- She could come home and find her brand-new car stolen and she doesn't have any theft insurance. This could be the car she was going to use to leave town the next day.
- Her apartment could be burned down.
- Her husband could have run off with the secretary and left her with nothing but bills.

Whether Falling Prey to Cruelty or Misfortune is used as plot, sub-plot, or incident, the elements of the beginning, middle, and end are the same:

BEGINNING: An Unfortunate has a really tough time of it, and things get tougher as a Cruelty or Misfortune come her way.

- Has a Cruelty or Misfortune befallen her before the story begins?
- How unfortunate will you make her? Is her whole life in chaos or just one aspect of it? (Watching rich people lose some money isn't as dramatic as watching a mother of three lose her last twenty dollars.)
- Will she face Cruelty or Misfortune? Which would be more dramatic for her?
- Are there other characters that are in the same boat as she is? Does she have a lot of reasons not to change her life?
- Is she trying to better herself? Has she made any progress?
- How will the Cruelty or Misfortune fall? Will she be humiliated?

MIDDLE: The Unfortunate deals with the Cruelty or Misfortune.

- How will she react to the Cruelty or Misfortune? Will she stand up for herself right away? Will she look for someone else to help her? Will she fall apart and feel sorry for herself?
- Will someone come to her rescue (even though she ultimately has to rescue herself)?
- Does she have any resources at all? (Family, friends, work, possessions, dreams, goals?)
- Is she about to give up on life altogether? What makes her push on?
- How many obstacles will you place in front of her once she decides to save herself?
- Are you working toward a happy or sad ending?

END: The Unfortunate succeeds or fails in putting herself back together.

- Will she end up in the same spot as she was in the beginning as if nothing has changed?
- Will she succeed or fail? How will you show this?
- Has she learned anything from her journey?
- What feeling will the audience have after the story?
- Have you kept the tone consistent throughout the entire story? (Don't lapse into making things easy on the character in the end; keep everything consistent.)
- Have you established a theme or lesson in this story? Why should a reader put herself through your character's hardship?

> "Being fortunate is based on how much peace you have, not how many luxuries or conveniences you have. Practice from the heart to make peace with what is, then life gives you more help to change things for the better."
>
> —DOC CHILDRE

Becoming Fortunate

Becoming Fortunate means having unexpected good fortune or luck. Just as Misfortune can come out of nowhere, so, too, can fortune.

In this situation the Unfortunate becomes the Fortunate. Something unexpectedly positive happens to a needy character:

- A teacher takes notice of a poor student and helps her find her way.
- A poor maid wins the lottery and uses it to help people.
- A man facing death is saved by an angel and feels reborn.
- A workaholic finds love and leaves his job for a simple yet very happy life in the mountains.

Whether Becoming Fortunate is used as plot, subplot, or incident, the elements of the beginning, middle, and end are the same:

BEGINNING: An Unfortunate is having a tough time. Things look like they are about to fall apart when fortune smiles upon him.

- What kind of tough time is the Unfortunate having? (Make sure it is not something that is temporary or easy to get out of.)
- Show us what is at stake and make us root for this character.
- How quickly does fortune come?
- Does the character know he's an Unfortunate? (He may be kidding himself into thinking his life is great so he can be in denial about his situation.)
- What kind of fortune does he receive? How?

MIDDLE: The fortune is a little more than he bargained for.

- Will he be able to handle it? Does he need to hire someone to manage it?
- How does his life change?

- Does he feel unworthy?
- Can he still be friends with his old buddies, or do they resent him now?
- Is he grateful for this fortune?
- Does it make him greedy?

END: The Unfortunate manages to keep things together. He has completely changed.

- Does he change for the better? Why? (Some people who win the lottery find their life hasn't gotten much better. They don't know how to manage their money, friends ask for money constantly, and family may resent them.)
- Does he want to go back to the way he was?
- Does he give something back to others?

EXAMPLES

King Lear, WILLIAM SHAKESPEARE

MISFORTUNE AS PLOT—An aging King invites Misfortune when he abdicates to his corrupt daughters and rejects his one loving and honest daughter.

The Grapes of Wrath, JOHN STEINBECK

MISFORTUNE AS PLOT—Driven off their Oklahoma farm during the dust bowl days of the Great Depression, the Joad family loads its belongings into a truck and joins thousands of other dispossessed farmers in the trek to California.

Schindler's List, STEVEN SPIELBERG

FORTUNE AND MISFORTUNE AS SUBPLOT—Oskar Schindler is a greedy German businessman who becomes an unlikely savior during the barbaric Nazi reign when he turns his factory into a refuge for Jews. The Jews have experienced Misfortune under the Nazi regime but Fortune in finding Mr. Schindler.

It Could Happen to You, JANE ANDERSON

FORTUNE AS PLOT—A police officer leaves a lottery ticket as a tip for a waitress. It is a winning ticket, and their lives change when they split the fortune.

Situations 15 & 16

REVOLT AND SUPPORT

"The first rule is to keep an untouched spirit. The second is to look things in the face and know them for what they are."

—MARCUS AURELIUS

Revolt

Revolt means to attempt to overthrow the authority of the state, to rebel, or to refuse to accept something.

This situation requires a Tyrant and a Conspirator. Revolt is the converse of the previous situation. Whereas Falling Prey to Cruelty or Misfortune mainly concerns one individual, Revolt concerns a group of people.

An individual may stand out in the group as a leader or there may be one individual who has suffered more than the rest of the group, but at the end of the day several characters are involved in the Revolt because the individual couldn't possibly do it all himself.

This situation is much more popular than the previous situation because it allows for more action, is masculine in nature, and is easier on the psyche of the writer. The characters are actively standing up for themselves instead of being beaten down every step of the way.

There are many reasons for Revolt, such as:

- injustice
- ideals or morals
- politics
- fairness
- greed
- power
- fame
- money
- humanitarianism

This situation lends itself to conspiracy among the group revolting—they must meet in secrecy, after all. Conspiracy lends itself to mystery, twists and turns, betrayals, and secrets. Those who the Main Character is conspiring with could tell the Tyrant what is going on at any moment. The Conspirator is dependent upon a group of people being honest with each other. This is where the mystery lies because we don't know until the very end what will happen. Will he be betrayed? Will everyone be loyal to the cause?

THE TYRANT

The Tyrant is a person who feels he needs to keep control over the situation, that it is his duty to protect those below him. He just doesn't understand that he is not God and that his word is not law. He would never allow another person to have an opinion about his actions or decisions because they are of no consequence. He knows best and he will let everyone know it.

The Tyrant must have resources to back up his behavior. If he's a king he'll have an army. If he's a parent he'll have money or fear to use as a weapon against family members. If he's a boss he'll have authority given to him by the company and all its resources at his disposal—his word will count for more than a secretary's.

THE CONSPIRATOR

The Conspirator is a man who feels cheated, harmed, oppressed, or neglected in some way. One of his needs in this situation is not being met because the Tyrant won't give it to him. He refuses to beg and instead questions, "Who is this Tyrant to have such power over me?"

The Conspirator is very driven by his want or belief, and he never wavers. If he has no family ties, he has nothing to live for other than himself. He may be willing to sacrifice himself to make a statement or sacrifice himself just to show the Tyrant he has no power over him. He will gladly give up his life.

On the other hand, the Conspirator doesn't have to be ethical at all. He can be just as bad as the Tyrant, only he doesn't hold as much power as the Tyrant does at this moment.

Whether Revolt is used as plot, subplot, or incident, the elements of the beginning, middle, and end are the same:

BEGINNING: The Tyrant exercises his power and therefore gives a reason for a Revolt. The Conspirator cannot take any more abuse.

- How does the Tyrant exercise his power? Does he stand to gain anything or does he just want to show off?

- How many people are abused?
- Does the Conspirator have any friends?
- What resources does the Conspirator have, if any?
- Is there another person in power who can gain something if there is a Revolt against the Tyrant?
- Is the Tyrant a king or boss type of figure or an intimate parental type of figure to the Conspirator?
- Will there be a lot of action or just one incident that pushes the Conspirator to the breaking point?
- Does the Tyrant care at all about others or is he a nasty person through and through? (It helps if he has one endearing quality.)
- What are the Tyrant's resources?

MIDDLE: The Conspirator gathers some forces. Mystery and secrets abound.

- What beliefs does the Conspirator have to keep him going? (He needs to be really motivated to bring a group of people together for a Revolt.)
- Does the Conspirator have any family members involved? Has the Tyrant hurt them?
- How trusting is the Conspirator? Will he talk to others easily about the Revolt or is he unapproachable?
- Is the Conspirator a little paranoid? With or without reason?
- Will the Conspirator gain or lose resources?
- How many obstacles will the Conspirator face?
- Does the Tyrant have any idea about the Revolt? Does he take it seriously?
- Will the Tyrant try to stop the Revolt?
- Will something interfere with the Conspirator's plans, adding more tension?

END: The Revolt takes place, and we see where the chips fall.

- Did anyone betray the cause?
- Who wins?
- Will the Conspirator survive? (Think about the ending to *Braveheart*.)
- Will the Tyrant survive? Is there another Tyrant waiting to take his place?
- Will the Conspirator become the next Tyrant?
- How has this situation changed the Conspirator?
- Did you use every opportunity for action? Can you add more?
- Is there the mystery of a possible betrayal?

"A cause may be inconvenient, but it's magnifi-
cent. It's like champagne or high heels, and one
must be prepared to suffer for it."

–ARNOLD BENNETT

Support

*Support, in this case, means to uphold by aid or help, to back up
as to support a friend, party, or belief.*

In this situation the Conspirator becomes the Supporter. He channels his energy into helping the one in power he agrees with rather
than fighting or revolting against the one in power he doesn't agree
with. Of course by its very nature this implies a democratic situation where it is not necessary to overthrow a Tyrant to be rid of him.
In a democratic situation, there is always another candidate to
choose.

In situations where democracy is not the case, such as with a
parent or boss, the Supporter can walk away and head for "green-
er pasture" somewhere else. He can always find someone who agrees
with his views to live or work in harmony with.

The Supporter can also be supporting himself. Perhaps the Tyrant
was his boss and now the Supporter has decided to start his own
business. In this way the situation turns out to be a blessing in disguise.

The Conflict comes when the Tyrant and Supporter run into each
other throughout the situation. They are now competing against
each other whether the Supporter is supporting himself or someone else.

Whether Support is used as plot, subplot, or incident, the elements
of the beginning, middle, and end are the same:

BEGINNING: A Supporter finds someone he can get behind or support. This
person needs his help in some way. A Tyrant is opposing them.

- Who will the Supporter meet first—the one he supports or the Tyrant?
- What type of Support is needed? Is there a type of support the Supporter would never give?
- How willing is the Supporter to sacrifice his needs for the one he is
supporting?
- How crucial is this support? Is something with far-reaching consequence at stake, like a major presidential election?

- Will there be other supporters for the Supporter to work with?
- How grateful for this support will the one supported be? Does recognition matter to the Supporter?

MIDDLE: The Supporter has a run-in with the Tyrant.

- Will the Tyrant fuel the Supporter's resolve or discourage him?
- How harsh is this run-in with the Tyrant? Does the Supporter get hurt?
- Does the Supporter question getting involved in all of this?
- Does the Tyrant question his ability to succeed? Will he up the stakes as a result?
- How does this encounter make the one supported feel? Does he even know this happened?
- What decisions does the Supporter make as a result of this run-in?

END: The Supporter accomplishes his goal of supporting the one he agrees with regardless of the outcome.

- Will the support given help to make this a successful ending?
- Will the Supporter be upset if things don't go his way? Will he see the good in a job well done for its own sake?
- What does the Tyrant do to push the final outcome? How does he contribute?
- Would the Supporter do it all again if given the chance?
- What has the Supporter learned from all of this?
- Is the one supported grateful?
- If the Supporter doesn't win, will he feel like a failure?

EXAMPLES

Braveheart, MEL GIBSON

REVOLT AS PLOT—William Wallace, a commoner, unites the thirteenth-century Scots in their battle to overthrow English rule.

The Patriot, ROLAND EMMERICH

REVOLT AS PLOT—Benjamin Martin is drawn into the American Revolutionary War against his will when a brutal British commander kills his son.

Dave, IVAN REITMAN

SUPPORT AS PLOT—A look-alike is hired to impersonate the President, who has suffered a stroke while having sex with a co-worker, rendering him a vegetable. The look-alike does everything he can to help the President and the country by agreeing to take on this role.

Primary Colors, MIKE NICHOLS

SUPPORT AS PLOT—An idealistic man joins the political campaign of a smooth-operator candidate for President of the United States.

> "Avoiding danger is no safer in the long run than
> outright exposure. Life is either a daring adven-
> ture, or nothing."
>
> —HELEN KELLER

Daring Enterprise

*Enterprise means an undertaking, especially one of some scope,
complication, and risk.*

This situation requires a Bold Leader, an Object, and an Adversary.
Within Daring Enterprise are two types: the Personal and the Objective.

In the Personal Daring Enterprise, the Object is emotionally connected to the Leader. Something very personal is at stake for him.
Think Search, Quest, Escape, and Rescue.

This type of Daring Enterprise is similar to a Quest where a hero
pursues a desired object that is seemingly out of his reach. It's as if
his whole life depends upon him finding the object. The enterprise
may be doomed to fail, but the hero pushes on because he is so personally connected to the Object and his desire for it is strong. This
connection has to be great to motivate him to take risks.

There are several reasons why he may desire the Object sought:

- He may have a sense of Honor, helping his friend or boss because they
  need his help. If it's important to them it's important to him.

- He may have a sense of Duty, like a cop who takes risks everyday as
  part of the job, especially when a partner is in need. The Object may be
  a criminal.

- He may have a sense of Powerlessness. Something like his child or a
  project of some sort is stolen from him and he wants it back.

- He may have a sense of Entitlement. He may be an archeologist who
  has spent his whole life looking for an artifact and has given up a lot in
  the process.

- He may have a sense of Freedom, like the men who carefully planned out their escape from Alcatraz. They were not fleeing the law like a fugitive in situation nine; they were on a quest for freedom and their lives were at stake.

The motivation here is always personal, hitting the hero right in the heart. He desires the Object, just as in the following Objective Enterprise, but he has personal reasons for finding it.

In the Objective Daring Enterprise the Object is *not* emotionally connected to the Leader. Think of a Gamble, a Treasure Hunt, an Investment, an Adventure, a War, and Politics.

The Bold Leader may want to take a Gamble because he wants an Object, but the reasons that motivate him are not personal and perhaps not noble. His whole life, or that of others, is not dependent upon him finding it; it is just something he wants at the time. Maybe he only wants it because his adversary wants it.

He may embark on the Daring Enterprise just to get the job done and become famous for having done it. He hasn't invested himself emotionally in the Object. He takes a Gamble, wins or loses, and moves on. His motivation is usually for personal gain, in a somewhat greedy sense. For example:

- He may seek something he believes will change his life, like a suitcase full of money, an ancient artifact he knows nothing about, or a mystical experience during an adventurous travel.

- He may seek something he believes will give him immortality, like taking a stand in a war and going down in history books. (Think of Achilles in *Troy*.)

- He may seek something he believes will give him more control, like a political position or weapons.

- He may unconsciously have a death wish so he takes risks because he just doesn't care anymore. (Think Mel Gibson in *Lethal Weapon*.)

THE BOLD LEADER

The Bold Leader is a man with a mission. He knows what he wants and will stop at nothing to get it. No one can deter him from his path. They may try to throw doubts his way, and they can make fun of him, but nothing will change his mind.

If it's personal, he needs this Object and can't imagine his life without it. If it's objective, he can't imagine turning down a shot at adventure.

He lives for the adrenaline rush of risk taking. He craves it. Once he has made up his mind to embark on the Daring Enterprise the Object is always foremost on his mind. He becomes preoccupied with it. Family and friends know better than to bother him with mundane tasks of everyday life.

THE ADVERSARY

The Adversary is someone who is either jealous or envious of the Bold Leader and will stop at nothing to keep the Bold Leader from reaching his goal. Ultimately, the Bold Leader is the Adversary's Object of obsession.

If he is jealous, he will want what the Bold Leader has—nice tools, great workers, financing, support, recognition and, ultimately, the Object. If he is the envious type, he will want to destroy what the Bold Leader has so no one can have it. He may even damage the Object—his envy is that destructive.

On the other hand, the Adversary is very similar to the Bold Leader in that he has an adventurous spirit and a willingness to take risks. He just lacks the moral fiber of the Bold Leader. There may even be a sort of respect between the two, as they know very few people would ever attempt to do what they do. And perhaps each one makes life more interesting and exciting for the other.

Whether Daring Enterprise is used as plot, subplot, or incident, the elements of the beginning, middle, and end are the same:

BEGINNING: A Bold Leader realizes there is an Object he desires. After careful investigation he thinks he knows where it is.

- What type of Object is it? Person? Place? Thing?
- How important is the Object to him? How will you show this?
- Where is the Object?
- Does the Object want to be found? If it's a person, does he want to be rescued or helped? If it's an Object, are there ancient spells upon it to keep thieves away?
- Are there any people around trying to cast doubt on him?
- When does the Adversary make himself known? How much power does he have?
- Why does the Adversary work against the Bold Leader?
- Is there more than one Adversary?

MIDDLE: The Bold Leader overcomes obstacles as he goes after the Object.

- Does the Object's location play a role in creating obstacles?
- How many resources will the Bold Leader need to get the Object?
- Are there any secondary characters working against the Bold Leader? Friends or family who don't support him?

- Does the Bold Leader become more determined to reach the Object when met with obstacles or does he have moments where he is about to give up?

- What kind of unexpected obstacles can you add to spice things up? Throw some obstacles in the Adversary's way, too.

END: The Bold Leader finds the Object. It was everything he dreamed it would be, or the victory is bittersweet as he realizes it doesn't bring him what he wanted.

- Is this a happy ending? Or does the Bold Leader realize the Object can't bring him happiness?

- Will the Bold Leader decide to leave the Object where it is? Or take it with him so he can reap the benefits? Does he abandon his original goal for a new one?

- What happens to the Adversary? Is he still trying to get the Object, vowing to return again someday when the Bold Leader least expects it?

- How does the story change the life of the Bold Leader? What happens to all those who helped him achieve his goal? Does he abandon them?

> "Without inner peace, it is impossible to have world peace."
>
> –THE DALAI LAMA

The Healing Journey

Healing is defined as restoring to health, to repair or cure someone or something.

The Healing Journey is when the Bold Leader becomes the Healer, whose motive is to heal herself or others. It is an inner journey of sorts to possibly find, preserve, or grow the self.

Whether she realizes it or not her actions help the community as a whole. As one person heals, others are influenced as they see firsthand that one can live a better, happier life.

She may want to find answers to the meaning of life or find a cure of some sort for whatever ails her or her community. Her search is not for material possessions, personal gain, or vanity but for a deeper sense of self or a better way of life. She knows there is something more to life and she sets out to find it. She may never know where the Object is but she is going out there to find it anyway. She may:

- go back to school
- open a healing practice
- see a psychologist or doctor
- travel to the rainforest to seek a cure
- take a sabbatical to get a much-needed rest
- offer self motivation seminars in the city
- go on a peace mission
- write an inspirational book

The drama and conflict come from her inner struggles with her decision to heal and how she follows through with it. People are generally not supported by family and friends when they embark on a journey such as this. This type of journey causes others to take a serious look at their lives and what they are doing or not doing for themselves as they watch the hero change her life and help others.

She will invariably doubt her decision and wonder if she is going mad. Everyone around her may have money and material possessions and seem happy. Why couldn't she be happy with those things? But she presses on and makes changes every day, doing things a little different than before, taking back her power and loving it!

Whether The Healing Journey is used as plot, subplot, or incident, the elements of the beginning, middle, and end are the same:

BEGINNING: A Healer sees a problem with herself, or others, that needs healing. She decides to do it.

- What is the problem? Is it with her or others? (Evelyn Couch, in *Fried Green Tomatoes*, is very unhappy with her life.)
- What is the theme?
- What motivates her? Is a family member involved, or is she just the type of person who would do this?
- Will others support her right away?
- Will she meet with resistance right away?
- Are there other characters around who can help her?
- What resources does she have? Her looks (*Erin Brockovich*)? Her mind? Her contacts? Her family? Money?
- What skills does she have?

MIDDLE: The Healer takes steps to heal the situation.

- What steps can she reasonably take? Unreasonably?
- How far do you want her to go?

- How can you make things difficult for her?
- What type of obstacles will she face? If the Healer is a woman, will her sex be an obstacle, or vice versa?
- Do other situations come up to be healed?
- What does she have to sacrifice? Time with her family? Her reputation?
- Does she lose allies?

END: The Healer is successful, at least in doing the work needed.

- The Healer does the work needed, but is she completely successful all the way around? (She could stop waste dumping in her town, only to find out there is a much larger problem.)
- How have others around her changed from this? Is anyone really helped?
- Have you brought the theme through the entire situation?
- Does she do it all on her own or do others come out at the end to help?
- If she is healing herself, how much has she changed? Or does she go back to the way things were because her friends and family don't like it and she has no where else to go? Will she be ostracized? Is healing unacceptable for her?

EXAMPLES

A Bug's Life,
JOHN LASSETER AND ANDREW STANTON

DARING ENTERPRISE AS PLOT—A misfit ant, looking for warriors to save his colony from grasshoppers, recruits a group of bugs that turn out to be an inept circus troop.

Raiders of the Lost Ark, STEVEN SPIELBERG

DARING ENTERPRISE AS PLOT—Archeologist and adventurer Indiana Jones is hired by the U.S. government to find the Ark of the Covenant before the Nazis can get it.

Smoke Signals, CHRIS EYRE

HEALING JOURNEY AS SUBPLOT—The story of two Native American boys, Victor and Thomas, on a Healing Journey. Through storytelling, Thomas makes every effort to connect with the people around him. Victor, in contrast, uses his quiet countenance to gain strength and confidence. When Victor's estranged father dies, the two men embark on an adventure to Phoenix to collect the ashes.

Erin Brockovich, STEVEN SODERBERGH

HEALING JOURNEY AS PLOT—An unemployed single mother becomes a legal assistant and almost single-handedly brings down a California power company accused of polluting a city's water supply. She finds self-esteem and life purpose.

"People wish to be settled: Only as far as they
are unsettled is there any hope for them."

–RALPH WALDO EMERSON

Abduction

Abduction means to carry off by force or to kidnap.

This situation requires a Guardian, a Victim, and an Abductor. In
rare cases the Guardian and Abductor are the same person, as in
romance novels where the hero kidnaps the heroine in order to save
her life.

Abduction is a loss for the Guardian. It's personal to her whether
she knows the Victim or not because it was her duty to protect the
Victim. If the Victim is harmed, she has failed.

There are three types of Abduction:

1. Victim is taken by force.
2. Victim is tricked into captivity.
3. Victim is willing to go.

In the first type, the Victim is completely innocent of the events leading up to his capture. He may have the ability to fight back, but he
doesn't know he has to. He is oblivious to what is happening and is
completely shocked when the Abduction comes. He may fight back
if things do not happen too quickly for him to ascertain the situation. The shock of what is happening may paralyze him. Usually
someone close to him has betrayed him, thus allowing for the element of surprise.

In the second type, the Victim is tricked into being captured.
He may be totally engrossed in something else and not see the
danger signs as a man approaches to ask him questions. Or he may
think he is just helping a little old lady cross the street when in reality a van full of thugs are waiting on the other side. Or he may

be under orders to perform a task and doesn't realize he's walking into a trap.

In the third type, the Victim wants to get away or escape. He may welcome the kidnappers and help them if he has to. For him, it is a way out of a bad situation, and he welcomes the surprise attack. If his situation is dire enough he may even fake his own abduction. Perhaps he wants a ransom paid so he can get some quick cash or he wants to flee the country and needs some help to do it.

The Guardian is usually not privy to this information. She just knows the Victim was kidnapped, and she assumes he was taken by force until something tells her otherwise. The Victim's personality and age will dictate how readily she will consider other scenarios. After all, abducted children are always assumed innocent of involvement in the act.

There are four possible reasons why this particular victim was selected, regardless of type:

1. The Victim was in the wrong place at the wrong time. In a foreign country, he may just have been the wrong nationality.

2. The Victim is worth a lot of money, and it is assumed a large ransom will be paid.

3. The Abductor has a mental illness and is obsessed with the Victim or what the Victim represents.

4. The Abductor perceives, however rightly, that the Victim or someone close to him has "wronged" him and he wants revenge.

THE GUARDIAN

The Guardian is someone who takes her job seriously because her job is her identity. Messing up and getting someone hurt is not an option. She may be a parent who sees herself as guardian to her children, a teacher, a policeman, bodyguard, or just a friend who feels responsible for the Victim.

She is used to being in control and having to watch out for others. To her, life would stop if she dropped the ball, so she keeps on juggling.

She usually has a mean streak, something that allows her to be tough when necessary. She has given up a lot to care for others, and when they are gone she's not sure what to do with herself.

THE ABDUCTOR

The Abductor is someone who only cares about himself or his cause. Nothing else matters to him—period. He can't be reasoned with or manipulated.

There are three types of Abductors—the Regretful, the Indifferent, and the Pawn.

The Regretful Abductor may realize what he has done is wrong—especially if the Victim comes to harm in the end. If he was obsessed with the Victim, he probably had feelings for her and just wanted her all to himself.

The Indifferent Abductor doesn't care who lives or dies; he just wants to reach his goal—money, fame, revenge. Even if he knows the Victim, he may not care what happens to her. She may be an acceptable casualty for his cause.

The Pawn Abductor is being used by a willing Victim to meet her goal—that of faking her Abduction or faking the Abduction of someone she knows. He may not be of much use at all and may not have a goal of his own. He is a follower, not a leader, and winds up getting himself into a lot of trouble as the Victim will usually set him up to take the fall for her.

Whether Abduction is used as plot, subplot, or incident, the elements of the beginning, middle, and end are the same:

BEGINNING: The Abductor selects a Victim and kidnaps her.

- Where is the Guardian during the event? Is she right there?
- What type of Victim and Abductor are they?
- Are there any witnesses to the Abduction?
- What type of relationship do the Guardian and Victim have? The Guardian and Abductor? How will you show this?
- Does it take place in a foreign country, thereby creating more conflict due to differing legal systems?
- What does the Abductor stand to gain?

MIDDLE: The Guardian moves full force to rescue the Victim. She faces many obstacles and surprises.

- What approach does the Guardian take when dealing with the Abductor? Do they ever talk?
- What skills and resources does the Guardian have to help her? (Foreshadow them if necessary.)
- How is the Victim holding up?
- What's at stake for the Guardian on a personal level?
- What surprises can you throw in to spice it up?
- Is the Guardian putting too much pressure on the Abductor?

END: The Guardian finds the Victim and Abductor.

- Is the Victim still alive in the end?
- Does the Abductor have a change of heart?
- How does the rescue take place? Does it show the Guardian's character growth? Did she not accept help in the first two acts but must learn to accept help now?
- Has the Victim changed forever? Will he ever be the same again?
- Does the Abductor survive the final confrontation?
- What will the Victim and Guardian do differently now? What have they learned?

> "Every parting is a form of death, as every reunion is a type of heaven."
>
> **—TYRON EDWARDS**

Reunion

Reunion is the act of being reunited or the coming together of those who have been separated.

In this situation the Guardian becomes the Facilitator who helps the Victim reunite with someone dear to him. (This corresponds to Polti's Recovery of Lost One.)

There are two different ways that reunions can occur. Both parties could be searching for the other, which will be a happy Reunion, or one party will not be interested in the Reunion at all, which will make it a difficult one.

There are many reasons why someone would not want to be reunited:

- A person may feel inadequate and unable to handle a Reunion and all the emotions that come with it.
- Sometimes a person may think they haven't accomplished enough and they don't want those from their past to find them.
- A person may not want to face all the memories that come up from seeing someone they haven't seen in many years.

Reunions can consist of:

- old friends coming together
- co-workers
- team members

- soul mates across lifetimes (like *Somewhere in Time* with Christopher Reeve)
- a long-lost biological parent and child
- siblings separated at birth
- a beloved teacher and student
- many family members coming together for a Reunion

Whether Reunion is used as plot, subplot, or incident, the elements of the beginning, middle, and end are the same:

BEGINNING: A Victim is missing someone, and she wants to be reunited.

- Why does the Victim want to be reunited with this person?
- What does the Victim hope to achieve with this Reunion? If she wants to find a long-lost parent, does she think she will be able to start a life with that parent?
- How does the Victim come to decide to be reunited? What prompts this search? Does something bad happen?
- Does anyone oppose this Reunion?
- Will anyone support her search?

MIDDLE: A Victim goes to a Facilitator to help her find the person she is looking for.

- How does she find the Facilitator?
- Will the Facilitator be eager to help? Or does he think it's a hard case?
- Does the Facilitator need to get permission from the Victim's guardian if she is under eighteen?
- Is the Facilitator genuine? Or a scam artist?
- Does the Victim have a lot of clues to give the Facilitator?
- Does the Victim want to be involved in the search?

END: The Victim finds the person she is looking for and it is either a happy or sorrowful Reunion.

- Will this be a happy Reunion? Why?
- What does the Victim learn from this experience? That the parents who raised her are all she really needs? Or her long-lost friend was never really a friend at all?
- Does the Victim feel betrayed? Why?
- Is the person found happy or upset about this? (In *Crossroads*, the chgaracter's birth mother wants nothing to do with her when she finds her.)
- Does the Facilitator stay to help the Victim with the news?
- How has the Victim's life changed?

EXAMPLES

Ransom, RON HOWARD

ABDUCTION AS PLOT—Tom, a rich airline owner, is shocked when his son is kidnapped. He pays the two million dollar ransom, but something goes wrong. So Tom turns the tide against the kidnappers.

Overboard, GARRY MARSHALL

ABDUCTION AS PLOT—Rich snob Joanna hires country carpenter Dean to build a closet on her yacht. When the two don't see eye to eye, Dean is left unpaid while Joanna sets sail. The following day, Joanna is fished out of the sea after falling overboard, suffering from amnesia. Dean finds her and tells her she's his wife so he can get a free housekeeper for a while as she works off the money she owes him.

Somewhere in Time, RICHARD MATHESON

REUNION AS PLOT—A Chicago playwright uses self-hypnosis to find the actress whose vintage portrait hangs in a grand hotel.

The Big Chill, LAWRENCE KASDAN

REUNION AS PLOT—A group of college friends reunite at the funeral of one of their friends.

> "Never try to solve all the problems at once—
> make them line up for you one by one."
>
> —RICHARD SLOMA

Enigma

Enigma means an action, mode of action, or thing that cannot be satisfactorily explained. It is puzzling.

This situation requires an Interrogator, a Seeker, and a Problem. An Enigma is an intriguing mental plotline par excellence, holding the audience's attention as they, too, try to solve the riddle or figure out the secret. It is what great mysteries are made of.

There are three types of Enigmas in stories—the Baffling Enigma, the Anticipating Enigma, and the Spiritual Enigma.

In the Baffling Enigma the reader either can't believe what has happened or can't figure out how it happened. It seems beyond explanation—though probable. For example, the girl was locked in the safe but, even though the safe was never opened, as the guard was watching it, she has escaped and managed to kill her husband. It's a magic trick of sorts. The audience reads on just to find out what the secret behind the trick is.

In the Anticipating Enigma the reader tries to figure out what happened or tries to solve the riddle, always anticipating what will come next. The Enigma seems clear-cut to the reader, even though she knows there will usually be a twist at the end revealing clues she missed.

The reader also thinks she knows who did it, but how he did it or the people who were involved may be a mystery to her. There is no "magical act" here, though.

The Spiritual Enigma is an Enigma that fosters inner growth in the Seeker. Think for instance of a Zen Koan. The Seeker has asked a question and in trying to figure it out has grown beyond measure. The answer doesn't even matter anymore; it has become irrelevant.

An example of a Zen Koan follows:

Bokuju, a great sage, was asked, "We have to dress and eat every day. How can we escape from that?" Bokuju answered, "We dress, we eat." "I do not understand," persisted the questioner. "Then put on your food and eat your dress!" replied Bokuju.

Ultimately the Enigma situation is a search for an answer; whether it is why something happened, how it happened, or the answer to a riddle does not matter. The Seeker is still seeking an answer of some sort, piecing the puzzle together as he goes along.

THE INTERROGATOR

The Interrogator is someone who loves to drive others crazy, in a sense. She loves to play games and is never forthcoming with answers. She tests people, pushing them to their breaking points. Many fall apart under her questioning. This only proves them unworthy of her help.

Or, in the case of many mythological stories, the Interrogator is like a trickster. She may be the prize to be claimed by the hero who can answer her riddle. She's not going to make things easy, as she values herself highly. She does not take pity on those who step forward and take a risk to win her favor. They find the answer or they don't, and they pay the price for it either way.

THE SEEKER

The Seeker is someone who aspires, searches, and investigates. He is an explorer, a hunter, and a scout. Questions drive him toward his goal. They stimulate his brain and fuel his heart. Without questions to answer, his life seems dull, boring, and lifeless.

He is the student who asks a question but doesn't want to accept the answer because then the search is over. His mind is always thinking, analyzing, and comparing. If he wants to know the meaning of life he will seek answers from several different holy men and weigh all the answers against each other, never fully accepting one at face value.

When he does give an opinion on something, people tend to listen because they know he didn't arrive at it lightly. He will explain how he came to his opinion, analyzing the facts, reading body language, and taking into account other people's opinions.

In a detective role, he can be very deceiving at times, acting like an innocent who doesn't understand much. But this is only a ploy to keep people talking—like *Columbo*. He notices everything, watches body language, and intuits things unsaid. He's a master of human behavior.

There are two types of Seekers—one who just sticks to the facts and one who allows his gut instinct to help him. They both start out with the facts, but if it comes down to deciding between two answers, the latter will go with his gut. The seeker can be a computer hacker, a CIA code breaker, or an analyst of some sort. Great intellectual pursuits are usually motivated through the desire to seek new ways of doing something or the desire to be the first one to figure something out.

Whether Enigma is used as plot, subplot, or incident, the elements of the beginning, middle, and end are the same:

BEGINNING: Something happens that causes the Seeker to approach an Interrogator. The Interrogator presents a riddle of some sort.

- What is the main cause? Is the Seeker personally involved in the Enigma or its outcome?
- How do the Seeker and Interrogator meet? Is the Interrogator hard to come by?
- What type of riddle is there? Baffling, Anticipating, or Spiritual?
- Is there more than one riddle?
- What resources does the Seeker have?
- What additional conflict stands in the way of the Seeker answering the riddle?

MIDDLE: The Seeker must overcome several obstacles and twists. He may think he has the answer but finds out he is wrong. The Interrogator makes things more difficult for him.

- What type of obstacles does the Seeker face? Internal fear-related obstacles? External events? Other characters trying to throw him off track?
- Can you throw in some red herrings to lead the reader astray and keep her guessing?
- Can you plant clues that are hidden enough to be revealed in the end, yet believable?
- Can you figure out the answer to the riddle before you plot out the middle? Then layer other characters into it to confuse things a bit?
- Can you up the stakes? Make the problem worse?

END: The Seeker solves the riddle and the Interrogator must pay up.

- What does the Seeker gain for his troubles? (Foreshadow it.)
- How does the Interrogator feel about the Seeker being successful?
- How does the Seeker feel? Is he itching to find the next riddle to solve? Or does he pat himself on the back for a while?

- Who is helped or saved by the Seeker?
- Are other characters shocked by the answer?
- Does the Seeker use any special talent or device to solve the riddle?
- Does the Seeker trick anyone to help him find the answer?

"I have a great belief in the fact that whenever
there is chaos, it creates wonderful thinking."

–SEPTIMA POINSETTE CLARK

Invention

*Invention is a new device, method, or process developed from
study and experimentation.*

In this situation the Seeker becomes the Inventor. Whereas Enigma
is about searching for an answer, Invention is about creating your
own answer to a problem.

A seemingly insurmountable problem has come into a character's life. She may go to others for help but they can't seem to help
her. She has to figure out a way to help herself. There is no other
option for her. This problem can be:

- PHYSICAL: She can't physically do something or get to a certain place
  so she has to invent something to help her accomplish the task.
- MENTAL: She can't figure something out so she has to learn a new way
  of going about the task. Perhaps she needs to be more creative in her
  thinking. She has to step outside of her own "box."
- EMOTIONAL: She can't see the truth right in front of her eyes because
  she is too emotionally involved. She needs to relax and try to gain an
  objective point of view to move forward.
- SPIRITUAL: She won't see the truth or the answer right in front of her
  because it may be too painful or it may shatter all her accepted beliefs.
  Perhaps she is a scientist who believed in Darwin's theory of evolution
  and is now faced with the possibility that the Bible is right.

At first she may rebel and ask why this is happening to her but in the
end she sees the growth this situation has offered her and wouldn't
have it any other way. Her life may be completely changed but it is
usually for the better. She has done something she never thought
possible, at least not for her to do.

Perhaps she needs to create a new way to help the homeless,
pregnant teens, or abandoned animals. Or she may need to create
a physical product.

The conflict comes from the naysayers who don't want to see her succeed. Perhaps they are scared of what will happen or how things will change if she does. Think of *The Time Machine* and *Frankenstein*.

Whether Invention is used as plot, subplot, or incident, the elements of the beginning, middle, and end are the same:

BEGINNING: An Inventor is faced with a seemingly insurmountable problem.

- What type of problem is this? Physical? Emotional? Mental? Spiritual?
- How does this problem present itself? Does someone else cause it and then ask her for help?
- Will the naysayers come out right away?
- Will the naysayers have any effect on her? Does she care about them or their opinions?
- How does she feel about this problem? Does she feel up to the task or try to get out of it?
- If she tries to get out of it, who or what pulls her back in?
- What is at stake if she doesn't figure things out or make the Invention?

MIDDLE: The Inventor is going about the task of inventing a solution to the problem when a naysayer interrupts her work.

- Do other naysayers agree with this naysayer? Does a whole group stand behind him?
- What do the naysayers want? Is one of their beliefs being challenged by the Inventor's work?
- Will someone threaten her safety?
- Will the Inventor get scared and stop working or press on?
- Is time running out and the Inventor can't bother with the naysayers?
- What type of ingenious approach does the Inventor take to solve the problem?

END: The Inventor solves the problem, but it may or may not effect and help others.

- How does the Inventor finally solve the problem? Was the answer right under her nose all along?
- Does anyone know she has invented a solution? Does the solution affect anyone else?
- Do the naysayers successfully stop her? (Think of *Contact* and how the Main Character travels on an alien device only to be treated like a fool by the government when she returns. No one will really know or benefit from what happened to her.)

- What happens to the naysayers? Are they made out to be fools, or do they get what they want in the end?
- Is the Inventor happy with her accomplishment? Does she wish she had done some things differently?
- What will the reader learn from this story? Will the reader's beliefs be challenged?

EXAMPLES

Contact, ROBERT ZEMECKIS

ENIGMA AS PLOT—Dr. Ellie Arroway finds conclusive radio proof of intelligent aliens, who send plans for a mysterious machine to be built.

Enigma, MICHAEL APTED

ENIGMA AS PLOT—During the heart of World War II, crypto analysts at Britain's code-breaking center have discovered, to their horror, that Nazi U-boats have changed their Enigma Code.

Frankenstein, MARY SHELLEY

INVENTION AS SUBPLOT—Dr. Frankenstein creates a human creature from stolen body parts. The creature turns into a monster when Dr. Frankenstein rejects him.

Cats and Dogs, LAWRENCE GUTERMAN

INVENTION AS SUBPLOT—A top-secret, high-tech war is going on between cats and dogs, of which humans are unaware. The cats want to destroy a new vaccine that, if the human scientist can develop it, would destroy all human allergies to dogs. The dogs want to stop the cats.

> "Don't wait for your ship to come in. Swim out to it."
>
> –UNKNOWN

Obtaining

Obtaining means to acquire or to succeed in gaining possession as the result of planning.

There are two types of Obtaining situations—Obtaining Through Selling, which requires a Solicitor and Adversary Who Is Refusing; and Obtaining Through Negotiation, which requires an Arbitrator and Opposing Parties.

In Obtaining Through Selling, the Solicitor has a goal of obtaining an objective or object but cannot reach this goal unless an Adversary agrees with her and buys into her presentation.

The Adversary stands as the obstacle to her objective. Even if he agrees to fund or be a part of her objective, he will have a hard time leaving her alone to do her job. He's like a venture capitalist who wants to be involved in every minute detail of the business—micromanaging it when he should just step aside.

In this type, the Solicitor wants to either sell an idea to the Adversary or she wants the Adversary to buy something so she can go out and obtain an object.

- She has the idea, it's already set in stone—now who wants to buy in?
- She wants to convert the Adversary into her way of thinking (like a missionary trying to convert the natives).

She may use:

- **RUSE:** something intended to misrepresent the true nature of an activity
- **TEMPTATION:** an inducement, especially to something evil, to try to get someone to do something wrong
- **LURE:** to attract by wiles or entice; something that attracts with the promise of pleasure or reward

In Obtaining Through Negotiation, the Opposing Party has a goal of obtaining an objective or object but cannot reach this goal unless another Opposing Party is willing to negotiate with him.

It's as if the hero needs to get across an alligator-infested lake and the Opposing Party has the only boat. Of course he wants way too much money to take him across, so an Arbitrator may step in to help the negotiation.

Usually the hero can negotiate for himself depending on how tough the Opposing Party is. Do they have any history of butting heads? One party may not want to help the other without great compensation. If they have a long history, the second Opposing Party will know exactly what to ask for in compensation—that which he knows the hero loves or values.

He may use:

- FORCE: the exertion of physical power or the operation of circumstances that permit no options

- CHARM: to attract strongly or irresistibly, to please

- DIPLOMACY: the art or practice of conducting international relations, as in negotiating alliances and agreements; tact and skill in dealing with people

THE SOLICITOR/ARBITRATOR

The Solicitor/Arbitrator is someone who cannot reach her goal without outside help. On the one hand she can be seen as not being self-sufficient; on the other she can be seen as someone who has learned to work with others, instead of against them, to reach her goals.

At times she can be hard on herself if she doesn't make a "sale" or if she doesn't believe in the product or ideal she is selling, but she always pushes on. She knows what she wants and is willing to do what ever it takes to get it.

She is driven by her desire for a specific objective or object, and desire can sometimes make one do crazy things. If she is conflicted about her tactics she will find the positive side to it, like the cigarette company executive who stated that cigarettes bring down elderly medical costs because so many smokers die early deaths and never make it to old age. Of course, if the Solicitor/Arbitrator is the hero in the story, she should not be so heinous.

Her beliefs are very strong; she has to believe in herself and her product or idea. She wants to meet her goal to possibly:

- get the funding she needs

- stop a war

- start a war
- save a life
- help the environment
- find her kidnapped child
- rescue someone in captivity
- make the big sale
- win her freedom

ADVERSARY/OPPOSING PARTY

The Adversary and Opposing Party are very similar. This is someone who enjoys saying "No," being confrontational, or playing devil's advocate. He knows what the Solicititor/Arbitrator wants and may enjoy exercising his power over her to just say "No." He may not care one way or the other about the Solicitor/Arbitrator's cause or objective, so he could easily say "Yes."

If he is ethical, he is looking for a reason to say yes and may try to help the Solicitor/Arbitrator phrase her request in the correct way or come up with a plan to make the request doable. It's like the politician who says he can vote for a bill if you take certain words out.

The Adversary is there to test the Solicitor/Arbitrator. How serious is she? How strong are her desires? How long will she keep it up? To what lengths will she go?

Whether Obtaining is used as plot, subplot, or incident, the elements of the beginning, middle, and end are the same:

BEGINNING: The Solicitor/Arbitrator realizes her desired objective or object and gets close to it. She has to approach either an Adversary who refuses or an Opposing Party.

- When does she meet the Adversary? Is he friendly?
- How will she approach the Adversary? What tactic will she use?
- Does she believe in what she is doing?
- Is the Solicitor the hero of the story?
- What is at stake for the Solicitor/Arbitrator? For the Adversary?
- Can you add other characters to spice things up?

MIDDLE: The Solicitor meets with the Adversary again.

- How will their second meeting be? Do they each have more ammunition to throw?

- Will an Arbitrator be needed? Are they at an impasse?
- What does the Solicitor do to sweeten the offer and get her way?
- Does the Adversary really care about the Solicitor or her objective?
- Does the Adversary try to turn the tables on the Solicitor? Is he successful?
- How far will the Solicitor go?

END: The Solicitor gets her way.

- At what cost does the Solicitor get her way? Does she have to give up something dear to her?
- How does she reach her object or objective?
- Is victory as sweet as she thought it would be?
- Is she satisfied now?
- How does the Adversary feel about it? Did he trick her?

"Growth demands a temporary surrender of security."

–GAIL SHEEHY

Letting Go

Letting Go means to give up or abandon, put aside, surrender, or release.

In this situation the Solicitor becomes the Liberator. Instead of trying to obtain more things or ideas, she lets go of the ones she has and becomes freer in the process. She gives up that which holds her back and ties her to things that make her unhappy—a dead-end job, a bad marriage, an unhealthy belief system. This is what the New Age movement is all about.

She possibly meets someone who seems to have obtained the peace she desires, but she learns that "obtain" is the wrong word to use. The person has let go.

Perhaps a stranger came to town to teach a seminar, which she attended, and now her friends and family think she has been taken over by a cult because her personality has changed that much.

Perhaps a housewife facing empty-nest syndrome learns how to let go of her kids as they go off to college and finds herself in the process.

A great theme here is how others may fear change so much that they will do anything to keep their family and friends exactly the throughout their lives. If one person steps out of the box it causes everyone they know to examine their own lives. This can be very frightening for some. Just watch the television show *Clean Sweep* on TLC and see how people fight to keep junk they will never use.

There may still be an Adversary in this situation, as many people around her may not want her to change or let go of her old self.

Whether Letting Go is used as plot, subplot, or incident, the elements of the beginning, middle, and end are the same:

BEGINNING: A Liberator is faced with losing something (kids, husband, job).

- What does she need to let go of? Why?
- Why won't she see that the best thing she can do is to let go?
- Why is she so attached to "it"?
- Do other characters want her to let it go? Will they be supportive?
- How will you show the inner struggle here? Or is she in complete denial?
- What incident pushes her to examine things?

MIDDLE: The Liberator realizes the only way for her to be happy or to move on is to let go. Can she do it?

- Will she accept the truth that she needs to let go? Or will she spend some time still trying to hold on? (If the kids go off to college, will she still try to get them to go to school closer to home?)
- Will anyone help her? Hinder her?
- Where does the realization take place? (Maybe use a location that adds irony or comic relief to the moment.)
- Does something from her past give her strength? Does she see an old diary of hers where she wrote down her dreams?

END: The Liberator lets go and enjoys the rewards of her decision.

- What kind of reward does she get?
- Does her life seem to be starting over again?
- Is she better off now?
- What is the message or theme here?
- Did she lose any relationships in the process?
- Does she want to go out and help others do the same now?

EXAMPLES

Contact, ROBERT ZEMECKIS

OBTAINING AS SUBPLOT—Dr. Ellie Arroway, after years of searching, finds conclusive radio proof of intelligent aliens, who send plans for a mysterious machine. When her funding is pulled she must travel around giving presentations to raise more funding.

Jurassic Park, MICHAEL CRICHTON

OBTAINING AS INCIDENT—A scientist clones dinosaurs to populate a theme park. He tries to obtain the endorsements of several objective scientists for his investors and insurance agent.

Practical Magic, ALICE HOFFMAN

LETTING GO AS SUBPLOT—The Owens sisters, Sally and Gillian, struggle to use their hereditary gift for practical magic to overcome the obstacles in discovering true love. Sally lets go and falls in love even though she's afraid of a curse.

Something to Talk About, LASSE HALLSTROM

LETTING GO AS PLOT—Grace discovers that her husband Eddie deceived her with another woman. After confronting him in the middle of the night, she decides to stay at her sister Emma Rae's house for a while, to make up her mind. Breaking out of her everyday life, she starts to question the authority of everyone, especially her father.

> "A family is a little kingdom, torn with factions
> and exposed to revolutions."
>
> –SAMUEL JOHNSON

Enmity of Kinsman

Enmity of Kinsman means to have a deep-seated, often mutual, hatred toward a relative.

This situation requires a Malevolent Kinsman and a Hated or Reciprocally Hating Kinsman.

There are two types of Enmity of Kinsman: the Reciprocal and the Nonreciprocal.

In Reciprocal Enmity both parties equally hate each other. They may see themselves as competing with each other for love, power, prestige, or any type of resource that comes from being part of a family. Whatever it is, it must be powerful enough to warrant the breaking of the strongest blood ties.

When both parties hate, there is also a sense of competition that only one can have what is desired. It may start out as one person hating, but soon the one hated becomes the hater as well. They both perceive a lack of resources—that if one has the other will go without. If they could only see the bigger picture they might be able to work out a way for them to both be happy. Unfortunately most of us are conditioned since birth to believe there is only a "limited supply left," as the ads tell us.

Perhaps a mother-in-law hates her daughter-in-law for taking her son away. Soon the daughter-in-law will grow to hate her for her meddling. They don't realize the son has enough love for both of them.

In Nonreciprocal Enmity, one party hates and the other party does not; thus one becomes a Victim. Perhaps the eldest son is going to inherit a large fortune from the father, leaving the younger son with nothing. The elder son is fine with the situation and has no reason to hate the younger brother. Or perhaps a daughter is receiving all the male attention lately and her mother feels way past her prime. The daughter has no reason to hate her mother but she may be the brunt of her mother's jokes, gossip, or sabotage.

Whatever it is, it causes great personal, internal stress for the one who hates. Not only does she feel hate but she may also feel some guilt for hating a family member so much. This guilt will have to be suppressed, and sometimes the only way to suppress it is to hate even more fiercely, to push the hated one into doing something wrong, which in turn validates the one who hates. "See how horrible she is, I knew I was right to hate her!"

A very sad example of Nonreciprocal Enmity is infanticide. The infant is completely innocent and for whatever reason (culture, sickness, responsibility, embarrassment) the parent doesn't want the child. In order to get rid of the infant, the parent must bring himself to first hate it, otherwise he could never follow through with it.

Enmity can be real or created. One can create Enmity by adding his own distorted perceptions. Perhaps a mother is very upset about her job and comes home with a scowl on her face. Her child may think her mother is out to get her and scowl back.

Enmity toward parents usually starts very early on. Children (teenagers and adults, too, for that matter) desperately need to feel accepted by their parents or caregiver. When this need is not met they may become hostile, aggressive, dependent, defensively independent, have low self-esteem, become emotionally unresponsive and unstable, and have a negative view of the world.

Enmity toward siblings is somewhat expected in its basic sense but can become abnormal. William Antonio Boyle, Ph.D., author of *Sibling Rivalry*, says:

> It isn't difficult to find the root cause of sibling rivalry. The problem is basically one of competition for limited or scarce resources. The scarce resources are usually the time, attention, love, and approval that the parents can give to each of their children.

We also assume that family is the most important thing in one's life, but that may not be the case. In spiritual stories or self-actualizing stories the family may be detrimental, and the one who hates or is hated may be the one trying to separate from the family.

For one character, learning to be part of a family is important; for another, it may be learning to be autonomous. In the television show *Frasier*, Frasier is learning to live with his father and become friends with his brother. But Ray, in the show *Everybody Loves Raymond*, is trying to separate from his parents and make his own decisions.

THE MALEVOLENT KINSMAN

The Malevolent Kinsman is someone who is insecure either in his standing in life or in his ability to meet his basic needs. He sees the world as having limited resources. He is a "glass is half empty" kind of guy. He is only concerned with himself and what he needs. Other people should just step aside because they don't need things as badly as he does. Everyone may have a tough life, but he's sure no one else in the history of the world has gone through what he has.

His family owes him—he has done a lot for them and now it's his turn to reap rewards. His family may see things differently. Perhaps he gathered the firewood once and now he complains that he did it all the time. This would make those who actually did the work very angry. Or maybe he did work hard all his life and now his family is telling him to wait another year to go away to school so his younger brother can go first. This may be very logical to the family for certain reasons, but the elder brother will feel very betrayed. Reasons usually don't matter to children; they tend to see things in black and white when it comes to siblings and rewards given out.

THE HATED OR RECIPROCALLY HATING KINSMAN

The Hated or Reciprocally Hating Kinsman usually doesn't know what he did wrong at first. If he doesn't hate back he may try to make things right. He wants to settle the dispute and make amends but it never seems to work. His kindness and sincerity may even anger the Malevolent Kinsman further. It's a no-win situation for him and his only choice is to leave the situation, but ultimately even that will be futile. Other family members must step in to help the Hated Kinsman if he chooses not to hate back.

If he does hate back, he is basically just like the Malevolent Kinsman except that he is more on the defensive than the offensive. He is retaliating to the actions of the Malevolent Kinsman and will forever be reacting to him, waiting to see what he will do next. The few times he comes out on the offensive only escalates the Malevolent Kinsman's anger.

Whether Enmity of Kinsman is used as plot, subplot, or incident, the elements of the beginning, middle, and end are the same:

BEGINNING: Something happens that turns one Kinsman against another.

- What pushes the Malevolent Kinsman over the edge? Does he create the perceived offense?

- How will the Hated Kinsman react? Will he hate back?
- How many other family members are involved?
- Will any family members help out and try to resolve the situation?
- Does the Malevolent Kinsman get angry with everyone in the family?
- Is there an object they are competing for?

MIDDLE: The Hated Kinsman either tries to resolve the situation or attacks the Malevolent Kinsman.

- Will either of these characters be likeable? How?
- Are they both in the wrong?
- Do we like the Hated Kinsman (even if he fights back) because he didn't start the feud?
- Does the Malevolent Kinsman even entertain the idea that he may have overreacted? Or is he totally not self-aware?
- What do the other family members do? How do they contribute to the problem?
- Is there an end in sight?

END: One or both of the Kinsmen are defeated.

- Does anyone really win in this type of situation?
- Is the family forever torn apart because of this?
- Does the Malevolent Kinsman ever grasp his "prize" even if he dies because of it?
- Do we feel pity for the Malevolent Kinsman in the end?
- Are any major life lessons learned? What does this situation say about families?

"To have no heroes is to have no aspiration, to live on the momentum of the past, to be thrown back upon routine, sensuality, and the narrow self."

—CHARLES HORTON COOLEY

Hero to Kinsman

The Hero of Kinsman is one who is regarded with ardent or adoring respect and devotion.

In this situation the Malevolent Kinsman becomes the Heroic Idol and the Hated Kinsman becomes the Admiring Kinsman.

Here, a usually younger kinsman looks up to another kinsman for his work, stature, good deeds, accomplishments, or strength. The Heroic Idol embodies whatever the Admiring Kinsman lacks or has yet to develop. The Admiring Kinsman wants to be around his object of admiration as much as possible but this may ultimately push the Heroic Idol away. Ultimately his weakness is not a threat to the Heroic Idol so the Admiring Kinsman is tolerated.

Hopefully the Heroic Idol takes a liking to the Admiring Kinsman and tries to teach him or guide him along the way. If he is ethical he will make sure to foster independence in the Admiring Kinsman so as to not make him dependent upon him. He is like the older brother who teaches his sibling to fish rather than making him watch. Or the Aunt who counsels her niece when she is lovesick and gives her advice that empowers her to stand on her own two feet, independent of love games.

The Conflict comes from other characters who don't like the Heroic Idol and can't see anything great about him or those who are jealous of the Heroic Idol—especially if their lover likes the Heroic Idol, as may be the case with movie stars as Heroic Idols.

The two do not have to be related but should be in the same "field," such as a boy who loves to play baseball would be interested in a talented baseball player.

Whether Hero to Kinsman is used as plot, subplot, or incident, the elements of the beginning, middle, and end are the same:

BEGINNING: An Admiring Kinsman finds a Heroic Idol to admire and tries to be around him.

- Why does the Admiring Kinsman look up to the Heroic Idol? Does he do something heroic?

- Does the Admiring Kinsman have any other role models? Has he been searching for one?

- How closely are they related?

- What does the Heroic Idol think of the Admiring Kinsman at first?

- How do they meet?

MIDDLE: The Heroic Idol finally agrees to help the Admiring Kinsman or at least let him be a small part of his life.

- Why does the Heroic Idol agree to help the Admiring Kinsman? Does he feel pity for him? See himself in him?

- How does this act of kindness make the Admiring Kinsman feel? Does he feel more important? Does he feel like he is the Heroic Idol's sidekick?

- Will the Heroic Idol abuse the relationship at all, taking advantage of the Admiring Kinsman?
- To what lengths does the Admiring Kinsman go to be with the Heroic Idol?
- Does the Admiring Kinsman's family support this relationship? Why?

END: The Admiring Kinsman either gets into trouble defending the Heroic Idol or in trying to emulate the Heroic Idol. The Heroic Idol saves him.

- Does the Admiring Kinsman defend or emulate the Heroic Idol? How?
- When does the Heroic Idol find out? Is it in time to stop him?
- What does the Heroic Idol sacrifice to help the Admiring Kinsman? (In the movie *Finding Forrester*, he sacrifices his privacy and solitude to come forward.)
- What is at stake for the Admiring Kinsman? Does he need to prove he can do it just like his Heroic Idol can?
- Is the Heroic Idol going to leave in the end? Or will they continue to work together?

EXAMPLES

The Man in the Iron Mask, ALEXANDER DUMAS

ENMITY OF KINSMAN AS PLOT—The cruel King Louis XIV of France has a secret twin brother whom he keeps imprisoned.

Hannah and Her Sisters, WOODY ALLEN

ENMITY OF KINSMAN AS SUBPLOT—During a Thanksgiving Day party we make acquaintance with a numerous and problematic family, mainly three sisters: Lee, Holly, and Hannah. The balance of the family begins to break up when Hannah's husband, Elliot, falls in love with Lee, who leaves her husband.

Finding Forrester, GUS VAN SANT

HERO TO KINSMAN AS PLOT—A teen writing prodigy finds a mentor in a reclusive author who comes to his aid when he's most needed.

Sweet November, PAT O'CONNOR

HERO TO KINSMAN AS SUBPLOT—Abner, a young boy without a father figure, comes to admire Nelson Moss, a career-minded man who quits his job to move in with Abner's spontaneous neighbor, Sara. Nelson does activities with the boy and keeps promises to him even when it interferes with his other plans.

"You wish to find out a person's weak points? Note the failings he has the quickest eye for in others. They may not be the very failings he is himself conscious of; but they will be their next-door neighbors. No man keeps such a jealous lookout as a rival."

–A.W. HARE AND D.C. HARE

Competition

Competition is the act of seeking, or endeavoring to gain, what another is endeavoring to gain at the same time; common strife for the same objects; strife for superiority; rivalry.

This situation requires an Exceptional Person, an Adversary, and an Object.

This situation is somewhat similar to the last situation (Enmity of Kinsman) in that two people are competing for something, but it is different in the fact that enmity is a type of hatred and the characters in this situation don't necessarily hate each other. In fact, in some cases they may enjoy the competition.

There are three types of Competition: Jealous Competition, Threatened Competition (usually between Superior and Inferior), and Desirous Competition (usually between two Ambitious people).

In Jealous Competition, two characters compete for the same Object. It's as if they have been waiting years to put one over on each other. They just need an excuse to engage in a battle, and almost any battle will do. Think of two brothers who haven't seen each other for a while coming home for Thanksgiving dinner. Old rivalries may rear their ugly head as the two compete for mother's attention at the dinner table. Perhaps they will see who can eat the most food.

Whatever the Object they seem to be seeking, in the end it may be completely forgotten if the Object was just a vehicle to get them into a conflict. They may fight over a woman but in the end may hardly care about her. They desire a fight more than they desire the reward. Both parties are equally jealous in this case from the start.

Rivalry in this situation is a pretext to the darker feelings that may lie beneath the surface of the rivals. This situation thus breeds a tragic ending, usually leaving the Object fought for unclaimed, though sometimes the Object is completely destroyed as their jealousy turns to envy ("If I can't have it, no one will!").

Threatened Competition covers competition that is between one who is an expert in the field of the Competition and one who is a novice in it. They are usually not related though they may be very close—before the Competition, that is.

The rivalry between them is usually started by the Inferior One. As she does better and better for herself she will gain the notice of the Superior One, who may then feel threatened by her.

Several relationship types can work for this, such as:

- Immortal Being and Mortal Being
- Magician/Sorceress and Ordinary Man
- Conqueror and Conquered
- King and Noble
- Teacher and Student
- Rich One and Poor One
- Honored Man and Suspected One
- Queen and Servant
- Scientist and Uneducated
- Book Smart Person and Street Smart Person (depends on Competition)

In Desirous Competition two ambitious people, who may be equally matched, are shooting for the same objective or goal at the same time. Once a desire is sparked within each person, it is only fueled more by the competition. As soon as one sees the other is interested, desires rise ever higher—especially if it is mingled with sincerity of a faith or a conviction. There are so many types of desire to pursue:

- Power
- Honor
- Fortune
- Glory
- Fame
- Distinction

THE EXCEPTIONAL PERSON

The Exceptional Person is the one who seems to be in possession of the Object, or at least close to possessing it. He seems to be on top of it all, yet he is not happy. He can feel the presence of the Adversary and therefore cannot truly enjoy his prize. He may not even want this prize. The mere fact that the Adversary wants it may make him want it. He is obsessed with the Adversary:

- What is he doing?
- Where is he going?
- What will he think?
- Does he want this?
- I want him to see me with it.

He may think his life would be better without the Adversary but he almost needs him to "feed" off of. They have a dependent relationship.

THE ADVERSARY

The Adversary is equally obsessed with the Exceptional Person:

- Why does he have it?
- How did he get it?
- I deserve it more!
- I'll show him, I'll take it and smash it to pieces.
- Who does he think he is?

The Adversary has more motivation to compete with the Exceptional Person because he has nothing to lose at this point, while the Exceptional Person has everything to lose. The Adversary will take any chance that comes his way, however small, to become the Exceptional Person. If he works really hard, he may actually earn and deserve the reward. If he resorts to trickery or any other manner of immoral device, the feud will continue endlessly. The two parties will never trust each other again.

Our sympathies may lie with either the Exceptional Person or the Adversary depending on the circumstandces.

Whether Competition is used as plot, subplot, or incident, the elements of the beginning, middle, and end are the same:

BEGINNING: The Exceptional Person seems to obtain the Object desired. The Adversary finds out.

- What is the Object? Do they really care about it or is it just a symbol to them?

- Are other people impressed by the Exceptional Person? How does this make the Adversary feel?
- Does the Adversary react right away or bide his time in secret?
- Does the Exceptional Person flaunt his "winnings"?
- Is anyone on the side of the Adversary?
- Are there any shady characters around who would like to exploit or aggravate the situation for their own benefit?

MIDDLE: The Adversary carries out his plan to win the Object and get back at the Exceptional Person.

- At what point does he make his intentions known to the Exceptional Person?
- How does the Exceptional Person react?
- If the Object is a person, what does she think about it?
- Will the rest of the family take sides?
- How far is the Adversary willing to go?
- What type of obstacles will the Adversary face? Will they escalate?
- Do the Exceptional Person and Adversary switch places for a while, with the Adversary becoming the Exceptional Person?

END: The Adversary and Exceptional Person have a "showdown" of sorts.

- Do they forget completely about the Object sought?
- Who wins? Or do they both fail?
- Do they learn anything from the experience? Are they better people in the end?
- What happens to the family as a unit?
- Do any other characters influence the outcome to their advantage?
- Does something life changing happens for one of the Rivals, making this feud seem silly? (She could find out she's having a baby or be diagnosed with a fatal disease.)

"Many people believe that humility is the opposite of pride, when, in fact, it is a point of equilibrium. The opposite of pride is actually a lack of self-esteem. A humble person is totally different from a person who cannot recognize and appreciate himself as part of the world's marvels."

—RABINO NILTON BONDER

Concession

To Concede means to yield, grant, or surrender.

In this situation, the Exceptional Person becomes the Sacrificer. He willingly allows the Adversary to win the Object sought. He sees how much the Adversary needs this win, not just the Object itself. The actual process of winning is what can foster growth in the Adversary.

The Sacrificer is comfortable with who he is. He is grateful for what he has and sees it as his duty to help others. There may be those around him who do not like the Adversary and try to get the Sacrificer to fight with him.

In the end it doesn't work unless the Adversary pushes things too far and completely tries to humiliate and embarrass the Sacrificer. If he crosses that imaginary line the Sacrificer may, temporarily, turn into the Exceptional Person and fight it out a bit. Sooner or later he sees the truth behind the Adversary's antics and vows to help him before he self-destructs.

The Sacrificer has much more power than the Adversary and can afford to give up an Object or two. He may receive benefits from his sacrifice if others see how altruistic he is being.

The conflict comes from the Adversary's self-destructive nature. Perhaps the Adversary has no self-esteem at all and cannot comprehend someone doing something out of the goodness of his heart—*the Sacrificer has to be lying*, he thinks to himself.

Whether Concession is used as plot, subplot, or incident, the elements of the beginning, middle, and end are the same:

BEGINNING: The Adversary and Sacrificer paths cross. They may already know each other.

- How long have they known each other? Do they live together?
- How did they meet?
- Is either of them happy to see the other?
- Have they always had the same interests, hobbies, or objectives?
- What does the Adversary want?
- Does the Sacrificer care anymore about the objective?

MIDDLE: The Adversary makes his objective known. The Sacrificer reacts.

- Will the Sacrificer fight with the Adversary at first?
- How long will this go on?

- Will the Sacrificer rise above the situation? Why? What's different?
- Is the Adversary a lot younger and inexperienced compared to the Sacrificer? Will this influence the Sacrificer's decision to concede?
- What is at stake for the Sacrificer? The Adversary?
- Is the Adversary being pushed or controlled by someone else into doing this? Is his life at stake?

END: The Sacrificer concedes to the Adversary and feels better for it.

- Will the Adversary know the Sacrificer "gave it" to him? Will this make him angry?
- Will the Adversary's pride be hurt?
- How will the other characters feel about this?
- Has the Adversary gained or learned anything from this?
- How has their relationship changed? Is it over, or stronger?

EXAMPLES

Wall Street, OLIVER STONE

COMPETITION AS SUBPLOT—Bud Fox is a Wall Street stockbroker with a strong desire to get to the top. He meets with his idol, Gordon Gekko, who tells him, "Greed is good." Taking this advice and working closely with Gekko, Fox soon finds himself swept into a world of shady business deals. He turns the tables on Gekko.

Adam's Rib, GEORGE CUKOR

COMPETITION AS PLOT—Married lawyers Adam and Amanda Bonner find themselves on opposite sides of the courtroom. Adam is prosecuting a high-profile murder case. Amanda acts as the defense attorney.

A League of Their Own, PENNY MARSHALL

CONCESSION AS INCIDENT—Two sisters join the first female professional baseball league and struggle to keep it afloat. Dottie lets Kit win the last game to help her self-esteem.

Casablanca, MICHAEL CURTIZ

CONCESSION AS INCIDENT—Rick Blaine's world is turned upside down when his lost love returns. On several occasions he allows people to win money and arguments with him to achieve his goals. He sets aside his feelings and competitive nature and allows his love to have the documents she seeks, even though there is nothing for him to gain from it but trouble.

> "Where there's Marriage without Love, there will
> be Love without Marriage."
>
> –BENJAMIN FRANKLIN

Adultery

*Adultery is a voluntary relationship between a married person
and a partner other than the lawful spouse.*

This situation requires Two Adulterers and a Betrayed Spouse.

Adultery occurs when a husband or wife is betrayed. There are
cases of infidelity, such as "swinging," where all parties know about
the affair and agree to it in some way, but Adultery, by contrast, has
the strong element of betrayal attached to it.

This feeling of betrayal is what adds the conflict to the situation and
fuels the fires of retribution. Betrayal can cause the average Joe to
do things he never thought he was capable of doing. It can lead to:

Murderous Adultery:

- the slaying of Wife or Husband by the Lover
- the slaying of Wife or Husband by the Spouse
- the slaying of Lover by Wife or Husband
- the slaying of Adulterer by Neighbors

Or:

- the Adulterer being ostracized from the community (especially depending on the time period of the story)
- the Adulterer being consumed with guilt, possibly becoming paranoid
  that the spouse knows
- the Lover being consumed with passion and wanting the Adulterer to
  marry him (as in *Fatal Attraction*)
- the Spouse finding out and holding it against the Adulterer to get something she wants (blackmail of sorts)
- the Lover being abandoned and alone

There may be social mores, sexist standards, religious laws, or even personal standards to add more conflict to the act of Adultery. The time period of the story is important here. In some places, even today, a woman is killed for sleeping with someone other than her husband.

But centuries ago, when Courtly Love existed, it was expected that the nobility would find lovers outside of their marriages. It is what made the great Knights great.

The audience can root for either the betrayed or the betrayer depending on a few factors:

- Is the betrayed Spouse nice and loving and the Lover "ugly" on the inside? (If so, the audience will root for the Spouse, and vice versa.)
- How long was the married couple together? (The longer the relationship, the more people will want to see the married couple stay together.)
- Are there any children involved?
- Why did they get married? Was it an arranged marriage or were they in love?
- Is there a large age difference between the married partners?
- Is the Spouse available sexually? Or too frigid?
- Is this the first time it's happened? Or is this a pattern of behavior?

The audience for this situation is like a jury. They want to know all the facts so they can figure out who to root for. This situation can really hit home for a lot of people, so you better make sure you are asking the audience to root for the most likeable character, otherwise you'll lose their interest.

THE ADULTERERS

The Adulterers can be wonderful or deceitful people. The reason for the affair and how they each feel about it afterward are the deciding factors.

Perhaps the cheating spouse isn't honest with the Lover about her marriage. Or the Lover manipulates the cheating Spouse, taking advantage of her while she is vulnerable. He could be a seducer who doesn't really care about her at all.

Either way the Adulterer is on the edge, unsure of herself and what she wants in life. Why did she get married? What changed since then? Is she having a midlife crisis? Why would she risk her marriage and security?

Something is so wrong in her life that she is willing to risk it all for this affair because she believes her rewards for it will be great. She will feel better somehow. She doesn't have the strength to face what is going on inside of her that makes her want to do this; she is

ng for the "high" this affair can bring. The Spouse represents
.ch "reality" for her and she would rather hide her pain in the
of a stranger.

THE BETRAYED SPOUSE

The Betrayed Spouse is usually overly secure in the relationship at
times and may not pay enough attention to the Cheating Spouse.
Adultery usually comes as a shock to him. It's easier for him to get
mad and retaliate than to look at what he may have done to cause
this affair. If only he would look closely he might see that the warning signs were there and he just didn't want to listen.

It's as if you have two people trying to run away from their feelings and the reality of home life rather than fix what is wrong.

The Betrayed Spouse feels completely justified in striking out.
He quickly takes on the role of Victim and gathers allies against the
Cheating Spouse—"See what she did to me!"

The question is, is he upset that his wife cheated or that this
Lover took his "property"? Many women mistake jealously for love
when in reality the man is only angry that someone else invaded his
territory.

Whether Adultery is used as plot, subplot, or incident, the elements
of the beginning, middle, and end are the same:

BEGINNING: Two Adulterers meet. The Cheating Spouse may not act just yet.

- Are the Adulterers or the Betrayed and Lover tied together in any way
  (co-workers, family members, some common project or responsibility)?
- What obstacles are in the way? Schedules? Other people? Time?
  Money?
- Are children involved?
- How long have the Betrayed Spouse and the Adulterer been married
  and in what shape is their marriage?
- Why is the Cheating Spouse considering cheating?
- What is at stake besides the marriage? Is the married couple work-
  ing on something together (buying a house, building a life, making
  friends, starting a business, being critiqued by the public eye)?

MIDDLE: The Adulterers have the affair.

- Is the Lover much better than the Betrayed Spouse? Is the Betrayed
  Spouse a horrible person?
- Where will audience loyalties be?
- What obstacles are in the way?

- How many times will the affair happen?
- Does the Cheating Spouse feel remorse?
- When does the Betrayed Spouse find out?
- Does the Betrayed Spouse care about the Spouse at all or just feel cheated? Does he want to save the marriage?
- What do family, friends, and co-workers think? Do they get involved?
- Do the Adulterers try to stop themselves from being exposed? What obstacles are in their way?

END: The Betrayed Spouse retaliates and someone may die.

- Does someone influence the Betrayed Spouse to strike back? Or does he make up his mind on his own?
- Is the Betrayed Spouse's response swift and quick or calculated and planned out?
- Will someone die? Who? How?
- Is there a lesson to be learned here?
- Is there a twist to the ending that may change the audience's loyalties? Did they root for the wrong person all along? (Perhaps they thought the Betrayed Spouse was a good man until, like a mystery, all the pieces fall into place and they see he is a horrible person.)

> "Nothing is more noble, nothing more venerable than fidelity. Faithfulness and truth are the most sacred excellences and endowments of the human mind."
>
> —CICERO

Fidelity

Fidelity is the unfailing fulfillment of one's duties and obligations and strict adherence to vows or promises.

In this situation the Adulterer becomes the Faithful Spouse who refuses to find another Lover after the loss of her spouse. This loss could stem from her spouse dying, going to prison, getting sick, divorcing her, or perhaps leaving her for his job.

She could feel guilty at the thought of being with someone new or possibly doesn't feel capable of being back out on the dating scene and clings to the memory of her former spouse.

She needs to find self-esteem and self-empowerment to get over her loss and get on with her life. She is much more than her title of

," and she needs to realize this. Hopefully she has friends, family, or even a stranger around to push her to go out and change her life. She may be afraid but she really has no choice in the matter; she can't bring her spouse back.

If her spouse is living and is in jail or just plain left her, she can't force him to come back. Her happiness shouldn't be dependent upon another human being. She has to learn how to make herself happy. She has to find out who she really is deep down inside. Maybe being in this situation is just what she needs.

Whether Fidelity is used as plot, subplot, or incident, the elements of the beginning, middle, and end are the same:

BEGINNING: The Faithful Spouse loses her spouse in some way.

- Does he pass away? Or does he leave her? Why?
- How does this make the Faithful Spouse feel? Is she in denial, thinking he will come back?
- What do other characters think about the situation? Are they giving her some time to get over the loss?
- Does the Faithful Spouse stay in the same house or apartment that she had with her spouse? Does she save his things like a shrine?
- How does she spend her long, lonely nights?
- How does she handle taking over the jobs her spouse used to do?

MIDDLE: The Faithful Spouse is forced to face her loneliness.

- Does she decide to go out and try to date? Or does she fall further into her isolated life?
- Does she have a job or other obligations to hide in?
- How is she pushed to face her loneliness? Do other characters push her?
- Does she have any family or close friends to visit?
- Does she try to date but find it to be too hard? Does she get discouraged easily?
- Does she feel guilty about thinking about moving on?

END: The Faithful Spouse cleans up her life and moves on.

- How does she move on? Go on a date? Clean up her house? Move? Get a new job? Start a new hobby? Do volunteer work?
- Does she realize love and happiness are found within?
- Does she find happiness with another man? Or in rediscovering herself?
- What is the theme here?

EXAMPLES

Unfaithful, ADRIAN LYNE

ADULTERY AS PLOT—The marriage of a couple living in the New York City suburbs goes dangerously awry when the wife indulges in an adulterous fling.

Fatal Attraction, ADRIAN LYNE

ADULTERY AS PLOT—A married man's one-night stand comes back to haunt him when that lover begins to stalk him and his family.

Men Don't Leave, PAUL BRICKMAN

FIDELITY AS SUBPLOT—A mother of two sons finds life considerably difficult on her own after the death of her beloved husband.

The Notebook, NICHOLAS SPARKS

FIDELITY AS SUBPLOT—An elderly man reads a story to an elderly woman with Alzheimer's in a nursing home. The story he reads follows two young lovers named Allie Hamilton and Noah Calhoun, who meet one evening at a carnival. It's clear this man is staying faithfully by his wife's side while she has Alzheimer's.

Situations 31 & 32

MADNESS AND GENIUS

> "It is much more comfortable to be mad and know it, than to be sane and have one's doubts."
>
> –GEORGE BROWN

Madness

Madness is the quality or condition of being insane and demounts fury and rage.

This situation requires a Madman and a Victim.

The Victim may or may not play a major role here. She may be killed in the opening scene, as is the case with many police dramas, or she may struggle to survive, as is the case with many horror movies such as *Halloween*.

Madness is a fearful mystery where it was once thought to be a form of possession. People have never been able to comprehend cruel acts committed for no apparent reason or cause. The Madman cannot be reasoned with. The Victim is either strong enough to protect herself or she isn't. It is survival of the fittest.

Why do these things happen? Because life is unpredictable — which is why audiences relate to these stories.

Metaphors abound here upon the Madman. Is he a symbol of society as he kills all the bad teenagers, allowing only the virginal female to survive? Does his costume say anything about sports violence as in the hockey mask of Jason? Is Freddy Krueger a symbol of a pedophile hiding out in a basement and hurting children when they are most vulnerable and scaring the kids from ever going to bed again?

MADMAN

There are two types of Madmen here: the Personal and the Stranger.

The Personal is someone known by the Victim in a somewhat intimate way — a family member, friend, teacher, or sibling, for example. He is someone the Victim has seen many times and knows on a first-name basis. This type brings up issues of trust because the Victim believes she is safe around this Madman. She lets her guard down and is more vulnerable. When the attack comes, it is even more painful for having known the Madman.

The Stranger is someone totally unknown by the Victim. This makes the act seem random and thus scares the audience even more. The Victim may have done something to set off the Madman, but she rarely realizes she has done anything wrong. She's just going about her day as if nothing is wrong until she feels that change in the air, as if she senses danger. This situation doesn't have any trust issues, because however nice she may be to a Stranger, she will never trust him 100 percent. Very often Victims who do seemingly "stupid" things later say that something told them not to trust the stranger but they didn't heed that inner warning.

VICTIM

There are two types of Victims: the Passive and the Aggressive.

The Passive Victim doesn't try to fight back. She may be in shock or thinks if she stays calm he'll eventually leave her alone and she'll survive. This Victim usually is killed at the beginning of this situation because we are dealing with a Madman, not a kidnapper.

The Aggressive Victim reacts quickly and tries to fight back. She may not even know she is fighting at all; it could just be an automatic reflex. The Victim usually makes it through the Climax and possibly saves herself in the end. She is dealing with a Madman who can't be reasoned with so she has to fight to save herself.

Whether Madness is used as plot, subplot, or incident, the elements of the beginning, middle, and end are the same:

BEGINNING: A Madman snaps and selects his Victim. The Victim is just going about her normal everyday routine.

- What makes the Madman snap?

- Why does the Madman select this Victim? Is she just in the wrong place at the wrong time or is there something more significant about her? (Remember how the Son of Sam killer wanted to hurt brunettes.)

- Will this Madman be Personal or a Stranger?

- Will the Madman have any supernatural powers? (A lot of B-horror films have a Madman who can't be killed, like Freddy Krueger.)

- What does the Madman symbolize? Will you use metaphors?

- Will the Victim be Passive or Aggressive? How big of a part will she play in this situation? (If you want her to save herself, she better have some aggressiveness in her even if we don't see it yet. She can be a very nice person until later when the Madman makes her do aggressive things in order to stay alive.)

- Does the Victim have a brief moment of opportunity to get away? Why doesn't she take it? Perhaps she doesn't know she's in any real danger yet or she's afraid someone else will get hurt? (In some horror films you'll see the Victim walk right by a policeman in the beginning, which really frustrates the audience.)

- How will the Madman first approach the Victim? Will he be violent right away or try to give the Victim a false sense of security? (Think of Ted Bundy and how he put a cast on his arm and begged a woman for help in moving a piece of furniture.)

- If the Madman is Personal, what makes his temper flare up with the Victim? Does he want control over her like a parent over a child?

- Is the Victim used to the Madman's displays of anger? Does she not take him seriously?

- Will the Victim survive the first scene?

MIDDLE: The Victim tries to escape. She tries to get help.

- If the Victim doesn't survive the first scene, a new Victim is selected.

- Will the Victim be offered another chance to escape only to lose it again?

- Will she get away temporarily? How does she get caught again? (Perhaps she's in the middle of nowhere and there is no place to go or she doesn't know where she is and walks in circles.)

- Why hasn't the Madman done away with the Victim yet? Is he waiting for something? Does he have a certain ritual he has to perform? Or is the Victim able to talk him out of it or get away from him, making him chase after her?

- Why hasn't anyone come to the Victim's aid?

- What obstacles will the Victim and Madman face here?

END: The Victim defends herself, but she can also receive outside help at the last moment.

- If the Victim survives, how will she defend herself? How will the Victim outsmart the Madman?

- If the Victim dies, how will the police or the Victim's family members catch the Madman?

- Will the Madman get away? (Think about the many horror films when the Madman disappears at the end. This has been overdone, so be careful.)

- Will the Madman be caught, yet get away with his crime? (Think of the Madmen who have falsely claimed insanity and kept themselves out of jail. Many psychological thrillers have Madmen who are very smart and cunning.)

• Is anyone else, besides the Victim, changed by this experience?

> "There is no great genius without some touch of madness."
>
> –LUCIUS ANNAEUS SENECA

Genius

Genius is distinguished mental superiority or uncommon intellectual power. It is the ability to invent and see things differently from everyone else.

In this situation the Madman becomes the Genius who tries to fit into the world but never really can. He is too smart, too creative, and too intense. He sees things no one else sees. He questions things no one else would think to question. This can freak people out, especially if he pushes them to expand their beliefs.

He is usually an eccentric man, not buying into the traditional ways of society. His mind is too busy thinking to be concerned with the mundane aspects of life. Albert Einstein had a closet full of suits that were exactly alike so he didn't have to think about what to wear everyday. Some possible Genius situations are:

• A man is in love, but the woman wants nothing to do with him or just can't handle him. (Think Vincent van Gogh.)

• The smartest man in the world lives as a bar bouncer while he tries to find a way to end world hunger. (This is a true story.)

• A great writer challenges the status quo and sparks a massive change in the "system."

The Genius knows he is important to the world but doesn't know how much of himself he'll have to sacrifice for the greater good. He may also wonder if the world is ready for him and his knowledge.

He has a sense of responsibility to others though he may at times think himself above them. He can't help it. He lives on a totally different wavelength. He may be in a room full of people yet feel extremely lonely. At times his genius is truly a curse for him, but he wouldn't give it up. It is his identity.

Whether Genius is used as plot, subplot, or incident, the elements of the beginning, middle, and end are the same:

BEGINNING: A Genius discovers something.

- How does he make this discovery?
- Is he happy about this discovery? Or is he worried that mankind may not be ready for it yet?
- Is there great responsibility with this discovery? Is he up to it? Does he care?
- Who does he tell first? Does he have any close friends to talk to, even if they don't always understand him?
- Is he always using big words and getting frustrated when others don't understand him?
- Does he enjoy being around college students?
- Does he try to fit into regular society? Or has he given that up?

MIDDLE: The Genius tries to get help and support for his discovery, or he tries to hide it.

- Does he hide the discovery only to have someone steal it anyway? Or does he decide to make it public right away?
- Will he be taken advantage of if he is not skilled in business matters?
- Will people think his discovery is a joke and not see it for what it is?
- What do his friends and family think?
- If he wants to fit in, how does he manage that along with this discovery?
- Does someone successfully steal his discovery?

END: The discovery helps a lot of people and is successful or it gets into the wrong hands and it harms people.

- Does the discovery help or hurt? How will the Genius deal with this? (Think *Jurassic Park*.)
- Has the Genius been able to fit in? If not, does he at least find one person he can relate to?
- Does he go out on the lecture circuit due to this discovery? Or become reclusive?
- How has he changed after this discovery?
- Does he go back to life as normal, for him, and try to make other discoveries? Or does he try to be "normal"?

EXAMPLES

Halloween, JOHN CARPENTER

MADNESS AS PLOT—A psychotic murderer institutionalized since childhood escapes on a mindless rampage.

The Silence of the Lambs, JONATHAN DEMME

MADNESS AS PLOT AND SUBPLOT—Clarice Starling, a young FBI agent, is assigned to help find a missing woman and save her from a psychopathic killer with the help of another killer.

Jurassic Park, STEVEN SPIELBERG

GENIUS AS SUBPLOT—Scientists clone dinosaurs to populate a theme park. A major security breakdown releases the dinosaurs.

Good Will Hunting, GUS VAN SANT

GENIUS AS PLOT—Will Hunting, a janitor at MIT, has a genius level gift for mathematics, but his traumatic childhood leaves him too closed up to truly develop it.

> "How true it is that our destinies are decided by nothing and that a small imprudence helped by some insignificant accident, as an acorn is fertilized by a drop of rain, may raise the trees on which perhaps we and others shall be crucified."
>
> —HENRI FREDERICK AMIEL

Imprudence

Imprudence is the condition of being unwise or indiscreet and lacking caution.

This situation requires the Imprudent and the Victim or Object Lost.

In this situation an Imprudent character has done something without thinking it through and has gotten himself, and possibly others, into trouble. This situation is based on the hasty actions of a character that have big consequences. It's as if this character has triggered a series of dominoes that twist and turn the story with each falling piece.

Imprudence is sparked by several distinct motives: Curiosity, Credulity, Jealousy, Passion, and Human Weakness, but the results of the Fatal Imprudence are interchangeable.

- Curiosity is a desire to know or learn about people or things that do not concern one.

- Credulity is to believe too readily, to be gullible.

- Jealousy is the desire to have something someone else has. (Unlike Envy, where one would destroy an object to keep someone else from having it.)

- Passion comes from strong emotions, desires, and needs.

- Human Weaknesses can be sleep, hunger, gluttony, lust, and childish simplicity.

Whatever the reason or motive for the Fatal Imprudence, the character has set off a chain reaction that no one can stop. He soon realizes he will have to pay the price for his actions.

THE IMPRUDENT

The Imprudent can be either a Fool or a Rebel. The Fool thinks he may, by some fluke, be above the law; the Rebel knows he is and demands it.

A Fool is the silly simpleton who doesn't understand the gravity of the situation. He makes a decision in haste because he has absolutely no idea of the differing consequences or results of it. He may expect good in others and be idealistic toward them, believing everything they say. People have a habit of bailing him out of jams, and he may have come to rely on always being saved, except this time that may not be possible. He takes risks and is irresponsible and reckless with no thought to the future.

A Rebel knows no boundaries. He does whatever he wants whenever he wants. Rules are made to be broken, and he will make decisions in haste because he believes things will always work out in his favor. It's not his fault if someone else is hurt by his decision; it's up to others to take care of themselves. He didn't force the choice upon him, fate did. It's fate's fault for leaving faulty outcomes at his feet. If his decision causes pain, he blames everyone but himself. He may be trying to do some good, so he can rationalize any decision he has to make. He may call it choosing the lesser of two evils.

VICTIM OR LOST OBJECT

The Victim or Lost Object is in the wrong place at the wrong time. Perhaps knowing the Imprudent is the Victim's only mistake in all of this, but there is nothing that can be done. Fate has taken over as far as the Victim or Lost Object is concerned.

The Imprudent one has done something that has either affected someone (or an Object) who is now a Victim of his actions. Perhaps the Imprudent one gets behind the wheel of his car while he is overly emotional and hits an innocent pedestrian. The Victim didn't do anything wrong; she was just walking down the street at the wrong time.

Of course the Imprudent one can also be the Victim of his own actions. He may be overcome with guilt for having hurt an innocent bystander.

Whether Imprudence is used as plot, subplot, or incident, the elements of the beginning, middle, and end are the same:

BEGINNING: The Imprudent receives a motivating force (curiosity, for example). He may be warned away.

- What type of Imprudent is in this situation?
- Do other characters see the disaster ahead and try to warn him?
- Are there other characters there to instigate the Imprudent?
- How many Victims are on the line?
- Why does the Imprudent act with such haste?
- What happened to make the Imprudent hasty? Is there a time element?

MIDDLE: The Imprudent makes a hasty decision and has to live with it.

- How do other characters react to his decision?
- How hard is the Victim hit?
- Does the Imprudent care about the Victim or Lost Object?
- Does the Imprudent take even a little bit of responsibility here?
- Did his choice set up several other choices for him to make? Is he spiraling out of control?
- Will another character try to bail him out?

END: The Imprudent is punished for his haste. The Victim gets justice or the Lost Object is found.

- Does the Imprudent punish himself? Or is he punished?
- What lesson is learned here?
- What do other characters do or feel about this event? Do they try to prevent it from happening again?
- Is the Imprudent humiliated at all? Or still blaming others?

> "When science discovers the center of the universe, a lot of people will be disappointed to find they are not it."
>
> —BERNARD BAILEY

Caution

To be cautious means to be careful, tentative, or restrained in behavior or decisions.

In this situation the Imprudent becomes the Cautious. He is someone who takes his time making decisions because he doesn't want to make the wrong choice. He knows he is not infallible. He doesn't have anything to prove and can therefore act or not act without pressure. He doesn't have a strong sense of pride that needs to be tended. If someone else steps up to make a decision ahead of him, that is fine.

The problem comes when he is unable to make a decision for fear of making the wrong one. He doesn't want to hurt anyone, so he procrastinates, waiting for the right time to make a decision. He wants all the facts before saying a word. Sometimes waiting is not an option, especially if someone is in danger right now and he needs to decide to help them. His procrastination can get the better of him, and he may inadvertently harm a Victim or Object because of it. Imagine if he has to cut the wires on a bomb and can't decide what to do!

He has to learn to act when appropriate, to stand up for what he believes and risk being assertive. True assertiveness is not aggressive; it sets boundaries against what is not wanted and allows in what is wanted. Without it one cannot create nor do anything of value in the world. To teach, one must say "I know;" to have, one must say "This is mine;" to create, one must say, "I am creative." If he focuses too much on being cautious he will never be assertive and others will not to listen to him.

The seven steps to ethical decision making (according to the Josephson Institute of Ethics, a nonprofit organization that works to improve the ethical quality of society) are:

1. stop and think
2. clarify goals
3. determine facts
4. develop options
5. consider consequences
6. choose
7. monitor and modify

The Cautious one gets into trouble with step six, choose—that is, if there is time enough to get to step six before a decision should be made.

This type of situation can be seen a lot in cop buddy movies where one cop is a loose cannon (Fatal Imprudence) and the other wants to do things slowly and figure things out. He feels his responsibilities more (Caution).

Whether Caution is used as plot, subplot, or incident, the elements of the beginning, middle, and end are the same:

BEGINNING: A Cautious character is faced with making a decision.

- Can he act?
- What is at stake? Is this too much pressure for him?
- Why does he hesitate?
- Are there other characters around who want to make the decision and grow impatient with him?
- Is he being set up by other characters?
- Is he being careful or afraid to act?
- How does this situation relate to other subplots?

MIDDLE: The Cautious character is still gathering information and weighing options.

- Are the consequences too big for him? (Think about *Star Trek* commanders having to decide to sacrifice a crewmember for the good of the whole.)
- Does he have anyone else to talk to about this? Someone he trusts? Advisors of some sort?
- What are other characters doing? Getting ready to mutiny?

END: The Cautious character makes a decision or is overthrown by someone else who does.

- Does he make a decision? Can he stand behind it?
- If not, how is he pushed aside? Is the wrong decision made by his replacement?
- What are the consequences of the decision?
- What is at stake for the Cautious character?
- Can a bad decision be corrected?

EXAMPLES

King Lear, WILLIAM SHAKESPEARE

IMPRUDENCE AS PLOT—An aging King makes a rash judgement and turns his kingdom over to his cruel, selfish daughters and sends away the only daughter who truly cares for him and for the kingdom.

Lethal Weapon, RICHARD DONNER

IMPRUDENCE AND CAUTION AS SUBPLOT—A veteran detective is partnered with a young detective who seems to have a suicidal death wish.

Crimson Tide, TONY SCOTT

CAUTION AND IMPRUDENCE AS PLOT—On a U.S. nuclear missile submarine, a young first officer stages a mutiny to prevent his trigger-happy captain from launching his missiles before confirming his orders to do so.

Little Women, LOUISA MAY ALCOTT

CAUTION AS SUBPLOT—Jo waits too long to decide to marry long-time friend, Laurie, and ends up losing him to her younger sister.

> "My attitude toward men who mess around is simple: If you find 'em kill 'em."
>
> –LORETTA LYNN

Crimes of Love

A crime is an unlawful, unjust, or senseless act. Crimes of Love involve passion and jealousy.

This situation requires a Lover, a Beloved, and possibly a Revealer.

In this situation a Lover has committed a crime with his Beloved of which there are two types: Voluntary and Involuntary.

Crimes of Love are crimes of the heart where unacceptable unions are desired. These desires are shunned by society as taboo and would only ostracize the participants if they commit the act. These crimes can be of relations or of taboos. Either the Lover and Beloved are related in some way or they are breaking a taboo by being together.

In the Involuntary Crime, the Lover does not know what he is doing is wrong until it is either too late or at the point of being too late.

The crime may have even been viciously planned by a third party, but this still doesn't take away from the shock and guilt of it all for the Lover.

There are many ways this type of crime can happen:

- discovery that one has married one's mother, daughter, or sister
- sleeping with the twin of a husband unknowingly
- not knowing someone is married
- not knowing the age of a partner
- not knowing the real sex of a partner
- abusing a spouse in a fit of rage, where the abuser just can't stop himself

Voluntary Crimes of Love have a twist in that they can be unrequited. In this case, the Beloved knows of their relationship to each other and isn't willing to break a taboo. This may not stop the advances of the Lover and usually makes for great comedic effect and shock.

Otherwise, both parties know what they are doing and may have some sense that it is wrong or socially unacceptable but just can't help themselves.

Some situations are:

- a parent in love with her child and vice versa

- a woman and her stepson enamored with each other

- a woman sleeping with both a father and a son

- a man loving his sister-in-law

- siblings in love

- an older woman and a very young man, and vice versa

- prostitution (still has some taboo)

- teacher and student

- homosexuality (which, at the writing of this book, is considered a taboo by many in the United States; several countries almost encourage it with strict anti-hate laws, so do your research)

- onanism (masturbation, which is still considered a taboo and rarely discussed openly)

Polti, who was writing in 1946, states that homosexuality is a crime. I have chosen to omit this as a crime, though there still is a taboo against it. Regardless of what anyone's opinion on this subject is, it does involve two consenting, unrelated adults. However, it is a very polarized subject for many people who consider it taboo.

It just depends on the time period of the story as to whether or not this is considered a criminal act by society. There were several periods in history where it was considered normal, especially when all the men were off to war for years at a time.

Do your research when it comes to using taboos. You might be surprised at what you will find. For example, in *Women in the Ancient World*, James C. Thompson says, "In ancient Athens a wife was a necessity in order to have legitimate children and heirs, but a man's normal desire for female companionship and sex was something to be satisfied outside of marriage. A woman's desire for male companionship was never given much thought."

There are many other taboos in existence, especially when it comes to love and sexuality, but I'll leave it up to you to research those. My advice with this is to read several authors who write the type of taboo you want to write about—there are limits, even within erotica. Also, think of the "*Jaws* technique," as we call it in screenwriting. In the film *Jaws* we hardly ever see the shark, and that is what makes the film so intense. The viewer's brain fills in the blanks and his imagination runs wild. You don't have to spell everything out for the reader.

THE LOVER

The Lover is someone who can love very deeply and passionately. He is in touch with his feelings and desires and doesn't mind taking risks … he just likes to know the facts. If he is caught in an Involuntary Crime of Love he may feel betrayed but can usually rationalize himself out of guilty feelings because he just didn't know any better. He will realize that he loved this person before he knew it was a "crime" to do so, and he may choose to keep on loving her no matter what happens.

If his crime is Voluntary, he has made his decision but may or may not care what other people think. It depends on his standing in the community. If he is a political figure, his entire career may be on the line, for example. He may make a decision to act one minute and then change his mind the next.

THE BELOVED

The Beloved one is in the same predicament as the Lover. She may be an involuntary participant as well, not realizing their relation, but when it comes to age, race, and marital status she knows what she is doing. The Lover is the hero of the story, so the Beloved would be the one concealing things from him in the case of Involuntary Crimes of Love.

When it comes to Voluntary Crimes of Love she may have just as much to lose as the Lover does. Her passion may be equal to that of the Lover or she may need convincing. Perhaps she's in a vulnerable place when the Lover comes knocking and it seems like the right thing to do at the time, but she later has regrets. She may think it will be easy for her to walk away but then later finds it's not so easy.

THE REVEALER

The Revealer may be present in cases of Involuntary Crimes of Love. Usually he is a somewhat innocent bystander who learns the truth about the union, but he can also be a Villain who revels in the thought of pushing the two together.

He may want to secretly try to get the two apart so nothing happens and no one has to know what happened. His heart may be clear and true and he just wants to help, but hiding the information from the Lovers could cause more harm than good.

Whether Crimes of Love is used as plot, subplot, or incident, the elements of the beginning, middle, and end are the same:

BEGINNING: The Lover meets his Beloved and pursues her.

- Will this be a chance meeting?
- Will this be an Involuntary Crime of Love or a Voluntary one?
- How does the Beloved feel at this point? Is she interested in the Lover?
- Will a Revealer be involved? You may need to foreshadow him here.
- What kind of family or societal obligations do the Lovers have?
- What could the Lovers lose from pursuing this union?

MIDDLE: The Lover meets many obstacles but finally gets the Beloved and may or may not act.

- What type of obstacles will the Lover face?
- Does the Beloved still need convincing? Or is she just as willing?
- If this is an Involuntary Crime of Love, will they almost figure things out on their own but get sidetracked? How will they find out the truth?
- How far will they go? Are they stopped before anything happens?
- Do higher stakes make it more pleasurable for them?
- How many other characters know about the union?

END: The Lover and Beloved are caught if Voluntary or learn the truth if Involuntary. Now they face the consequences of their actions.

- Did anyone betray them?
- Will the Lover or Beloved be driven to Shakespearian-style suicide?
- Will the Lover and Beloved stop seeing each other?
- What do other characters think? Will they know about it?
- Do the Lovers lose everything because of this?
- Will both Lovers survive? Will they be attacked for their differences?
- Will there be a happy ending?

> "Love is that condition in which the happiness of
> another person is essential to your own."
>
> –ROBERT HEINLEIN

Sacrifice for Love

*Sacrifice for Love means to give up something held dear for the
sake of something loved.*

In this situation the Lover becomes the Sacrificer. His needs and desires are not as important as the well-being of the Beloved. He won't
risk hurting her in any way, so he does what he can for her from a
distance and leaves her alone. He is at peace with himself and allows his compassion for others to grow.

In time, the Beloved may pursue him. The circumstances keeping them apart have hopefully changed; otherwise, they may both
need to make a Sacrifice for Love. But this Sacrifice will be made
by two loving individuals who know what they are getting into. They
are not acting from intense passion in the heat of the moment.

They will still have obstacles to overcome but they will try to get
through them together. They are in love, and that is the most important thing at the moment.

Whether Sacrifice for Love is used as plot, subplot, or incident, the
elements of the beginning, middle, and end are the same:

BEGINNING: The Lover meets the Beloved and wants to pursue her.

- Where and how do they meet? Is it memorable? Romantic?
- Does he pursue her?
- What makes him hesitate to pursue her further? What does he learn?
- Why does he fall in love so quickly? Is it fate? Does she remind him of
  someone else?
- How does the Beloved feel?
- What influence do other characters have? Society? Taboos?
- In what ways are the lovers the same? Different (class, age, race)?

MIDDLE: The Lover helps the Beloved but stays out of her life as much as
possible. He develops himself as a human being.

- Why does the Lover stay out of her life?

- Does the Beloved want him in her life? Is she heartbroken? Does she think he's shy?
- How does he develop himself? Why? To be better for her?
- Does she date other men?
- Do other characters reinforce their separation?
- How does he help her?

END: The Beloved pursues the Lover and they face their obstacles together.

- Why does the Beloved pursue the Lover now? What happens?
- Is she afraid of rejection? Is he?
- Is he happy? Does he return her advances?
- How many obstacles do they face?
- Are they successful?
- What do other characters think or do?

EXAMPLES

The Crying Game, NEIL JORDAN

CRIMES OF LOVE AS SUBPLOT—A British soldier is kidnapped by IRA terrorists. He befriends one of his captors, who is drawn into the soldier's world. Taboos abound.

Oedipus Rex, SOPHOCLES

CRIMES OF LOVE AS PLOT—Oedipus kills his father and sleeps with his mother. When Oedipus learns what he has done, he chooses exile, leaving Creon to be king.

Titanic, JAMES CAMERON

SACRIFICE AS INCIDENT—In a romantic tale, a rich girl and poor boy meet on the ill-fated voyage of the "unsinkable" ship. He sacrifices himself in the end for her.

Better Off Dead, SAVAGE STEVE HOLLAND

SACRIFICE AS SUBPLOT—A teenager has to deal with his girlfriend dumping him at the same time as several family crises break out. An exchange student next door helps him try to win his girlfriend's heart back even though she is in love with him. She sacrifices her feelings for his happiness.

"This is his first punishment, that by the verdict of his own heart no guilty man is acquitted."

–JUVENAL

Slaying of Loved One

To slay means to kill violently with intention.

This situation requires a Slayer, a Victim, and a Reason.

There are two types of slayings: the Unrecognized Victim and the Recognized Victim. The decision to slay or not slay a kinsman in cold blood is what this situation is all about; therefore, the kinsman will always be recognized before the actual slaying takes place.

SLAYER AND UNRECOGNIZED VICTIM

Even though this situation is about the Slaying of a Loved One, the Victim can be unrecognized as a loved one to the Slayer. It is not unusual, especially in ancient times, to not know a person's parentage or to not recognize a distant relative. Today with adoption, divorce, and multiple marriages it is also not uncommon to be ignorant of one's extended family tree.

In this type of situation, the Slayer is usually at the point of slaying a child, parent, sibling, or other relative and learns they are related before committing the act. (You can have the Slayer commit the act before finding out he is related to his Victim if your story calls for it.)

Once this is revealed to him, he won't follow through with the Slaying, but guilt still overwhelms him at what might have been. He plays over in his mind how the Victim was supposed to die and what he was about to do. He is horrified at the thought of it.

He knows he will have to face up to whoever wanted him to slay the Victim, but he doesn't care much for himself at the moment. He may even be angry at the one who ordered the Slaying, wondering if he knew the Slayer was related to the Victim—especially if you have him follow through with the Slaying before he finds out they are related.

SLAYER AND RECOGNIZED VICTIM

Here the Slayer knows the Victim is related to him. They are usually a close relation, but he knows he has to make this sacrifice. He believes there is no way around it. He may:

- feel it is his duty to do it
- have taken a vow or oath to do it and is afraid of breaking that vow or oath, especially if it was to God (Think self-preservation.)
- feel it is a necessity—other lives may be at stake
- have been blackmailed into doing it
- do it for reasons of state, egoism, honor, or passion

His standing in the community will also be a factor as well as the time period. If a King in ancient times sacrificed his daughter to ensure a battle will be won, that may be considered noble. Today it would be considered a criminal act.

THE VICTIM

The Unrecognized Victim may not have a large roll in the story at all. The Slayer will want to protect the Victim if the Victim is still alive. Once the Slayer learns they are related, he and the story will most likely be focused on retaliating against the one who ordered the Slaying. That threat is not going to go away and must be dealt with. If the Slayer fails, another Slayer will be sent in his place to finish the job.

The Recognized Victim may play a larger role if he is not killed right away. The Slayer's internal process of deciding to have a relative slain will most likely be examined. There may also be several other characters who act as the Slayer's conscience, pleading with him not to do it.

THE REASON

The Reason is a valid, credible motivation for the Slaying to be completed. This is the most important piece, as the whole story depends on the reader believing there is no other choice or course of action for the Slayer to take.

The reason may only be valid and credible to the one ordering the Slaying. Perhaps a paranoid king suspects the Victim of plotting against him. He should have some evidence to support this even if others don't accept that evidence.

Whether Slaying of Loved One is used as plot, subplot, or incident, the elements of the beginning, middle, and end are the same:

BEGINNING: The Slayer learns that he must slay someone and he agrees to do his duty, or the Slayer attempts to slay someone out of hatred.

- Does the Slayer know he is related to the Victim yet?
- Does he know anything about her?
- Is the Victim helpless?
- Does the Victim find out about it now or later on?
- How much of the planning is left for him to decide? The more he has to plan, the guiltier he will feel later on.
- Are there any other family members who find out about this?
- Does the Slayer think this is a necessary sacrifice?
- Does he agree with it?
- Why can't the Slayer get someone else to do the dirty work? Is it his duty? His oath? Does he want to do it?
- Does the Slayer interact with the Victim in the days before the act?

MIDDLE: In Unrecognized Slaying, the Slayer finds the Victim and is about to slay her when he realizes the Victim is a relative and he stops. In Recognized Slaying, the Slayer prepares for the Slaying. Others may try to get in his way.

- Unrecognized: How does the Slayer find out about his relationship to the Victim? Does another character tell him? (This will happen before the Slaying takes place.)
- Unrecognized: Does the Slayer believe the news when he first finds out? Does he still move forward to commit the Slaying for a moment or two while he decides if he believes the news?
- Unrecognized: What does the Victim do to save herself? Or is she willing to be sacrificed for the seemingly greater good?
- Unrecognized: What is at stake for the Slayer if he doesn't follow through?
- Recognized: How does the Slayer feel about preparing for the Slaying? Does he try to come up with a merciful way to sacrifice the Victim?
- Recognized: Do other characters get in his way? Do they try to make him feel guilty?
- Recognized: What is at stake if he doesn't carry out his duty?
- Recognized: Will he have any contact with the Victim beforehand? Will he grant a last wish?

END: The Unrecognized Slayer saves the Victim and faces the consequences of his actions. He may be on the run himself now. The Recognized Slayer does his duty and faces his own conscience. He may be driven to end his own life.

- Unrecognized: Will this Slaying can end on a happy note? (The Recognized doesn't, unless someone comes along to rescue the Victim.)
- Unrecognized: Will the Victim help the Slayer get away?
- Unrecognized: Will the Victim have to give up her life as she knows it and go on the run? Does everyone still want her sacrificed?
- Recognized: Will the rest of the family reject the Slayer for the Slaying? Will they be afraid of him?
- Recognized: Will the Slayer drive himself crazy with guilt? Or will he suppress his feelings?
- Recognized: If the Slayer sacrificed his loved one for a cause or specific favor, how will he react if the cause is unsuccessful or the favor is not granted?

> "He who believes is strong; he who doubts is weak.
> Strong convictions precede great actions."
>
> —LOUISA MAY ALCOTT

Conviction

Conviction is the strong persuasion or belief in something.

In this situation the Slayer becomes the Challenger. He challenges the status quo, questions his vows and oaths, and won't abide rules or laws that harm.

He won't blindly follow what he is told to do. He questions the validity of it all, especially when asked to slay another. He is usually aware of his relationship to the intended Victim and that familial bond is what breaks the spell of obedience cast upon him. This situation does not require that they be related, however. The Victim may resemble a family member or friend.

The Victim in this situation can also be a large group of people. Perhaps an entire workforce is being taken advantage of and the Challenger is one of them or is the one called on to do the dirty work of taking advantage of them.

To him it seems as if his whole world has come crashing down. Everything he has believed to be true is now questioned. He has believed so many things—has his whole life been a lie?

He may become idealistic, thinking he can change the world or open everyone's eyes to the fallacy of the governing laws, but this usually gets him killed, fired, or ostracized in the end, as most people fear change. But he stands up for what he believes in until the end.

Whether Conviction is used as plot, subplot, or incident, the elements of the beginning, middle, and end are the same:

BEGINNING: The Challenger is asked to harm a relative or close friend. He is torn between following the rules he always had and his love for his family.

- What type of relationship does he have to the Victim?
- Is the Victim a large group of people?
- Is he already a little fed up with the status quo? Has something else happened prior to this situation?
- How many people has he harmed, however lightly, before this?
- Are other characters pressuring him to proceed?
- How do the Victim and Challenger meet?
- What is he supposed to do to the Victim?

MIDDLE: The Challenger may attempt to harm the Victim but cannot go through with it. He saves the Victim instead and places himself in jeopardy.

- What is at stake for the Challenger? Will he lose everything?
- What does the Victim think of the Challenger? Is he angry even though the Challenger saved him?
- Will the Victim help the Challenger now?
- Will the Victim want revenge against the Challenger? Or his boss?
- Are any other characters involved? Perhaps other Slayers who come after the Challenger? Or those who don't want change?

END: The Challenger stands up for what he believes in but may wind up sacrificing himself.

- How does the Challenger make a stand? (He doesn't just save the Victim and disappear. He wants to be heard.)
- Is the Victim helping him?
- Will the Challenger get out of this situation unharmed?
- Will his boss be brought to justice?
- What will others stand to gain if he succeeds? (Think about *Norma Rae* and unionization.)
- Are we left with the sense that his stand will have a long-lasting effect on future generations?

EXAMPLES

Sophie's Choice, WILLIAM STYRON

SLAYING OF LOVED ONE AS SUBPLOT—Sophie is the survivor of Nazi concentration camps and has to deal with the choice she was forced to make—to sacrifice one of her children to the Nazis.

Iphigenia at Aulis, EURIPIDES

SLAYING OF LOVED ONE AS PLOT—The Greek army is about to set sail to a great battle, but the winds refuse to blow. King Agamemnon has a message from the gods to sacrifice his daughter, Iphigenia, to make the winds blow again.

Norma Rae, MARTIN RITT

CONVICTION AS PLOT—A young single mother and textile worker agrees to help unionize her mill despite the problems and dangers involved.

The Transporter, LOUIS LETERRIER

CONVICTION AS PLOT—Frank Martin hires himself out as a mercenary who transports goods, no questions asked. Frank notices his current "package" is moving, so he looks inside the bag and finds a beautiful, gagged woman. When his employer tests his convictions, he decides to help the woman.

> "You find true joy and happiness in life when you give and give and go on giving and never count the cost."
>
> —EILEEN CADDY

Self-Sacrifice

Self-Sacrifice is a noble, generous, and unselfish act.

This situation requires a Hero, an Object, and a Thing Sacrificed. There are three types of Sacrifice: One is selfish in motive—Sacrifice for Passions—while the other two are selfless—Sacrifice for Ideal and Sacrifice for Kindred.

THING SACRIFICED

The Thing Sacrificed can be either selfish or selfless in nature.

Self-Sacrifice can be a wonderful thing when done with pure intentions. But there are times when the motive of a character that shows Self-Sacrifice may be to make another character feel guilty or obligated to her. If she is a self-proclaimed caretaker or martyr who finds her worth only in giving to receive, she is using Self-Sacrifice as a device to manipulate others. Very often those close to her won't want to accept gifts and help from her because they know there are strings attached. Think of Ray Romano's mother in *Everybody Loves Raymond* as an example of this. She sacrifices for the family to fulfill her passion to be needed.

This Selfish Sacrifice for Passion generally falls into the sacrificing for one's own interest or to manipulate others.

Passion can cause one to act impulsively or without logic:

- sacrificing sacred vows for a passion
- sacrificing honor due to temptation
- sacrificing health for a passion
- sacrificing of one's fortune for a passion

True Self-Sacrifice involves a hero with pure intentions, someone who for political or religious reasons, honor, or piety decides to make a sacrifice. This could be sacrifice of:

- ties
- interests
- ambition
- goals
- love
- happiness
- modesty
- life itself

Sacrificing for ideals consists of:

- sacrificing to keep one's word
- sacrificing for one's people
- sacrificing for one's faith

Sacrificing for kindred consists of:

- sacrificing for one's friends
- sacrificing for one's parents or siblings
- sacrificing for the happiness of a child

THE HERO

The Hero in the Idealistic and Kindred types is pure in intentions when he makes the decision to sacrifice something. He may be a rogue at every other moment, but when he stands his ground here, he is true to his word. He will fight until his last breath. Other characters may hate him, but they can't help admire him when he makes the ultimate sacrifice, perhaps a sacrifice they didn't have the courage to make.

The Hero in the Passionate type of sacrifice is more on the selfish side. He either wants to manipulate others into doing something for him or he lets his desires get the better of him and he sacrifices things he really doesn't have the right to sacrifice. Perhaps he is a married man who sacrifices his life savings on a gambling spree. Or a priest who sacrifices his vow to the church because he wants to be with a woman he just met.

OBJECT

The Object is the object sacrificed for. It is the Ideal, Kindred, or Passion desired. It can be tangible or intangible; either way, it is important to the Hero.

Whether Self-Sacrifice is used as plot, subplot, or incident, the elements of the beginning, middle, and end are the same:

BEGINNING: The Hero is placed in a position to sacrifice something for the Object. He's not sure what to do.

- What type of Object is it?
- How deeply connected to the thing sacrificed is the Hero?
- Will any other characters offer to help him?
- Will the Hero try to find a way out of making the sacrifice at first?
- What does the Hero want to gain by making the sacrifice? Will he change a nation (Idealistic)? Save someone's life (Kindred)? Fulfill a desire (Passion)?
- What makes the Hero capable of making a sacrifice?
- Does the Hero have any special abilities?

MIDDLE: The Hero decides to make the sacrifice and takes a chance.

- Will the Hero face any obstacles to making the sacrifice? Will another character try to stop him?
- Will all his obstacles be internal? Will he doubt himself?
- If the Hero is Passionate, will he consider the consequences of his actions?
- How will other characters react?
- Will the Hero confide in someone about what he is going to do?
- Will the Hero make any last-ditch efforts to avoid the sacrifice?

END: The Hero faces the consequences of his actions.

- Did the Hero survive the ordeal?
- Did he create the outcome he desired, even if he sacrificed himself?
- If the Hero is Passionate, will he be able to pick up the pieces and get his life back together? Does he even want to?
- Will another character be inspired and pick up where the Hero left off?
- What is learned from this sacrifice?

> "Hunger, love, pain, fear are some of those inner forces which rule the individual's instinct for self-preservation."
>
> —ALBERT EINSTEIN

Self-Preservation

Self-Preservation means to protect from injury or harm and to keep safe.

In this situation the Hero becomes the Preserver. She values herself and her life and won't give it up without a fight. She realizes that true love starts with loving the self. Everyone else around her may feign being in love, but sooner or later their insecurities will come out. True love is secure.

Self-love is often too neglected, even in spiritual disciplines. We are taught to be unconditionally loving toward others, but this is impossible until we love ourselves completely, otherwise the love generated can only be conditional. Self-love is a great gift to society because it heals. Self-love does not mean one is selfish; it means taking the time to heal and work on yourself so you can be able to be there for others. Love is giving something of yourself; it is all about being open. This cannot be accomplished until one has gone inside and developed a resource to give.

How can a woman who has been abused since childhood raise children without abusing them? Can she find or build enough resources within herself to unconditionally love her future children? If she heals her pain and takes care of herself, she can be one of the best mothers in the world. There is always hope, but she needs this opportunity to help herself first.

This Hero won't try to help others prematurely. Many times people do not want help to begin with. She will sit back and wait until the time is right. She will be available when needed but doesn't push to help because that would only be a selfish need to make herself useful or to be the savior of the other person. She is a leader and a teacher who guides others when ready.

The Conflict comes from her struggle to keep distractions and possible guilty feelings about focusing on herself away long enough to find out who she is:

• What does she want out of life?

• What are her goals and desires?

• What is her pain?

If the situation arises for her to sacrifice herself for another she won't do it. Usually this is not a life-or-death situation. Others may want her to sacrifice her time or resources. She is learning how to say "No" instead of putting her needs aside.

This situation is similar to the Healing Journey, but here she is more self-centered and self-focused. She will not be seeking a cure or object of some sort; instead she is seeking her true self and protecting that self. Many mothers can understand this dilemma, as they are asked to put everything about who they are as a person aside to raise their children. They are asked to live for their kids.

Whether Self-Preservation is used as plot, subplot, or incident, the elements of the beginning, middle, and end are the same:

BEGINNING: The Hero realizes she needs to make a change in her life. She begins to go inward and heal herself.

- What brought about this realization? Did she get a disease or have an accident?
- How does she begin the Healing Journey? Does she meet someone else who has done it? Does she go to a seminar?
- Does she feel guilty? Does she have responsibilities?
- Can others survive without her? Will they let her out of her pre-scribed role?
- Does she need to "freak out" in front of others to let them know she is serious about this?

MIDDLE: The Hero is faced with many obstacles to test her inner resolve. She is continuously tempted to go back to her old way of relating to the world.

- Why is she tempted? What is her weakness (for example, do her kids barge in on her writing time)?
- Does it seem easier at times for her to just go back to the way things were?
- What makes her keep going? Does she have an Object that reminds her to change, like an alcoholic carrying around the top to the last beer he drank?
- What will she have to give up to keep going? (Some alcoholics have to give up all their old friends.)
- How many obstacles will she face?

END: She is a changed person and is now available to help others.

- Are others happy now that she has made a change? Do they accept her new way of living? Or do they want the Hero to go back to the way she was before?
- Does she care what others think anymore? Can they still make her feel guilty?
- Is she happy about the changes she made?
- What will she do now with her new resources? Help others do the same thing?
- How will you show her metamorphosis?
- Will others even know she made a change or found herself? (Think *The Bridges of Madison County*.)

EXAMPLES

Pirates of the Caribbean:
The Curse of the Black Pearl, GORE VERBINSKI

SACRIFICE FOR PASSION AS PLOT—Pirate Jack Sparrow sets out to save a governor's daughter from fellow pirates, with the hopes that it will give him the opportunity to regain the ship that was stolen from him. He sacrifices his freedom and fortune to come to the aid of his comrades. His partner sacrifices everything he has for the damsel in distress.

The Bridges of Madison County,
ROBERT JAMES WALLER

SACRIFICE FOR KINDRED AND SELF-PRESERVATION AS PLOT—Photographer Robert Kincaid wanders into the life of housewife Francesca Johnson for four days in the 1960s. She falls in love with him, remembering the woman she used to be and learning about herself (Self-Preservation) but sacrifices her feelings for the sake of kindred.

Safe, TODD HAYNES

SELF-PRESERVATION AS PLOT—A housewife becomes sick, claiming she's become sensitive to the common toxins in today's world: exhaust, fumes, aerosol spray. Her physician examines her and can find nothing wrong. She decides to leave everything to go to a New Age retreat center. She tries to heal herself.

Something to Talk About, LASSE HALLSTROM

SELF-PRESERVATION AS PLOT—Grace discovers that her husband Eddie has been cheating on her with another woman. After confronting him in the middle of the night on the street, she decides to leave him and move in with her sister on their parents' farm. She questions the authority of everyone, especially her father, as she breaks away from her old life and tries to start a new one.

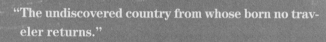

> "The undiscovered country from whose born no traveler returns."
>
> –WILLIAM SHAKESPEARE

Discovery of Dishonor of Loved One

Discovery is a revelation, disclosure, or exposure of something previously unknown by the discoverer.

This situation requires a Discoverer and a Guilty One. It is similar to Slaying of Loved One in the psychological struggle it offers, but the high ideal of the hero is replaced with the lash of shame.

In this situation, the hero discovers the shame of a loved one, usually an immediate family member—father, mother, child, spouse—but the shame can also come from a romantic partner or friend.

The shame may be something the Guilty One is currently doing, like a child doing drugs or a mother working as a stripper. Or it can be something from the past that was kept hidden only to be revealed to the Discoverer at the worst possible time, like a politician running for office who finds out his uncle is an embezzler so he has to bow out of a political race.

THE DISCOVERER

The Discoverer is someone who has something to lose from the discovery, whether it's his own respect for a parent or the social standing and respect he has worked so hard for. He can't believe what he has discovered at first and may think his whole life is crashing before his eyes.

He may question others in the family to confirm his suspicions or he may go to the Guilty One right away and confront her. His concern will either be for the welfare of the Guilty One or for himself.

This will show us his true character—is he concerned for others? Will he stand behind the Guilty One or try to hide what was done?

THE GUILTY ONE

The Guilty One may be noble or selfish. Her act is shameful, but if she did it to help someone else, she is a sympathetic character. She may have had to do it to put food on the table for her children.

If she did it without regard for anyone else and only because it was something she wanted to do, she is being selfish. Did she consider the consequences at all? Was she oblivious?

Whether Discovery of Dishonor of Loved One is used as plot, subplot, or incident, the elements of the beginning, middle, and end are the same:

BEGINNING: The Discoverer gets a hint about the Guilty One's act. He decides to look into it further.

- Will he believe what he finds out right away? Or will he need some convincing?
- To what degree will this shame hurt him? Emotionally? Socially?
- How close is he to the Guilty One?
- Is the Guilty One remorseful or does she stand behind what she's done?
- Does the Guilty One have any shame about it? Or is all about how the Discoverer feels? (We can't control how other people react to events.)
- Will the Discoverer talk to others about it?
- Did the Guilty One do it for the Discoverer? (Think of a mother doing things in order to feed her child. This way the Discoverer would have some guilt, too.)

MIDDLE: The Discoverer confronts the Guilty One.

- Will the Guilty One admit to it right away?
- Does the Discoverer have trouble confronting the Guilty One?
- How does the Guilty One react? Does she make things worse?
- Will any other character be involved at this point?
- What does the Discoverer want to do? Send the Guilty One away? Pay her off? Hide what was done? Distance himself from her?
- Will the Guilty One agree to handle the situation in the way the Discoverer wants? Will she be difficult?

END: The Discoverer deals with the consequences of the Guilty One's actions whether he wants to or not. The Guilty One either cooperates or doesn't.

- Did the Discoverer manage to effectively deal with the situation? Or did things get worse?
- Has the Guilty One been rejected by the rest of the family for what she did? Do they find out?
- Will the Guilty One and Discoverer ever have a relationship again?
- Will the Discoverer forgive the Guilty One?
- Has the Discoverer learned anything from this experience? What about the Guilty One?

> "Morality regulates the acts of man as a private individual; honor, his acts as a public man."
>
> —ESTEBAN ECHEVERRIA

Discovery of Honor of Loved One

Honor is integrity, esteem, merit, respect, and admiration.

In this situation the Guilty One becomes the Honored One. The Discoverer always thought the Honored One was a loser, a joke, or a misfit of sorts, but now he knows he was wrong. He is the one who feels guilty now because of his assumptions.

The Honored One usually did good things without trying to get credit for them. She may have been a volunteer, a philanthropist, a big sister for a troubled kid, an animal rescuer, a master athlete, or student who won awards without telling the rest of the family.

Sometimes these things are not discovered until after the Honored One dies—like the cranky old lady who turns out to be the person who sent the Discoverer money when he desperately needed it.

This type of Discovery seems to change the Discoverer forever. His whole view of the world and of people has changed. His assumptions were wrong after all—how many other assumptions of his are wrong? He may strive to be a better person from now on and give people a chance.

The Conflict comes from his dealings with others. He may have been very cynical and brash with others. Now he will try to change. Will others let him?

Whether Discovery of Honor of Loved One is used as plot, subplot, or incident, the elements of the beginning, middle, and end are the same:

BEGINNING: The Discoverer learns he was wrong about someone and feels guilty about it, even though he may suppress his guilt.

- How does he learn he was wrong? What happens?
- Is the Honored One still alive? If so, is she still living near the Discoverer?
- Are they related? How close are/were they?
- Will the Discoverer visit the Honored One?
- Will the Honored One take that visit? Or is she cynical about him?
- What is at stake here? The relationship? Why does the Discoverer want this relationship now that he has this new information?
- Why did the Honored One keep it a secret? Or did she leave it out in the open?

MIDDLE: The Discoverer tries to make it up to the Honored One.

- How does he try to make it up to her?
- Will the Honored One respond yet? If she is dead, will he make it up to her family or children, for example?
- How hard does the Honored One make it on the Discoverer?
- Is the Honored One mad that the Discoverer found out about her?
- What obstacles keep him from making up with her?

END: The Discoverer tries to be more like the Honored One.

- Why does the Discoverer want to be more like the Honored One? Was he inspired? Did she make him take a good, hard look at himself?
- Will he ever be as good as the Honored One?
- Will he find his own way of being honorable? What does he excel at?
- Will the Honored One help him? Forgive him? How has their relationship changed?
- How has the Discoverer changed? Is he much better off?
- Is he happy?

EXAMPLES

The Prince of Tides, PAT CONROY

DISCOVERY OF DISHONOR OF LOVED ONE AS PLOT—Tom is unhappy with his life. When his sister Savannah attempts suicide, her psychologist, Dr. Susan Lowenstein, consults him. Patiently and cautiously she uncovers the terrible secret hidden in Tom and Savannah's childhood.

Striptease, ANDREW BERGMAN

DISCOVERY OF DISHONOR OF LOVED ONE AS SUBPLOT—After losing her job, Erin loses custody of her child to her deadbeat ex-husband. To make the money she needs to appeal the verdict, she takes a job at a strip bar and tries to keep this knowledge from her child.

As Good As It Gets, JAMES L. BROOKS

DISCOVERY OF HONOR OF LOVED ONE AS INCIDENT—A single mother/waitress, a misanthropic author, and a gay artist form an unlikely friendship. The author gives the mother the money she needs and helps the gay artist he originally hated.

Courage Under Fire, EDWARD ZWICK

DISCOVERY OF HONOR OF LOVED ONE AS PLOT—The pilot of a rescue copter, Captain Karen Emma Walden, dies shortly before her crew is rescued from a crash in Desert Storm. Lieutenant Colonel Nathaniel Serling is assigned to investigate and award her the Medal of Honor for her bravery in holding her crew together against the Iraqis. Conflicting accounts from some of her crew cause him to question whether she deserves it or not. He doesn't believe she is honorable until the real facts later present themselves.

> "Pleasure of love lasts but a moment, Pain of love
> lasts a lifetime."
>
> —JEAN-PIERRE CLARIS DE FLORIAN

Obstacles to Love

*Obstacles to Love are those that stand in the way of or thwart
progress toward loving.*

Two Lovers and an Obstacle are required. In this situation two Lovers
are either being kept apart or in the process of being kept apart,
where they still see each other intermittently.

They both passionately want to be with each other and can't
imagine life any other way. Each one believes in the other's love so
completely that they will attempt to surmount any obstacle thrown
in their path. There is no doubt in either one's mind about the love
they share.

The love between them is true and it cannot be easily cast aside.
They know this type of love comes along only once in a lifetime,
and they will do or give up whatever it takes to keep this love alive.

If the Lovers have done a lot of soul searching, then their union
will be one of long-lasting happiness. If not, they may self-destruct
as their problems, hang-ups, and insecurities come out. Very often
stories of soul mates start out with wondrous rapture between the
couple only to see them quickly crash. The people in these unions
have a lot of unfinished baggage to deal with before they can commit to another at such a deep level, and the relationship must or
should end—at least for the time being. (Think of *A Streetcar Named
Desire*—Stanley has a lot of growing up to do.)

In most great love stories, the Lovers don't have much baggage
left to keep them apart. It is only outside circumstance that con-
spires against them.

THE LOVERS

The Lovers are both very passionate people, even if one seems shy at first. They have the capacity to open their hearts fully to another and be exposed and vulnerable. They can be intense and possibly jealous at times but deep down they care about each other's well being above their own.

Everyone has this capacity to find true love; it's just that most of us won't let our guard down to give it entrance. The Lovers have learned how to do just that, and they find the rewards are great and well worth the risk.

OBSTACLES

Unfortunately, seemingly insurmountable Obstacles are in the way of the Lovers' union:

Obstacles Created by others include:

- their race
- their class
- their age differences
- relatives feel they are too young
- relatives oppose due to family feud, or one or more relatives hate the Beloved because of this
- relatives have promised the woman to another
- the man is called away to war
- relatives feel man doesn't make enough money
- relatives feel the woman isn't good enough, especially if he has high social standing
- the death of a family member forces woman to care for other relatives
- gossip
- jealousy (Others may be jealous of their love and wish to destroy it; the Lover's happiness only reminds the others of how unhappy they are, and misery loves company.)

Obstacles created by the couple inlcude:

- poor health
- religious vows
- distance between them
- previous marriages
- titles that require certain types of marriages
- fear of the love they share and its power
- incompatible temperament between the Lovers

- low self-esteem; feeling unworthy of the Lover
- misunderstandings
- differing goals pulling them in different directions
- jealousy
- hate: Did the Beloved do something to cause this hatred:
  - Did he kill the Lover's father or other family member?
  - Is she related to someone who hurt the Lover's family member?
  - Did he treat her family poorly before they met?
  - Did he refuse the love of one of her relatives before meeting her?
  - Do her brothers hate him for something he did or didn't do in the past?

Whether Obstacles to Love is used as plot, subplot, or incident, the elements of the beginning, middle, and end are the same:

BEGINNING: A Lover finds his Beloved.

- Will they fall in love right away?
- Will anyone try to stop them yet?
- What Obstacle to Love are you setting up here?
- Is one Lover more swayed by relatives or the potential Obstacle to Love than the other? Can you foreshadow this?
- Do either of the Lovers have any baggage that will get in the way?
- Are there any other lovers on the sidelines, waiting to catch the eye of one of the Lovers?
- Does anyone stand to gain if the Lovers are kept apart? Or brought together?
- How will the Lovers first meet? (Make it memorable.)

MIDDLE: The Lovers announce their plans and Obstacles to Love are thrown their way.

- Are the Lovers afraid to make their love known? Why?
- Who will oppose their plans?
- What type of Obstacles to Love will you give them? Will the time period come into play here?
- What will the Lovers have to give up to keep the relationship going in light of the Obstacles to Love?
- Are both Lovers equally strong to fight the Obstacles? Or will one have to be strong for both of them?

END: The Lovers either conquer the Obstacles to Love or face defeat together.

- If the Lovers don't conquer the Obstacles to Love, will they wind up like Romeo and Juliet, sacrificing their lives for love?

- How will they overcome the Obstacles to Love? Will they have to give up something they hold dear? Will they have to give up their identity and move to a foreign land?

- Will anyone try to help them?

- Will a loved one betray them?

- Will the Lover sacrifice himself to save his Beloved?

- Do we leave the Lovers knowing they will be fine? Or is there a question mark in the end?

> "Love is a force that connects us to every strand of the universe, an unconditional state that characterizes human nature, a form of knowledge that is always there for us if only we can open ourselves to it."
>
> —EMILY HILBURN SELL

Unconditional Love

Unconditional Love means to love absolutely, completely, and without conditions of any type.

In this situation the Lover is so overwhelmed by the offer of love that he may not fully accept it. It may take him years to process the effects of being in the presence of such a wonderful gift of love and light. It's as if he has seen an angel in the flesh and his world has been totally turned upside down.

Unconditional Love has the power to change the world. Unfortunately, few ever experience it. To be accepted and validated, as if one were the most important being on the planet, breaks down all defenses. It is to be looked at as if one truly were made in the image of God. If you have ever visited a spiritual guru, you will understand this. There is a woman named Ammachi who travels around the world hugging people for free. Many leave her arms in tears completely overwhelmed by her presence. This situation is about dealing with such a transcendental experience and its effects.

This experience can also come from a true martial arts master, many of whom are very spiritual people. The discipline of martial arts leaves them with the power and discernment to hold their center at all times.

It can also come from the love of a parent who sacrifices all to help, comfort, or accept a child no matter what happens in life.

The Conflict comes because this type of love can also be way too much for one to handle if one has a lot of trauma or issues to deal with. In the face of so much love and acceptance, one's true self tries to emerge and all the pain of the past comes up to be healed so this can happen. Have you ever been so angry at someone only to have them forgive you and stop the cycle of anger cold? It can be off-putting.

The experience also can evoke such ecstasy that the character may seek it out like a drug, becoming dependent upon the "guru" or person who makes him feel this way, when he should be learning how to embody the love himself. He may also get involved with a cult, as he wants to be around people who have shared such an experience. He doesn't know how to be discerning.

Whether Unconditional Love is used as plot, subplot, or incident, the elements of the beginning, middle, and end are the same:

BEGINNING: The Lover experiences Unconditional Love and is overwhelmed by it.

- How does this take place?

- Does the Lover run from it? Why? Where to?

- Does the experience play over and over again in his mind?

- Does he become obsessed with the experience? Does he tell everyone he meets about it?

- Has his personality changed at all yet? Is this just temporary, as his daily responsibilities will pull him back into reality?

MIDDLE: The Lover longs to feel that love again, but his problems and pain cause Obstacles for him.

- Does he try to ignore his pain? Or push it away? (He may not realize that healing his issues is what will help reach the Unconditional Love experience within himself.)

- Does he long for a community of people who understand what he went through? Will he get involved in a cult as a result?

- What do other characters think of his experience? Will his family even listen or will it frighten them?

END: The Lover returns to his old ways or is reborn.

- Will the Lover return to his old ways? Why?
- If not, how will you show his rebirth?
- Has he learned discernment?
- Is he strong enough to go back to his old life and be in the world, just not of it? (This means to keep himself centered at all times no matter what is going on around him. Think of martial arts masters.)
- What will he do with his life now? (This type of situation sparks a complete 180-degree turn in the Lover's way of thinking and relating to the world.)

EXAMPLES

The Age of Innocence, EDITH WHARTON

OBSTACLES TO LOVE AS PLOT—Society scion Newland Archer is engaged to May Welland, but his well-ordered life is upset when he meets May's unconventional cousin and falls deeply in love with her. Societal mores prevent them from being together.

Romeo and Juliet, WILLIAM SHAKESPEARE

OBSTACLES TO LOVE AS PLOT—The Montagues and Capulets are two families of Renaissance Italy that have hated each other for years, but the son of one family and the daughter of the other fall desperately in love and secretly marry.

Holy Smoke!, JANE CAMPION

UNCONDITIONAL LOVE AS SUBPLOT—While on a journey of discovery in exotic India, beautiful Ruth Barron falls under the influence of a charismatic religious guru. Her parents hire P. J. Waters, a macho cult deprogrammer, to confront Ruth in a remote desert hideaway.

Dying Young, JOEL SCHUMACHER

UNCONDITIONAL LOVE AS SUBPLOT—Hilary O'Neil is looking for a new start and a new job. She begins to work as a private nurse for a young man suffering from blood cancer. The two slowly fall in love, all the while knowing their love cannot last because he is going to die. Hilary can't deny the love they feel for each other so she takes a chance. Knowing he will leave her, she has to love him unconditionally.

Situations | 45 & 46

CONFLICT WITH A GOD AND SUPERNATURAL OCCURRENCE

> "Great spirits have always encountered violent opposition from mediocre minds. The latter cannot understand it when a man does not thoughtlessly submit to hereditary prejudices but honestly and courageously uses his intelligence."
>
> —ALBERT EINSTEIN

Conflict With a God

Conflict is a state of disharmony between incompatible or antithetical persons, ideas, or interests.

This situation requires a Mortal and an Immortal. By its very nature this situation can set up a variety of religious and spiritual questions to use as the theme. How the other characters in this story react to the Mortal will show their belief systems and may also show those of the writer. Things to consider:

- Which religions are represented?
- How are they represented?
- Who are the "good guys"?
- Is the Mortal likeable or an antihero of sorts?

The first question one should ask is, "Is this situation about religion, spirituality, or both?" Religion is a set of beliefs, values, and practices based on the teachings of a religious leader. Religion is usually inherited from one's family, but it can change as one matures. Spirituality is about a personal relationship with the divine. It is an inner exploration of the soul that gives way to a personal theology. Spiritually is developed; it is not a set of beliefs one is born into.

The main Conflict here is with the Mortal:

- struggling against a deity
- involved in strife with believers in a god

- in controversy with a deity—doing what a deity commands
- being punished for contempt of a deity
- being punished for pride before a god
- having rivalry with a god, like a doctor who wants to save a life, for example

Mythological stories and fables are ripe with this type of situation, but modern stories will often use this situation as an inner Conflict without externalizing the deity into a physical form.

THE MORTAL

The Mortal is someone who questions life. He doesn't blindly believe what he is told to believe. He may have the same religion as everyone else in his community, but his views about that religion may be heretic.

If the deity asks him to do something, he will usually question it to make sure he is doing the right thing. Depending on his beliefs he may have a fear of the "devil" and therefore not want to be misled or tricked into doing something wrong.

Other Mortals may not believe in the devil at all, at least not as an outside force who tries to trick others but as an inside force or shadow self within the person who has done wrong.

Either way, he has a spiritual or religious belief that he adheres to. His beliefs may be open for discussion or he may fervently fight any opposition to his beliefs. Just because one is spiritual or religious does not mean one is enlightened.

THE IMMORTAL

The Immortal can be a physical presence in the story or an inner voice or consciousness of the Mortal. She can be a god, angel, muse, or concept, such as love or beauty.

The Immortal can be Loving or Vengeful. She can demand obedience in the Mortal and threaten with a type of punishment that will last for all eternity. She can be forgiving and patient with the Mortal and try to give him the answers and help he seeks.

Either way the Immortal will, at least once, give the Mortal a sign of some sort that they should be working together. In some cases the Mortal could have made the sign up himself, which leaves him with a sense of doubt. The Mortal needs something to hang onto when things get rough.

Whether Conflict With a God is used as plot, subplot, or incident, the elements of the beginning, middle, and end are the same:

BEGINNING: A Mortal is in Conflict with a god.

- Will this be a spiritual or religious Conflict? Or both?
- Is the Mortal in Conflict with the god or with other characters who don't approve of his actions regarding his relationship with his god?
- Is the Mortal in Conflict because he doesn't want to carry out the Immortal's request?
- How will the rest of the characters react?
- Will a concrete belief system be part of the story?
- Will the Mortal have help or support from anyone?
- Will other gods get involved?
- How do the god and Mortal come to know each other at this level?

MIDDLE: The Mortal voices his Conflict and gets himself into trouble.

- Will he get into trouble with the other characters? Or with the god?
- What options does the Mortal have?
- What price will the Mortal pay if he doesn't overcome this conflict in favor of the god?
- What will the Mortal have to sacrifice? Are both options equally devastating for him?
- Will anyone defend him?
- How powerful is the god?
- Are there other gods around? Can he go to one of them?
- If this is an internal Conflict, how will you show it?
- Are other characters going through the same thing?

END: The Mortal resolves his Conflict and pays the price.

- Did he succeed in getting help?
- Will he stick to his beliefs even in the face of death?
- Will the god admire his conviction in the end and spare him?
- Will anyone come to his rescue?
- How do the other characters react after witnessing his punishment? Are they more fearful?
- If he is not punished, does this make other characters question their beliefs?
- If there is internal Conflict, how will you show it is or is not resolved in the end? (Think subtext.)
- What is the ultimate message you are trying to convey to your reader with this situation? Is there a moral to the story?

Supernatural Occurrence

*Supernatural means being outside the natural world, attributed
to a power that seems to violate natural forces.*

In this situation, the Mortal becomes the Gifted One. There are two
types: the Receiver and the Witness.

The Receiver is one who directly receives the gift. She works
in concert with the "god force" and has reached a different level
than most people. She can possibly see other realms of existence,
predict the future, feel the presence of ghosts and angels, know
what others are thinking or feeling, walk through walls (think *X-
Men*), do laying on of hands for healing, or touch objects and
"read" them.

Usually this is somewhat unexpected by the Gifted One. Something may have happened to tune her into this new way of viewing
the world, such as:

- a near-death experience
- a jolt to her electrical system
- a fall
- something inherited (maybe she had a relative in touch with the supernatural)
- having this gift since childhood but it was suppressed until now

Whatever it is, it has opened her up and changed her life forever.
Her old identity is gone and she must now learn how to cope with
her expanded view of the world. She may fight it, but this will only
cause her pain and sorrow. After all, she would be denying not only
a gift but a huge part of who she is. She would also be denying all
those people she could possibly be helping if she would just come
to terms with her newfound gift. Imagine what it would be like to all
of a sudden see ghosts. (Some would say we all have these abilities.
Just take a look at the many books on Remote Viewing, a psychic
viewing technique developed by the military.)

The Witness is created when the Gifted One witnesses someone
else with the "gift" and has to deal with it. Will she be able to accept
what she sees? How will her life change?

The Witness usually has an open mind to start with but still has trouble comprehending these events. Her mind has to expand to accept what is happening or it will shut down and try to be in denial as it searches for a logical explanation to hang onto. Imagine what it would be like to find out your friend could read every thought in your mind!

Whether Supernatural Occurrence is used as plot, subplot, or incident, the elements of the beginning, middle, and end are the same:

BEGINNING: The Gifted One receives or witnesses a supernatural event and can't readily accept it.

- Does she witness or receive? Why?
- What do other characters think about this?
- What is at stake for her? Her whole belief system?
- Does she run away?
- Is she in denial?
- What does she stand to gain from this experience?
- Can she find a support group? A metaphysical group or store to go to? A psychic to talk to?

MIDDLE: The Gifted One struggles.

- What obstacles are in her way? Emotional? Mental? Spiritual?
- Are others jealous of her?
- Do family members disown her?
- Does she think she's a freak? Or, if she witnessed it, does she think what she saw was wrong or bad?
- Will she come around a little bit only to be pulled back into denial again and again?

END: The Gifted One accepts or masters the gift. As a Witness, she learns to accept what she saw. As a Receiver, she learns to master her gift.

- What has she gained from this experience?
- How do other characters react? (Usually, once she accepts it, it is easier for them to accept it.)
- Does she help people with it now?
- Does she find a group she fits in with? (Think about the *X-Men* movies and the school the kids went to.)
- Is she happy?

EXAMPLES

Signs, M. NIGHT SHYAMALAN

CONFLICT WITH A GOD AS SUBPLOT—After the death of his wife in a freak accident, Reverend Graham Hess questions his faith and leaves the church. Months later, he discovers a gigantic crop circle in his yard. This starts happening all around the world and everyone awaits the coming of aliens.

The Messenger: The Story of Joan of Arc, LUC BESSON

CONFLICT WITH A GOD AS INCIDENT—A young girl receives a vision that compels her to rid France of its oppressors. Many turn on her and think she is doing the work of the devil. The Conflict With a God comes in moments of doubt as people question her and her voices.

City of Angels, BRAD SILBERLING

SUPERNATURAL OCCURRENCE AS PLOT—Seth, an angel, finds his job difficult as he falls in love with Maggie, a beautiful heart surgeon. She becomes interested in Seth, and soon his immortal state becomes an obstacle rather than a gift, as she can't even conceive of someone like him.

The Sixth Sense, M. NIGHT SHYAMALAN

SUPERNATURAL OCCURRENCE AS PLOT—A boy who communicates with spirits that don't know they're dead seeks the help of a disheartened child psychologist.

Situations 47 & 48

MISTAKEN JUDGMENT AND INTUITIVE JUDGMENT

"Knowing a great deal is not the same as being smart; intelligence is not information alone but also judgment, the manner in which information is collected and used."

—CARL SAGAN

Mistaken Judgment

To be Mistaken means to be wrong or incorrect in opinion, understanding, or perception.

This situation requires a Mistaken One, the Victim of the mistake, and a possible Instigator of the mistake.

This situation is all about mistaken understandings and perceptions, which can be:

- jealousy in the mind of the Mistaken One or instigated by third party
- false suspicion in the form of misunderstanding or lack of faith
- false suspicion allowed to fall on the innocent who may or may not be an enemy
- false suspicion thrown by guilty upon a second Victim
- error provoked by an enemy
- indifference
- allowing false suspicions upon oneself to save a friend

There are three types of Mistaken Judgments in this situation: the Instigated, the Incidental, and the Psychogenic.

In the Instigated type of Mistaken Judgment a third party, or traitor, instigates the whole error in judgment. The Instigator:

- may be full of hatred for the Mistaken One or the Victim
- may have some sort of self-interest
- may be jealous himself
- may just want the Mistaken One and Victim to break up or part ways

for some reason, or wants to set up an innocent person to take the fall
for another

In the Incidental type of Mistaken Judgment, the Mistaken One is
led, by mere chance, into erroneous judgment. He may:

- hear a rumor by mere chance; perhaps he wasn't supposed to be where
  he was or when he was at the time
- hear or see something out of context and make assumptions about it
- watch a movie about adultery and start comparing the plot to his own
  life situation
- talk to a friend or family member who is committing adultery and start
  to question recent events with his own wife

In the Psychogenic type of Mistaken Judgment, the Mistaken Judgment originates in the Mistaken One's mind. He becomes suspicious
or paranoid for no apparent reason. Nothing has given him any reason to feel this way; it is an inner conflict that drives him. He may:

- be so happy that he becomes afraid something will take his happiness
  away
- be afraid he may do something to ruin everything and winds up making
  an erroneous judgment about himself; he may seek to fulfill this judgment
  in order to prove himself right
- be afraid God will take everything away from him if he is too successful (think of George Costanza in *Seinfeld*)

THE MISTAKEN ONE

The Mistaken One can be a very nice, gullible person who just
doesn't know any better. He may trust others quickly and believe
what he is told. Gossip and rumors may be a fun pastime for him, and
he doesn't realize it's wrong.

Or he may be a ruthless, smart person who just doesn't care who
gets hurt by his accusations. He can be cold and calculating or open
and available, only to turn around and stab someone in the back.

THE VICTIM

The Victim can be an innocent bystander or a conniving back-
stabber, but either way he is not guilty of the "crime" he is accused of.

He may fight back or trust in the legal system to vindicate him.
If this is a love triangle, he may try to prove his loyalty. Hopefully, this
is the first time he is accused of something he didn't do and the relationship can withstand it. If it has been going on for a while now,
the Victim may be fed up with the accusations and just leave. This
may incite the Mistaken One into a jealous rage.

Whether Mistaken Judgment is used as plot, subplot, or incident, the beginning, middle, and end are the same:

BEGINNING: The Mistaken One comes to believe the Victim is the guilty one.

- What makes him believe this?
- How well does he know the Victim?
- Which one of the three types of Mistaken Judgment is this?
- What do other characters think of the Mistaken One? If he is wrong will they come after him? This gives him motivation to stick to his guns when he identifies the Guilty One.
- If this is about jealousy, is it completely unfounded or is there some truth to it (for example, is his wife attracted to another man but never acts on it)?
- When does he confront the Victim?

MIDDLE: The Victim lashes back at the Mistaken One and tries to get others on her side.

- Will she find anyone to help her?
- Will she cause the Mistaken One to doubt himself?
- Who will others side with?
- How public does this become? Is it kept private?
- Is the Victim a well-known or important person?
- Is there in instigator? Does the Victim know about him? Will he cause any more trouble? Give an ultimatum to the Victim?
- How does the Mistaken One react to the Victim's pleas or threats?
- If this is a case of the Victim drawing suspicions upon himself, why doesn't he come clean? What is his motivation to keep the lie going? Is anyone else accused along with him?

END: The Mistaken One learns that he is wrong and either recants his story or denies he is wrong.

- Did the Victim get off the hook?
- Will the Mistaken One change his mind? Why?
- How will the situation resolve itself? Are there any tragic endings?
- Will the Victim take back control of her life and situation?
- If he drew suspicions upon himself, does he reveal that now? How?
- Has the Mistaken One learned anything from this experience? If so, what?

"Trust your hunches. They're usually based on facts
filed away just below the conscious level."

–DR. JOYCE BROTHERS

Intuitive Judgment

*To be intuitive means to know without the use of rational process-
es. It is immediate insight.*

In this situation the Mistaken One becomes the Intuitive One who
knows the truth of the matter regardless of what others may try to
make him believe. He is like the master detective who looks at more
than just the obvious clues.

He always "knows" when and where to look deeper, where to
place his focus. He doesn't just examine everything deeply; he picks
one clue out of hundreds to examine and turns up a great lead that
breaks the case wide open. He trusts himself above all else and won't
be swayed from his mission. Everyone may be annoyed with him,
but he doesn't care. Saving face is not important to him; truth is.

He can also be a parent who watches after his teenager, making
sure she is safe. He can be a teacher who gets involved with his kids
and knows when one of them needs some extra help. He may wind
up with too much trouble to handle, though.

Whether Intuitive Judgment is used as plot, subplot, or incident, the
beginning, middle, and end are the same:

BEGINNING: The Intuitive One finds out about an incident and is called to
investigate it.

- What kind of incident is he called to investigate? Does he have cre-
dentials to be investigating?

- Does he like being called upon?

- Does it come at a bad time for him, like a detective on vacation who
doesn't want to be bothered? Or a mother who is in the middle of something and has to stop to investigate what her child is doing at school?

- What does he stand to gain or lose by investigating?

- Do other characters admire him or resent him?

- How did he learn about his intuitive gift?

MIDDLE: He examines clues or goes on a hunt for the truth.

- Why does he get involved? Is it personal?

- How hard is it to find the clues he needs? Are some clues red herrings?

- Does he tell anyone about his findings yet? Can he trust anyone?

- How many obstacles will he face? What kinds?

- Do other characters think he is stupid?

- What makes him so great at this?

END: He finds the truth and deals with the consequences of it. If he is helping someone else, he has to get them to face the truth.

- Is he trying to figure out a murder or something like that?

- Is he trying to help someone and eventually presents them with the truth to help them move on (for example, investigating a cheating spouse, finding out how a loved one died, recovering a lost treasure)?

- How does he feel at the end of it all? Is he eager for the next investigation? Or does he want out?

- What did he gain from this experience?

EXAMPLES

Once Upon a Crime, EUGENE LEVY

MISTAKEN JUDGMENT AS PLOT—Phoebe and fellow American Julian meet in Rome, find a lost dog, and agree to return it to Monte Carlo to split the reward. Discovering the dog's owner dead, they panic and become fugitives. Several other victims of misfortune also become suspects, as Mistaken Judgment comes upon everyone.

Othello, WILLIAM SHAKESPEARE

MISTAKEN JUDGMENT AS PLOT—Iago was passed over for promotion in the Venetian army. He decides to avenge himself on his commander Othello. When Othello marries Desdemona, Iago decides to plant and nurture the seeds of jealousy in his commander. To achieve this, he manipulates Othello into believing that Desdemona is having an affair, which he mistakenly believes.

Death on the Nile, AGATHA CHRISTIE

INTUITIVE JUDGMENT AS SUBPLOT—A murder is committed on a Nile steamer, but the infamous Hercule Poirot is on board.

The Pink Panther, BLAKE EDWARDS

INTUITIVE JUDGMENT AS INCIDENT—In the first movie starring Peter Sellers, the bumbling Inspector Clouseau tries to catch a jewel thief who is right under his nose. He is totally inept but a moment of intuition toward the end places him at the right place at the right time to solve the case.

REMORSE AND EMPATHY

> "Maybe all one can do is hope to end up with the
> right regrets."
>
> —ARTHUR MILLER

Remorse

*Remorse is anguish arising from repentance for past misdeeds
or bitter regrets.*

This situation requires a Culprit, a Victim or Sin, and an Interrogator.

This situation is about an inner feeling of Remorse and Guilt that
may or may not be suppressed.

If these feelings are suppressed, the Culprit won't let his guard
down. He refuses to think about or face what he has done. He needs
people or events to open his eyes and prepare the way for his Remorse to come into his consciousness.

If these feelings are unsuppressed, he openly feels his Guilt and
Remorse because the feelings are at the surface and accessible. He
may also be afraid of punishment and therefore not be willing to confess. He may search for a way to justify what he did, especially if he
was ordered to do it by a higher authority, like a soldier in battle.

The other characters around him act as a consciousness barom-
eter. They may unknowingly make him feel guiltier through their
casual conversations, driving him mad.

The Sin he commits is grave; it is not a Sin against a silly little
societal custom but a Sin that he knows without a doubt to be wrong,
such as:

- murder
- treachery
- treason
- lies
- destroying someone who didn't deserve it

THE CULPRIT

The Culprit is someone who has committed some kind of Sin, whether there is a Victim involved or not. He knows right from wrong yet commits the act anyway. He may have been ordered to do so, but sometimes orders should be questioned.

If he suppresses his emotions, he is somewhat hard-hearted and out of touch with his feelings. He may feel the need to put on a strong front for others, especially if he is a leader of some sort. Perhaps he convinces himself subconsciously that he must push on for the good of his men, that he can't dwell in the past and be an effective leader.

He may think he is above the law and shouldn't have to feel any Remorse for what he has done, but it still eats away at him, little by little, until something makes him snap.

If he doesn't suppress his emotions, he is in touch with his feelings and has no problem experiencing them. They may make him feel alive. It can be addicting at times to feel very passionately about something.

He knows what he has done is wrong and, even if he can justify it, still feels Remorse and Guilt. It may haunt him relentlessly until he confesses to someone, anyone. Even then it may not be enough to stop the intense feelings welling up inside of him. He may search and search for a way to relieve himself of this Guilt, but he knows he can't undo what has been done. If there is a Victim available to forgive him and does so, he may find some peace with himself.

His whole life will change from this experience. If he can survive his Remorse and Guilt he will probably spend the rest of his life trying to do good for others to make up for it.

THE VICTIM OR SIN

The Victim or Sin relates to the regretful event for the Culprit. The character has either harmed someone in some way or has committed a Sin in his own eyes. The Sin may not seem bad to someone else, but to the Culprit it is a major offense. This is where his back-story may come into play—what roles or rules did his mother give him? Was he taught it was a Sin to talk back to elders? Perhaps he stays in a bad work relationship because he's afraid to speak up to his boss—until one day he just snaps.

THE INTERROGATOR

The Interrogator pushes the Culprit to confess. He is usually only concerned with solving the "crime" and making someone pay for it, but he can also be an enemy of the Culprit who wants to punish him.

He may follow the Culprit around making his life miserable, interviewing all of his friends and relatives. He may spread rumors, trying to draw someone out of the woodwork to testify against the Culprit. He can be very ruthless, especially if he has a "holier-than-thou" attitude.

Whether Remorse is used as plot, subplot, or incident, the beginning, middle, and end are the same:

BEGINNING: A Culprit commits a Sin of some sort that he knows is wrong.

- Does anyone try to stop him?
- Will he experience his feelings of Remorse right away or suppress them?
- Is he ashamed to show his face?
- Do other characters know what he did?
- Does he want to undo it? Or does he justify it?
- Does he try to redeem himself right away to no avail?
- What happens to make him think about it more and more? Does a new character come into the picture to remind him of the deed?

MIDDLE: The Interrogator comes and pesters the Culprit.

- Is the Interrogator ethical? Or out for blood?
- How does the Culprit react to him? Does his mental state get worse?
- Will the Culprit try to avoid the Interrogator?
- Will other characters get suspicious now that the Interrogator is around? Will the Culprit start acting differently?
- How does the Culprit answer to the Interrogator?
- Is there a punishment at stake that keeps the Culprit from confessing?

END: The Culprit ends things.

- Will the Culprit end his life? Or lose his mind? Or will he confess?
- How does confession make him feel?
- Does he get punished?
- How do other characters react?
- Can the Culprit make amends?
- Will the Interrogator be exposed if he is an enemy out for blood? Will this make others take pity on the Culprit?

"The great gift of human beings is that we have the power of empathy."

–MERYL STREEP

Empathy

Empathy is deeply understanding and feeling another's situation, emotions, pain, and motives.

In this situation the Culprit becomes the Empath who is unable to commit a "crime." She feels things so deeply, especially another's pain, she is just not capable of hurting anyone or anything. It would be like hurting herself. Compassion may come and go when things get tough, but true Empathy is something that never leaves.

She couldn't kill a fly let alone a human being. Witnessing someone else do harm makes her feel sick. She just can't understand how someone can hurt another living creature.

When she is ordered to do harm or is placed in a position to harm, she just can't do it no matter the cost to herself. (Her parents may ask her to kill a pig for dinner, for example.)

Others can't understand her behavior and she may feel like there is something terribly wrong with her at times. But when others need help or sympathy, she is the first one they come to. Most likely she won't live in a culture that values her gift and she will suffer greatly for it. She may learn to criticize herself for being so sensitive, as most people around will probably do.

Her Sin is not against another but usually against herself. She may starve rather than steal food from another or put herself down for her compassionate nature. Sensitive people are not honored in this day and age.

She may also be in a position to watch a loved one or friend become self-destructive. This too is painful for her. She, hopefully, has developed the patience to deal with it.

Whether Empathy is used as plot, subplot, or incident, the elements of the beginning, middle, and end are the same:

BEGINNING: The Empath is asked to do harm and she refuses. Or she witnesses harm and wants to stop it.

- How did she get into this situation?
- Does she have the patience for this?
- Does she feel hopeless?
- Does she have any plan of attack on how to deal with this situation? Has she done this before?
- Will she ask others for help?
- What do other characters think of her?

MIDDLE: The Empath is in trouble for refusing to harm or for trying to stop harm.

- What is at stake for her? Will she be punished?
- What does she do if someone else comes along and does the harm right in front of her (perhaps a brother comes in and kills the pig for dinner)?
- Will she feel like there is something wrong with her? Or with others?
- Does she have any special place to go to be herself? To be alone?
- Does she try to hide her sensitive nature when around peers?

END: The Empath wins or loses but usually remains true to herself.

- Does she win or lose?
- Did she remain true to herself or give in to what others expect of her? Did she harden her heart?
- Is she happy about her decision and actions?
- What do other characters think of her now?
- Would she give up being sensitive?

EXAMPLES

Hercules, HOMER

REMORSE AS SUBPLOT—Hercules is the son of Zeus and a mortal woman. Zeus's wife Hera is jealous and causes Hercules to go mad and kill his wife and children. The remorseful Hercules decides to use his superhuman strength to aid humanity.

The Fisher King, TERRY GILLIAM

REMORSE AS SUBPLOT—A talk DJ inadvertently convinces a psycho to blow away restaurant patrons and himself when the psycho calls in for advice. After three years of wallowing in his Remorse, he is attacked and almost set on fire, but a street person rescues him.

Seven Years in Tibet, HEINRICH HARRER

EMPATHY AS INCIDENT—This is the true story of Heinrich Harrer, an Austrian mountain climber who became friends with the Dalai Lama at the time of China's takeover of Tibet. The monks hold up the building of a temple to move worms out of the way by hand because they don't want to harm them.

Resurrection, STEPHEN GYLLENHAAL

EMPATHY AS PLOT—After a woman is crippled in an auto accident, she suddenly develops the power to feel the pain of others and heal it.

Situations 51 & 52

LOSS OF A LOVED ONE AND RESCUE OF A LOVED ONE

> "The beauty of the world has two edges, one of laughter, one of anguish, cutting the heart asunder."
>
> –VIRGINIA WOOLF

Loss of a Loved One

Loss is the condition of being deprived or bereaved of something or someone.

This situation requires a Kinsman Slain, a Kinsman Spectator, and an Executioner.

This situation is all about mourning. A Loved One has died and the surviving family members are trying to come to terms with their loss. The Slaying may have come about in several different ways:

- A Kinsman Spectator may have witnessed the Slaying but was unable to do anything about it.
- A Kinsman Spectator may have helped to bring misfortune upon one's people through secrecy and as a result many were slain.
- A Kinsman Spectator may have divined the death of a Loved One.
- A Kinsman Spectator learns about the death of a Loved One after it has happened.

His kin may seek revenge, but that is not the only focus of this situation. It is the feelings and reactions to losing the Love One that are the focus. The despair, grief, guilt, and helplessness make this dramatic.

How the kinsmen react is what this situation is about, especially if one of the kinsman witnessed the event. Things to consider:

- How do they handle the funeral?
- How do they handle hearing the news?
- What sort of problems does this bring them?
- Did the Kinsman Slain have a spouse and children?
- Will anyone seek revenge?

- Was it an accident?
- Do the kinsmen start to question God?
- Do the kinsmen try to understand and explore what death is?
- Are there any kinsmen who are glad the Kinsman Slain is dead?

THE KINSMAN SLAIN

The Kinsman Slain was someone who is usually deeply loved by his fellow kinsman, at least most of them. This is what makes it so tragic, because he may have:

- done good deeds
- helped out kinsmen when they needed him
- been a mentor to younger kinsmen, teaching them about life
- tried to live a good decent life, keeping to himself
- done some foolish things in his life but was still very charming
- had some endearing quality about him that others are drawn to

KINSMAN SPECTATOR

There may or may not be a Kinsman Spectator of the Slaying. If there is, most of the situation will probably be about how this Kinsman Spectator handles what she saw. She may:

- be paralyzed with fear and terror
- be numb and unable to face what happened
- go into shock
- change her whole personality
- lose faith in people and those that are supposed to be there to protect, causing her to become ever vigilant
- give up things she once held dear

THE EXECUTIONER

The Executioner is usually not the main focus of the story, as the main focus is on the loss of the Kinsman Slain. There is usually not a great deal of mystery surrounding the Kinsman's death. The cause of death is usually pretty clear. Once the Slaying takes place, the Executioner doesn't play much of a role in the story. In fact, the Slaying itself may never be seen. Perhaps the story opens with a mother getting a phone call about her son's death and we later hear from the Kinsman Spectator.

The Executioner may be an inanimate object such as drugs, a vehicle, or a rusty nail that infected the Kinsman.

The Executioner may even be the Kinsman Spectator if he is the one to bring misfortune to his kinsmen. Perhaps he is behind the wheel of the car that crashes, Slaying his fellow Kinsman.

Whether Loss of a Loved One is used as plot, subplot, or incident, the elements of the beginning, middle, and end are the same:

BEGINNING: A Kinsman is slain.

- Will the Executioner be shown?
- Will the Executioner be a person or an object?
- Will another Kinsman be there to witness it?
- Is the Slaying an accident? Or premeditated?
- Why is the Kinsman Slain? Did he do something wrong?
- How do other characters feel about it?
- Did he have any surviving children?
- Was he supposed to achieve greatness? Help a large group of people? Was he important?

MIDDLE: The Kinsman reacts to the Slaying.

- Will he seek revenge?
- Will he try to fill the Kinsman Slain's shoes? Carry on where he left off?
- Will he put himself in jeopardy now?
- Will he act differently? Lose his mind on some level?
- What will the rest of the family do? How will they deal with this? Are they afraid for the Kinsman?

END: The Kinsman comes to terms with the Slaying and gets on with life.

- Did he seek revenge? Was he successful?
- Has he found a way to let the pain go and get on with his life? How?
- Does he have to face other family members? Are they upset with him for moving on?
- How has his life changed?
- What will he do now?
- Is there anyone he can help who might be like the Kinsman Slain?

"It is not because things are difficult that we do not dare; it is because we do not dare that they are difficult."

–LUCIUS ANNAEUS SENECA

Rescue of a Loved One

To rescue means to set free from danger or imprisonment.

In this situation the Kinsman Spectator becomes the Rescuing Kinsman.

Whereas in the previous situation the Kinsman Spectator was helpless, in this situation she is able to pull herself together, gather her resources, and plan a rescue. Think of *Finding Nemo* and how the father fish rescues his son.

She is willing to do whatever it takes because the Kinsman means that much to her. They have family ties, but their relationship goes deeper than that.

She may not know how strong and resourceful she is until she has to step up and help him. This situation may be just what she needed to pull her out of her shell and force her into seeing how great and strong she really is.

Whether Rescue of a Loved One is used as plot, subplot, or incident, the elements of the beginning, middle, and end are the same:

BEGINNING: A Kinsman is threatened and the Rescuing Kinsman witnesses it.

- Why doesn't she jump in and rescue right now? What is the danger?
- Why does she want to rescue him? Is he her child?
- What does she stand to gain by rescuing?
- What is at stake?
- Where does the rescue have to take place? Does the place add more drama and make it harder to rescue?
- Do other characters want to help?

MIDDLE: The Rescuing Kinsman puts a plan together.

- Is she good at putting together plans? Or bad at it?
- Does she like to just jump in and do things even though the timing may be wrong?
- Will other characters help her?
- Is she in this alone?
- Does the Threatened Kinsman want her help?
- Is the rescue one of just giving money?

END: The Rescuing Kinsman rescues the Threatened Kinsman.

- How does the rescue take place?
- Are there any problems? What goes wrong?

- Is she successful? Are there any sacrifices made?
- Is the Threatened Kinsman happy and grateful?
- How does the Rescuing Kinsman feel about herself now?
- What do other characters think?
- What will the Rescuing Kinsman do now?

EXAMPLES

While I Was Gone, SUE MILLER

LOSS OF A LOVED ONE AS SUBPLOT—When she was in her twenties, Jo Becker discovered the body of her murdered best friend. She spends the next thirty years trying to come to terms with what happened without letting it ruin her marriage and relationship with her daughters.

The Big Chill, LAWRENCE KASDAN

LOSS OF A LOVED ONE AS SUBPLOT—At the funeral of one of their friends, a group of people who attended college together reunite.

The Last of the Mohicans, JAMES FENIMORE COOPER

RESCUE OF A LOVED ONE AS PLOT—Three trappers protect a British Colonel's daughter in the midst of the French and Indian War.

Finding Nemo, ANDREW STANTON AND LEE UNKRICH

RESCUE OF A LOVED ONE AS PLOT—Marlin is a widower who takes care of his only son Nemo. On Nemo's first day of school he's captured by a scuba diver and taken to live in a dentist office's fish tank. Marlin sets off to find Nemo at all costs.

> "Chaos and Order are not enemies, only opposites."
>
> –RICHARD GARRIOTT

Odd Couple

Odd means deviating from what is ordinary, usual, or expected.

This situation requires a Hero, a close Opposite Hero, and an Event that brings them together.

Two characters that are completely different in almost every way are forced to work together to achieve a common goal. Their differing styles and opinions cause much of the obstacles they face in the story and place their goal in jeopardy until they learn to work together and accept the other's way of being and working. Think about:

- the two buddy cops who can't stand working together but are forced to do so by the captain; one is soft, caring, and educated; the other is hard, tough, and street-smart

- the tough outdoorsman and city girl who fall in love and try to make it work

- the neat freak who has to live with the sloppy dirt-a-holic after his divorce (*The Odd Couple* television series)

These characters can differ in many ways, such as:

- occupation
- history and upbringing
- education
- philosophy
- hobbies
- morals
- goals and aspirations
- ways of living
- social interactions with others

- class or social standing
- money and culture

THE HERO

The Hero likes things done a certain way. Whatever the focus of the story is, the Hero knows a definite way to go about reaching his goal and he doesn't want to deviate from his way at all. He may not know any other way and therefore feels uncomfortable if someone forces him to do things another way. His pride could be at stake as well as his self-esteem if he has to admit he doesn't know how to do it another way.

He takes a "my way or the highway" approach to the job at hand, but that won't work. If he wants to reach the goal he will have to learn to let go a little and work in a team.

He may genuinely feel his way is the right way and not want to change because he believes his way will save the day. He will then want to convince or change his partner, which only makes matters worse.

OPPOSITE HERO

The Opposite Hero feels the exact same way as the Hero. She knows her way is the right way and she wants to convince or change the Hero. She will also have to learn to work in a team to get the job done.

Both the Hero and the Opposite Hero may get frustrated and try to use guilt, manipulation, or any other psychological game to change the other, but in the end it doesn't work too well and may only be temporary. Sooner or later, the one who tried to change will get very angry and lash out.

THE EVENT

The Event is something that happens that forces the two Heroes to be together in some way. There must be a compelling reason for both Heroes to be involved with this event so neither Hero can just walk away. Something about this event connects them—they have the same boss, live in the same apartment building, know the same man who needs help—anything at all can connect them.

Perhaps they are forced to work together on a project or they will be fired. Or think of *As Good As It Gets* and how the artistic gay man and his obnoxious, obsessive-compulsive, older neighbor are forced to interact and help each other out. Or think of the television show *The Odd Couple* and how Oscar is forced to take in his friend when his wife kicks him out on the street.

Whether Odd Couple is used as plot, subplot, or incident, the elements of the beginning, middle, and end are the same:

BEGINNING: A Hero meets an Opposite Hero and they clash.

- Are both equally unhappy with the situation? Or is one eager to work with the other at first?
- In what way are they opposites?
- Is either willing to try to change at this point? Or do they clash right away?
- Will anyone else get involved to try to help them?
- What Event makes them work together? It can't be easy for them to just walk away from each other.

MIDDLE: The Hero and Opposite Hero create their own obstacles toward reaching their goal.

- How will you use their opposing force against them? How will you turn it into Conflict that puts the goal in jeopardy?
- Will they find a way to work together or fight the whole time?
- Can an intermediary help them work things out?
- Do any other characters come to help? Are they like the Hero or the Opposite Hero?

END: The Hero and Opposite Hero manage to work together for once and reach the goal.

- Did one of them concede and do it the other one's way? Or did they both work together?
- What brought about this change?
- Did one character grow from being around the other? Did both of them grow?
- What did they learn from this?
- Would they work together again?

"The truth is that our finest moments are most likely to occur when we are feeling deeply uncomfortable, unhappy, or unfulfilled. For it is only in such moments, propelled by our discomfort, that we are likely to step out of our ruts and start searching for different ways or truer answers."

–M. SCOTT PECK

Fish Out of Water

A Fish Out of Water is a misfit who is unable to adjust to his environment or circumstances or is considered to be disturbingly different from others.

In this situation, the Hero is in conflict with an opposing Situation. She doesn't fit in where she is pushed to go, or at least feels that way. This could either be a simple issue of self-esteem for her, with everyone else thinking she fits in just fine, or she really could be out of her element. Why should she fit in? She should be allowed to be herself.

Whatever the reason, the Hero is in a situation that feels extremely uncomfortable for her. She may not know how to act, what to say, how to dress, who to talk to, and what is or is not acceptable where she is.

Her secondary goal may be to get out of the situation as quickly as possible, but she probably has to be there to get something that will lead her to her goal. She could be seeking information or trying to make a contact. Something very important awaits her within the situation or she wouldn't be going there at all.

She could snap under the pressure depending upon her personality and defensiveness, especially if someone makes fun of her.

Whether Fish Out of Water is used as plot, subplot, or incident, the elements of the beginning, middle, and end are the same:

BEGINNING: The Hero finds out she has to go somewhere she absolutely does not want to go.

- What compels her to go? Will it bring her closer to her goal?
- Why doesn't she feel like she'll fit in?
- Can she bring anyone with her for support?
- Will others make fun of her?
- How does she get herself excited to go?

MIDDLE: The Hero goes and feels completely out of place.

- Where does the Event take place? Can you change the place to make it more awkward for her?
- Is she able to fit in a little bit?
- Is it funny to see her in this situation?
- Does she get in little jabs at people without them realizing she is putting them down?

- Does she blow her cover?
- Will she be able to go back?

END: The Hero gets through the Event and finds the information that leads her to her goal.

- Does she receive help to get to her goal? Or does she do it all by herself?
- Does she embrace her differences?
- Does she have a newfound respect for the place or people she didn't fit in with?
- How has she changed from this?
- Are there any other places she wants to go now to see if she can fit in?
- Has she gotten a sense of humor from going through this?

EXAMPLES

Romancing the Stone, ROBERT ZEMECKIS

ODD COUPLE AS SUBPLOT—A girl from the big city meets a reckless soldier of fortune while lost in the jungle.

48 Hrs., WALTER HILL

ODD COUPLE AS SUBPLOT—A hard-nosed cop reluctantly teams up with a wisecracking criminal temporarily paroled to him in order to track down a killer.

Miss Congeniality, DONALD PETRIE

FISH OUT OF WATER AS PLOT—A tomboyish FBI agent goes undercover in the Miss United States beauty pageant to prevent a group from bombing the event.

Coyote Ugly, DAVID MCNALLY

FISH OUT OF WATER AS INCIDENT—A shy, small-town girl in her early twenties goes to New York City to pursue a dream of becoming a songwriter. She gets a job at a nightclub called Coyote Ugly where she struggles to fit in.

Situation 55

BLANK SITUATION TEMPLATE

> "There is no doubt that creativity is the most important human resource of all. Without creativity, there would be no progress, and we would be forever repeating the same patterns."
>
> —EDWARD DE BONO

Blank Situation Template

The above quote says it all about this situation. I want you to have the freedom to design your own situations if your story calls for it. While using situations that have been done and are known to work is a great way to write, there should always be some room for personal creativity.

Perhaps there are situations found only in certain cultures or certain fields of expertise. It would be impossible to include them all here, so I've come up with a blank situation template you can use to help flesh out a new situation if you need to.

SITUATION TEMPLATE

- What is your reasoning for creating this situation?
- Are you absolutely sure you can't use one of the situations already outlined?
- Will this situation be a plot, subplot, or incident?
- What is at stake for the hero? Or what is the hero's dilemma at the beginning of the situation? What needs to be solved? Or is this a Slice of Life situation? If so, what is the point of this situation? What do you want to convey?
- Can you piece together a beginning, middle, and end? (If you don't want a beginning, middle, or end, you don't need a situation. Just watch a film like *Before Sunrise* or *Daughters of the Dust* to get a feel of stories without the beginning, middle, and end structure.)
- Find the beginning: What does the hero want? What is his objective?

- Find the middle: What does the hero do to get it?
- Find the end: How does the hero get it?
- What do other characters think about this situation and what the hero wants? Will anyone try to stop the hero?
- Is there a clear-cut antagonist? What does the antagonist want? Is the antagonist human? Or something intangible?
- What type of obstacles can you put in the hero's way? How many? Will they escalate as he gets closer to the goal?
- How does the hero change during this situation? Does this situation cause another situation to happen?
- Does the hero or reader learn from this situation? Or is it just a fun ride?
- Will you have a theme?
- Will a smaller character become the heroic character during this situation? Will characters switch places?
- Will a sidekick character come onto the scene to help the hero?
- Will the hero want to share the spotlight with someone else? (In some cultures it is not acceptable for one person to take all the credit for something. In America it is the achievement of the individual that matters, but in other countries it is the achievement of the whole of society or family that matters. They don't want to stand out.)
- Could you use an antihero?

As you create, here is some food for thought:

"Sometimes the situation is only a problem because it is looked at in a certain way. Looked at in another way, the right course of action may be so obvious that the problem no longer exists."

—EDWARD DE BONO

Part 4

FINISHING TOUCHES

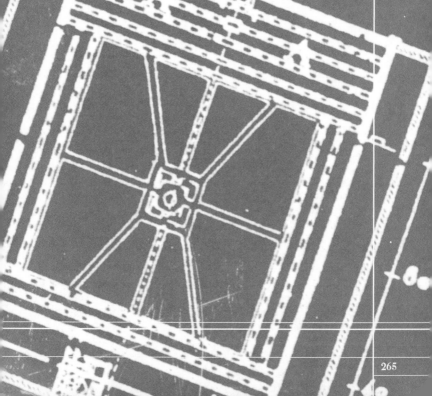

Research

"He who does not research has nothing to teach."

—ANONYMOUS PROVERB

Now that you have your story decisions made, sit back and examine the story for the following to see if there are any areas in particular that you would like to research:

- location
- setting
- place
- time period
- background
- facts
- class distinctions
- character history
- religion and beliefs
- customs
- supporting characters

Importance of Researching

Whether you're writing a character-driven story or a plot-driven one, research can only help to add depth to your scenes. It can uncover details that bring out mood, tone, and style, making your manuscript stand above others. In fact, all of the famous authors I know have told me the secret to great writing is *research*!

Filter what you will learn through research into your story—not by preaching or teaching but by sporadically placing this information into your scenes and dialogue where it is organic to the flow of your story.

In other words, find creative ways to convey your research to the reader; don't just dump several rambling pages of research into a chapter. If you do that, it will keep the story from moving forward, and it will bore the reader.

When research is completed before the major writing begins, you will see when you are constructing your scenes that you have so much more to add to make the characters come alive.

For example, there was a time at the start of industrialization when women slaved for hours in lace factories as a way to make a living. You can use this information to go from:

A redheaded girl walks into the room. She wears a green dress.

to:

A redheaded maid timidly walks into the ballroom. Her green dress is speckled with purple stains from the lace factory where she works during the day. Her darkened fingertips, perpetually stained with the horrid-smelling dye that never quite rinses off, brand her "lower class" for all to see.

Class, setting, work, character history, and time period have all added to the second version.

If you are writing a period piece you might look into:

• what people wore during the time of your story

• what they did for employment

• what their superstitions were

• what their social mores said about them

• whether or not a war was going on at the time

• how people traveled

• whether or not there was a threat of plague

• what rights and freedoms women had (the heroine may not be allowed to own land or walk around at night unescorted)

Conducting Research

Narrow down your research as much as possible by getting very specific about what you need to know. For example, find three books on the subject and skim through them. You don't have to read the entire book. Take a look at chapter headings and read the introductory chapter to find out what is included within each book.

Other ideas for research can be to:

• Go to a museum and buy brochures of places and artifacts to bring home.

• Read books on the time period, etc. of your story's setting.

• Read poetry to see how it often transports us to places, giving us a "felt sense" of them, the way most history books cannot.

- Read anyone that inspires you or helps you get into the mood of your particular story. For example, you can read women's poetry to get into the mind of your heroine (try Dorothy Parker, for instance) or read a story from a particular era, such as the Victorian era, if you are trying to capture that time period.

- Use the power of the Internet. I use www.dogpile.com search engine. It gives you the top ten results for over ten other search engines.

- Read autobiographies to help develop your character's family history and backstory.

- Look back at aspects of your life that might add to your story:
    - What experiences did you have that stand out?
    - What did you learn once upon a time, but may have forgotten about?
    - What did you play at as a child?
    - Did you ever take dance lessons? Or play sports?
    - What did you want to learn but didn't?

Setting, Background, and Place

The next sections talk about Setting, Background, and Place. Background is the broader space where a story takes place and Setting is where the actual scene is set up. Place is how the setting is conveyed.

For example, the Background could be Egypt and the Setting could then be the Pyramids, a café, or the desert.

Editors are always looking for manuscripts that either take place in settings they haven't seen before or convey a strong sense of place. So broaden your horizons and take time to learn about new towns, countries, or even unusual groups that people belong to (the Polar Bear Club, for example). Let your imagination go.

Place gives you a sense of the story and the characters. For example, if the Background is Egypt and the Setting is a café, the Place is the style of the café and the people who inhabit it.

If this café is a French café, it will have a very different feel or sense of place than if it were a Spanish café or a café inside a bordello. All of the people who work there would dress, act, and speak differently, and the design and decoration would be drastically different between the two.

My point is this: Be specific and it will help your creativity along. Once you describe the café as a Spanish café, your mind may start working:

- What if the waiter didn't speak English?

- What if a local girl comes in selling roses and interrupts their conversation just as he's about to confess something?

- What if, instead of having just some nameless guy sitting behind the heroine get mistakenly stabbed to death instead of her, you add some details to that nameless guy to make him more personal and real to the reader? This will only heighten the emotional response to the stabbing for the reader. Perhaps you make the stabbing victim the popular yet humble strolling café musician who plays Spanish tunes for the patrons.

Each "What if" adds a little more color to the scene and makes it much more real for the reader. Think about some more details.

Go over the following list to see if there are any creative opportunities you are missing in your story (though not all of the following will apply to your particular story).

LOCATION

- **GEOGRAPHICAL BACKGROUND:** What country, town, or state is the story set in? Are there mountains or deserts nearby?

- **SETTING:** What type of building, land, house, etc. dominates the storyline? Is there one setting that is extremely important? If so, think about researching it thoroughly so you have the details you need for your scenes.

- **PLACE:** What are the specifics of the setting? Play with the setting and change the atmosphere a bit. Picture a house—now picture Liberace living in it. Then picture a monk living there. Very different!

- **CLIMATE:** Is it cold, hot, dry, tropical? Can the climate affect the outcome of the story or add some more conflict and drama? Does the hero hate the snow?

TIME PERIOD

- **CLOTHING STYLES:** Clothing styles can be very important to your characters. In some time periods clothing was the only way to tell if someone was rich or poor, as there were no cars or fancy watches as status symbols.

- **MANNERISMS:** Does the hero act as men of his time period are accustomed to act? Does the heroine play the part of her sex or challenge it?

- **MORALITIES:** Can your heroine safely be alone with the hero before they are married?

- **INVENTIONS:** Don't put a car into a scene if cars haven't been invented yet! But also know the accomplishments of the time period you are working in, as many ancient civilizations had what we consider advanced technology, like running water for example.

- **LIFE EXPECTANCY:** How long did characters in your time period live? Will the heroine's parents still be around? Is she close to "normal" death even though she may only be twenty-nine?

- **GENDER ISSUES:** The heroines in many Victorian novels couldn't leave the house unescorted because of the time period. This meant that if the heroine snuck out to see the hero, she was risking everything.

FACTS

- **NAMES:** Will you choose a name for its meaning? Chandra means "moon." (See *The Writer's Digest Character Naming Sourcebook* by Sherrilyn Kenyon for more ideas.)
- **HISTORY:** What happened before the time period of your story? Don't have characters talk about an event that hasn't happened yet in their world.
- **WORDS AND SLANG:** For futuristic novels, you can make up your own slang; otherwise, research what common slang was for your time period. Perhaps the rich had different slang than the poor?
- **POLITICAL CLIMATE:** A democratic government will affect the people and their lives much differently than a dictatorship will.
- **LAWS:** Do any laws interfere with a character's goals?
- **CLASS:** As in lower, middle, upper. Know what situations and living conditions class divisions would create for your characters. Don't give a grocery clerk a mansion to live in unless it is a conscious choice on your part. During World War II, Hollywood specifically chose to show American characters living way above their class to help boost morale on the one hand and give Americans a true fantasy world to escape to when they came to the movies.
- **CHARACTER HISTORY:** Can you use your family history? Can you model any of your characters after someone you already know? Watch strangers and get some character idiosyncrasies.
- **RELIGION AND BELIEFS:** Do your characters have conflicting beliefs? Can that add drama to the story?

Questions

- Do you travel or sightsee? Would any of the places you have been to enrich your story?
- Do you read nonfiction books about other countries and cultures?
- What places interested you as a child?
- Are there any groups you can research for an unusual setting, such as the Polar Bear Club?
- Can your story stay in the same place you have chosen but be in a different time period for that place?
- Will changing time periods be more challenging for the characters, adding more conflict?

- Did you teach your readers something new? (Many readers love to learn, so take the time to get your facts right.)
- Can you get creative when selecting the backgrounds and settings for your story? (You don't have to write science fiction to invent your own background. You can create your own island in the Pacific or a town outside a well-known city.)
- Can you visit local museums or historical homes and buildings?
- Are there any subjects that are new to you that you would like to research?
- Can you spend some time at the library when you're developing your plot so you'll have tons of research books at your disposal?

Index

E

F

G

Get more great instruction from Writer's Digest Books!

THE 3 A.M. EPIPHANY
by Brian Kiteley

Push your writing to the limit and discover creative break-throughs by following Brian Kiteley's thought-provoking instruction and practicing the more than 200 challenging writing exercises found in this elegant, sophisticated book.
ISBN 1-58297-351-2 paperback, 272 pages, #10980-K

THE WRITER'S BOOK OF MATCHES
by the Staff of Fresh Boiled Peanuts, a Literary Journal

Beginning and professional writers can open this book anytime, anywhere to ignite a flash of inspiration and a bounty of fresh ideas. Over 1,001 creative prompts are waiting to be used as story starters, imagination-stretching exercises, and writer's block breakers.
ISBN 1-58297-411-X, paperback, 272 pages, #11030-K

WRITE GREAT FICTION: PLOT & STRUCTURE
by James Scott Bell

An award-winning author of suspense novels and thrillers offers clear, concise information to help you create a believable and engaging plot. There are examples from popular novels, comprehensive checklists, and practical hands-on guidance to help you write great fiction!
ISBN #1-58297-297-X, paperback, 240 pages, #10942-K

20 MASTER PLOTS
by Ronald Tobias

Build page-turning plots from just a spark of an idea! This book examines plots that occur again and again throughout fiction and provides instruction and examples for adapting these basic themes to your own work. *ISBN 1-58297-239-7, paperback, 240 pages, #10889-K*

45 MASTER CHARACTERS
by Victoria Schmidt

Create memorable, true-to-life characters for your novel, script, or screenplay with the help of archetypical models and their characteristics. Examples of cross-cultural model characters from television, movies, and history will help you create complex and compelling stories.
ISBN 1-58297-069-6, hardcover, 256 pages, #10752-K

FIRST DRAFT IN 30 DAYS
By Karen Wiesner

Outline your novel or short story and have a completed working draft in as little as thirty days! This book's instruction works for any genre and is customizable to individual style. It includes interactive worksheets, flexible schedules to keep you focused, sample worksheets, brainstorming techniques, and goal sheets keep your career on track!
ISBN 1-58297-296-6, paperback, 224 pages, #10944-K

ROBERT'S RULES OF WRITING
by Robert Masello

Established author Robert Masello offers 101 unconventional lessons for every fiction author, journalist, screenwriter, and nonfiction writer. Improve your work and your chances of getting published with fresh, irreverent advice from one of the best in the business.
ISBN 1-58297-326-1, paperback, 224 pages, #10962-K

PAGE AFTER PAGE
by Heather Sellers

Ninety percent of beginning writers stop practicing their craft before they have a chance to discover their talents. This essential and encouraging guide by veteran writer and teacher Heather Sellers will help you build an ongoing writing life through engaging exercises that will shape your life and help you achieve your goals. *ISBN 1-58297-312-1, hardcover, 240 pages, #10948-K*

These and other fine Writer's Digest books are available at your local bookstore, online supplier, or by calling 1-800-448-0915.